SURVEYING THE INTERIOR

Environmental Arts and Humanities Series

SURVEYING THE INTERIOR

Literary Cartographers and the Sense of Place

RICK VAN NOY

University of Nevada Press ▲▲ Reno Las Vegas

Environmental Arts and Humanities Series
Series Editors: Scott Slovic and Michael P. Cohen
University of Nevada Press, Reno, Nevada 89557 USA
Copyright © 2003 by University of Nevada Press
Manufactured in the United States of America
Design by Carrie House
Library of Congress Cataloging-in-Publication Data
Van Noy, Rick, 1966–
Surveying the interior : literary cartographers and the sense of
place / Rick Van Noy.
p. cm. — (Environmental arts and humanities series)
Includes bibliographical references and index.
ISBN 0-87417-548-8 (hardcover : alk. paper)
1. American literature—19th century—History and criticism.
2. Nature in literature. 3. Thoreau, Henry David, 1817–1862—
Knowledge—Cartography. 4. Powell, John Wesley, 1834–
1902—Knowledge—Cartography. 5. Stegner, Wallace Earle,
1909–1993—Knowledge—Cartography. 6. King, Clarence, 1842–
1901—Knowledge—Cartography. 7. Cartography—United
States—History. 8. Environmental protection in literature.
9. Surveying—United States—History. 10. Place (Philosophy)
in literature. 11. Wilderness areas in literature. 12. Landscape in
literature. I. Title. II. Series.
PS163 .V36 2003
810.9'36—dc21   2003000205

First Printing
12 11 10 09 08 07 06 05 04 03
5 4 3 2 1

Frontispiece: High Adirondack Peaks and Wild Forest: Westward from Basin Mountain. It was drawn by surveyor of the
Adirondacks, Verplanck Colvin, and appeared in his *Report on
the Progress of the Adirondack Land Survey to the Year 1886.*

For Catherine

The only true voyage of discovery is not to go to new places, but to have other eyes. — MARCEL PROUST

C O N T E N T S

ILLUSTRATIONS

Because I grew up on one, geographical borders have always fascinated me. The Delaware River formed the natural border of my childhood. From my bedroom window I could see it and another state. We lived on the New Jersey side just up from where George Washington crossed on Christmas night in 1776 and marched south to Trenton to surprise the boozing Hessians. I can remember locating where I lived on maps. There, the free-flowing river was a smooth static line, but my border moved.

When I grew up and moved away, I heard a lifetime of New Jersey jokes, "what exit" and the like. But the perception of where I had lived from those who didn't know it differed vastly from the place I had experienced. Like Mark Twain, I learned (though not on a steamboat) to read and navigate the river, knowing its submerged rocks, snags, and bends. Words like reef, rapids, weir, and eddy entered my vocabulary, as did the names of certain locales: John's Island, Scudder's Falls, Snuffy's—places otherwise invisible except to residents of the river, or "river rats." And I knew the terrain on the other side of my house, exploring the hills of a park that I thought stretched on forever. I discovered new places in those woods, but also came to know each path as I retraced my steps, remembering what sections would be muddy after rain, and what trails would take me home. I knew the curve of the creeks not like the back of my hand, as the cliché goes, but like the creases of my palm; I knew where they joined with the river to form a branch of the tree. On maps, the Delaware was a large tree, with roots in the Atlantic Ocean, limbs in Pennsylvania and New York, and my house in a fold of the trunk. However, I could navigate by the map in my mind rather than through the lines on paper.

I've been prone to a geographic imagination, so I was drawn to the surveyors in this book. Like many explorers, I once journeyed to a place, actually moved there, because it looked good on the map, but "found" myself lost. Being placed usually involves a long and even linguistic association with a landscape; familiarity breeds affection and, with that positive bond, a sense of place. The literary cartographers I write about have surveyed spaces that looked inviting on official maps but came to sense the ways that the map, with its two-dimensional representation of landscape, failed to communicate the places they traveled through. Their maps *present* a landscape, but their writing about place retraces the steps that the surveyor took to gain his initial vista, *re-presents* the place as it was experienced.

This project began during a period of reading the work of Wallace Stegner and discovering his fascination with explorers and literary cartographers as he tried to come to terms with the interrelations of the American Western lands—their history, literature, and borders—and his own life and "place." In a way, I'm out to test Stegner's thesis that "no place, not even a wild place, is a place until it has had that human attention that at its highest reach we call poetry" (LS 205). A place could require poetry because it is more than the sum of its physical objects. The synthesis of placed experience—the sights, stories, feelings, and concepts—gives us what we call the sense of place. To bring it into being, we need a complex intersection of cartography and literature, a charting of interior and exterior landscapes.

My project has been informed by the emerging field of literary scholarship that has paid attention to place, ecocriticism. Ecocritics wish to foreground what has too long been considered mere background or "setting." By bringing the natural world into sharper focus, ecocritics hope to converge on new relationships between natural places and human culture. At best, writing about place tries to establish an attentiveness to and respect for the landscapes we live in and the ways we live in them. For the ecocritic, attention to places may lead to attachment to them, and attachment may lead not only to the reader's awareness of their importance, but to the protection of those represented places. When attentively read, the representation of place can tell us about our behavior, values, and history: the maps that have guided us to this point—the ones in our hands and in our minds—so we can ask where they have navigated us.

My topic is inherently interdisciplinary, as I study people who were both scientists and writers; they bring together a knowledge of how the natural world works with some understanding of how it could be represented. To study the interactions between humans and their environment requires some acquaintance with geology, geography, cartography, philosophy, psychology, anthropology, art, and history. Though I can claim no depth in these fields, I have borrowed from all of them in learning more about how maps and writing represent the world and its inhabitants. I bring a literary and critical perspective to texts such as those by John Wesley Powell and Clarence King that have received very little attention from literary critics, in order to see them as part of a continuum of writing about the land that leads to writers such as Wallace Stegner, Edward Abbey, and Barry Lopez.

This study was also set in motion by Kent Ryden's *Mapping the Invisible Landscape: Folklore, Writing and the Sense of Place* (1993) from which I have drawn to learn how maps communicate—or fail to communicate—a sense of place. Yet, whereas Ryden discusses an "invisible landscape," the cultural attachments to place communicated through folklore and writing, I locate an "interior landscape," one also existing in the minds of people, but one projected upon the landscape by the surveyor according to pre-existing cultural and historical values such as the sublime. Ryden discusses well-known literary cartographers—Thoreau, Berry, Lopez—but my project is the first, as far as I know, to examine the writing by actual surveyors and mappers, who were writers only *after* they were scientists, and to look at them with the same glasses I use for Thoreau and Wallace Stegner. Like Ryden, I want to show that maps don't tell the full story, but I want to get the mappers themselves to tell it.

There are histories of American surveying and exploration, such as William Goetzmann's *Exploration and Empire* (1966) or Richard Bartlett's *Great Surveys of the American West* (1962), but none that adequately account for the literary and rhetorical devices used by these literary cartographers, within their historical context, to communicate a changing and evolving sense of place. There have also been studies, such as Bruce Greenfield's *Narrating Discovery* (1992), of how mappers colonize space, but they are not this book. Although I'm aware of the colonizing objectives that names and maps pursued, I'm primarily interested in how maps and "mapping" strategies express a powerful desire to know and live on the land. It is precisely the way maps did *not* yet take "possession" of the land that I am interested in.[1]

My project has also benefited from the growing body of historians who write about the environment. Their work stems from a present day concern for the well-being of the natural environment and a desire to understand how human attitudes toward it have changed. In a broad sense, my examination of nineteenth- and twentieth-century surveyors is a study of historical attitudes toward nature. As a reader of American literature, I try to point out how these particular texts, in their particular historical circumstances, comment upon the ways Americans have represented and understood American places.

Though on a smaller scale, I see this book as attempting to account for the presence of the sublime in the way Leo Marx explained the pastoral. In *The Machine in the Garden,* Marx describes how American writers faced a paradox. Americans defined themselves by the availability of free and untamed land, but that vision was continually receding. To deal with the contradiction, American writers imported the pastoral to reconcile art with nature, machine with garden, allaying fears about progress with fantasies of inexhaustible beauty. The surveyors in this book faced a similar problem: they were to map wild and unknown areas, but mapping disturbed both that initial allure and, ultimately, because of the purpose of their expeditions, that place. The map was the machine in this garden, and the sublime was brought in as a way to express a wild (even eternal) space within a known (if soon to be altered) place.

Certainly, just because a writer evokes a map does not make that writer a literary cartographer, no more than evoking plants makes one a literary naturalist. But the four writers I have concentrated on in this book are all concerned both with what it is to map or survey a place *and* what it is to write and explain it—to create literature, depth and meaning, to explore the spatial narrative of the map. At one end are cartographers who wanted to write (Powell and King); at the other, writers who wanted to map (literal or not) their places (Thoreau and Stegner). Some readers may find the inclusion of Wallace Stegner a stretch. Though he wrote about surveyors, he was not one of them. Rather, he was one of the first to "survey" the early writing on Western lands, and when he turned to write about it, he wanted to know all the perceptions of the geographical environment that preceded him. If surveyors through their boundary making establish an initial conceptual framework for places, Stegner inherited their "boundaries" when starting his exploration of the accumulated "fictions" that construct and chart our places. In proceeding from the surveyors to Stegner, it will also seem as if I'm proceeding from the epistemological to the moralistic, but such a movement, I believe, reflects a concern of these literary cartographers and one of Stegner himself: Once we come to know a place in a certain way, how should we behave toward it?

ACKNOWLEDGMENTS

A book on places wouldn't be possible without some special people and their *places*. I wish to thank the following people for housing me during certain key moments when parts of this project were either written or being formed: Elene Van Noy for Titusville, New Jersey; Richard and Debra Van Noy for Lawrenceville, New Jersey; Jennifer and Richard Cochran for Hinesburg, Vermont and Chagrin Falls, Ohio; Fred Abell for Seattle, Washington; Moira Baker for Radford, Virginia; and Clay and Beth Rankin for "the cottage" in Gates Mills, Ohio.

I also want thank some people who gave valuable *time*. Gretchen Van Noy shared time in one of those places. I am grateful to the staff of several libraries and to the interest they showed toward my project: the special collections departments at Stanford University, Virginia Polytechnic Institute, Appalachian State University, and Case Western Reserve University (CWRU). Sue Hanson of CWRU Special Collections found maps and old surveyors' tracts that I couldn't have known existed. Mike Partington of CWRU helped me track down needed information and sources, as did Bud Bennett of Radford University.

I am grateful to Rosemary Guruswamy who helped make time available during my first year and to other Radford University English faculty who acknowledged the importance of this project when I wasn't sure where it was going or how it would be finished. Don Samson provided valuable help with my teaching. I owe Jim Minick recognition for "Creases" and Justin Askins appreciation for looking at several of these chapters.

Michael Bryson gave valuable comments and influenced my own thinking about the epistemologies of maps and the rhetoric of science. Readers who are familiar with it will detect a strong influence of John Tallmadge's essay on Clarence King and John Wesley Powell. To him I am grateful. I also want to thank Gary Lee Stonum, for his help with the sublime; Roger Salomon, for his mentoring and continual encouragement; Ted Steinberg, who pointed me in useful directions; and Suzanne Ferguson, in whom some of Stegner's patience and wisdom as a teacher has been passed on. Their insights are throughout this project and have undoubtedly made it better. Karla Ambruster offered excellent advice for the final stages of revision, as did Richard Francaviglia and Roger Balm. Monica Micelli showed faith in the book from the start and advocated for it. I'm grateful for her work and for that of the staff at the University of Nevada Press. Kim Green provided a steady hand as copyeditor.

A condensed version of my argument was previously published and revised for this volume. "Surveying the Sublime: Literary Cartographers and the Spirit of Place" appeared in *The Greening of Literary Scholarship,* edited by Steven Rosendale and published by the University of Iowa Press (2002). Some material in the conclusion was originally published as "A Plate Tectonics of Language: Geology as Vernacular Science" in *John McPhee and the Art of Literary Non-Fiction,* Susan N. Maher and O. Alan Weltzien, editors (2003). Thoreau's "handbill" (Figure 2.3) appears courtesy of Henry W. and Albert A. Berg Collection of English and American Literature, The New York Public Library, Astor, Lenox, and Tilden Foundations. Thoreau's original survey map (Figure 2.2) appears courtesy of The Concord Free Public Library.

Finally, I should also thank the people who shared time with this project: my son Sam, who accompanied me on trips to the library and diversions through the woods, and with whom I hope to revisit many of these places; my daughter Elliot, who surveys our house and yard intently and attentively, increasing attachment to it for her and me; and most of all, my wife Catherine, who was there all the while this project consumed me, who stirs the soil under my feet, and who I met after much traveling—and helped me to see.

SURVEYING THE INTERIOR

Introduction
Surveying the Height of Our Mountains, the Country of Our Mind

It is not down in any map; true places never are. —Herman Melville

To those devoid of imagination, a blank place on the map is a useless waste; to others, the most valuable part. —Aldo Leopold

In his opening to the chapter "The Country of the Mind," from *Arctic Dreams,* Barry Lopez tells us that "the daily cycle of tides" on Pingok Island is "hard to read" (252). You can measure the vertical rise of these tides, he writes, "with a fingertip" (252). On the corresponding page is a map of Pingok Island, its coastline not rising and falling, but rather frozen on the two-dimensional surface of the page. Below that map, Lopez provides the cartographic coordinates, as if to underscore a way of measuring different from human touch. But the map of Pingok Island, too, can be hard to read, depending on what we wish to know. It provides an outline of the coast and a position relative to other islands and landforms, but little else about the place is revealed. It is difficult to map as well; Lopez tells us later in the chapter that the shoreline changes due to ice flows. He says that the island is also difficult to photograph, blanketed as it often is in snow. Yet it "emerges in June, resplendent with flowers and insects and birds" (255). That aspect of the Arctic he learns not by looking down at maps or photographs, but through an "an old business, walking slowly over the land with an appreciation of its immediacy to the senses and in anticipation of what lies hidden in it" (254).

If asked to describe the Arctic, many would use words like *bleak, vast, stark,* even *monotonous.* But this impression, Lopez writes, is gained by "staring at empty maps of the region or from traveling around in it by airplane," perspectives that contract and compress the land. "The orderliness, simplicity, and clarity of the presentation" of maps, Lopez writes, is "seductive" but also misleading, "altering the relationship between space and time" (280, 284). This aerial view, he tells us, "is a great temptation; but to learn anything of the land, to have any sense of the relevancy of the pertinent maps, you must walk away from the planes. You must get off into the country and sleep on the ground, or take an afternoon walk to take a tussock apart" (285). Lopez takes us on such walks, adding depth to dull landscape, narrating "the unsummarized dimensions of a deeper landscape" (286).

In unfolding that landscape, Lopez inserts one more set of maps into the chapter to show that Eskimos related their "maps" of their region to European explorers from memory. The artifacts they produced were almost identical to those created with modern cartographic devices, even while tracing out a "scaled replica of the region" on the ground (287). He presents, therefore, not only the physical maps travelers and explorers hold in their hands, but the intricate "mnemonic maps" of the country natives hold in their minds: the maps made from high panoramic views and the "maps" made while kneeling on the ground, carving contours in the sand.

This book is about writers and mappers. Like *Arctic Dreams,* it is concerned with geographical perception and understanding, with the way landscapes are mapped onto paper and "mapped" into thought and memory, and with the challenge facing the writer who would write about such landscapes. I try to use *map* (without quotation marks) to mean literally the piece of paper with a spatial narrative, using "map" (with quotation marks) to talk about other cultural and personal landscapes we hold in our minds. In everyday usage, the term *map* and its surveying correlatives are frequently used metaphorically; we map out plans, take a lay of the land, and chart a course. When someone loses focus or does something disorderly, that person is said to be "all over the map." Likewise, the spatial imagery of borders, boundaries, frontiers, horizons, and margins also pervades academic language.[1] Perhaps a reason for the widespread use of spatial terms as metaphors is that all experience takes *place* at a point in space. In order to comprehend the widespread use of cartographic metaphors and our "maps," we must examine the circumstances in which our lives and minds touch ground, circumstances that have always driven literature.

As Lawrence Buell notes in *The Environmental Imagination* (1995), for many of us, "regional terrain organizes itself . . . in the guise of maps and highways; rarely do we bring its topography, system of watercourses, vegetation zones, and atmospheric patterns into focus" when we drive or fly rapidly by them. Insulated from their existence, we do not feel their influence or relevance. The challenge, "for those interested in assuming it," becomes a *re-placing* of ourselves within the physical environment that our pre-scientific ancestors had to know experientially (108).

The literary cartographers in this book began with the map as their goal, but they seemed to sense that the challenge of knowing a place involved a more complex and thorough kind of environmental reading, the perceptual shift required to move from the abstract to the particular. They first conceived space cartographically, then experienced it as sublime on its way to being known more intimately—as a place. For how else to know places and live well in them, except by learning from the examples and stories of those who attempted to know them before we did?

In their writing, these authors both struggle with and exploit the basic problem of all maps: the reduction of the "real"—with various elevations, vegetation, and geologies—onto the limited space of the flat, blank, textureless sheet. When this move is initiated, a "literary cartography" may be said to emerge. As Graham Huggan writes in *Territorial Disputes*, a literary cartography is fundamentally concerned with the process of representation, but whereas the cartographic function of maps addresses how the land is controlled or spatialized, the symbolic representation of landscapes in literature questions how landscape is perceived or experienced (31). A literary cartography not only examines how maps function in literary texts (for example, as metaphors for possession), or how maps in themselves can tell a story, but also how literature can be used for cartographic means: to control, order, or limn a place. Maps can both "facilitate the relation between a real and a represented world" or they can intensify the distance between them, highlighting the ideological problems associated with differing cultural perceptions of space and the epistemological problems having to do with mimesis (31). For Kent Ryden in *Mapping the Invisible Landscape*, a literary cartography must "concentrate on trying to portray both the exterior, visible landscape—the world that can be mapped with mathematics and surveying equipment—and, more important, the interior, invisible landscape that lies atop it" (52). For Ryden, a place is much more than a point on a piece of paper or on the planet. It is "anchored to a specific location" by a set of map coordinates but it is also the landscape and story that is found there (38).

To learn all there is to know of a place, writers can contemplate how it would look on the map, but they must also turn away from the map and try to conceptualize in language. Language is also a way of abstracting, but it valorizes, provokes the image-making faculty, and stimulates the senses. Words give space a different form and shape from maps, making a "deep" space in the mind, evoking the "sense of place" in ways the surveyor's maps never can. Words also allow these literary cartographers to express how they were changed by their places, how the interior landscape they came with—the grid, the sublime—had to be adjusted to what was really there, and to what took *place* there.

All of us try to orient ourselves in our surroundings. Surveyors represent humanity's boldest attempt to pinpoint locations, to bring untrammeled space into some contours of definition, and to tie it all to the coordinate system that unifies the globe. In locating their place in the world, they are preoccupied with a fundamental question about where we are ("*Where* are we?" Thoreau implores on Mount Katahdin, after making "contact"), though they aren't equipped to answer unless they combine theolodites with theology, cartography with literature.

In his *PrairyErth*, William Least Heat-Moon writes about a more profound and complex sense of place than maps, stereotypes about the prairie, or the flyover view from an airplane acknowledge. Chase County, Kansas, is the geographical center of the United States. If you fold a map of the forty-eight states north to south then east to west, Least Heat-Moon writes, the creases would cross through it (10). He begins this way to summon the cartographic imagination and to recognize that Chase County is and was shaped by cartographic practices: the national geological surveys and Thomas Jefferson's grid. Least Heat-Moon divides his book into twelve sections, each section a gloss on one of the quadrangles of the U.S. Geological Survey (USGS) maps that cover Chase County. The idea came to him as he laid them out on the floor of his home, thinking on this "paper land," their outlines forming "a kind of grid such as an archaeologist lays over ground he will excavate. Wasn't I a kind of digger of shards?" Least Heat-Moon is there to "test the grid," to grasp the "deep map" (the book's subtitle). He hopes for a "topographic map of words that would open inch by inch to show its long miles." Where are the connections beyond the grid, he asks: "Were they themselves the only links we can truly understand? Could they lead into the dark loomings that draw me here?" (15).

The surveyors in this book wondered about maps and the grid even as they went about applying them, wondered about their own connections to the land through maps and the "loomings" beneath them. My title refers to surveyors who have set out literally to map the interior of the United States but have also in important ways mapped the interiors of their own consciousnesses. The first three were active in imposing the grid system on the U.S. landscape, but all of them sensed the ways that system failed to represent the places they experienced. I begin with Henry David Thoreau who, before he was a writer, was a skilled surveyor and cartographer. I then discuss the writings of two former directors of the USGS during the nineteenth century, Clarence King and John Wesley Powell. I locate the sites where the surveyor's view of landscape as quantifiable and measurable gives way to more qualitative and subjective ways of knowing. Finally, I examine the writing of Wallace Stegner who, although not a surveyor himself, wrote about surveyors—including King and Powell—geographical boundaries, and the "deep maps" that bind people to places.

Ironically, these "boundary makers" would come to think about place not as it is bounded or measured from a position of distance, but considered environmentally, where one is *included in* and not *separate from* the surrounding landscape. They set out to "know" their places empirically, but experience them phenomenologically and describe them in a more multidimensional and layered sense of place than the map angle of vision can provide. Because they are surveyors, they tend to look at landscape as an elaborate geometrical system, out of which they may draw useful information. The natural world exists for them as a space to be inventoried for resources or for routes—in, out, across. Yet, in their attention to where things are and how they represent them, they also raise epistemological problems about knowing and sensing place. They have focused on mapping locations but have become "lost," challenging the acquisitive sense that the mapper presumes. Their shock at recognizing lostness often brings on a new discovery: With the techniques they use to calibrate landscapes, they've never been "found" in any meaningful way. Although the map for them is first envisioned as a means to know and represent the unknown land, it is later seen as an incomplete form, incapable of accounting for their complex and diverse responses to nature. The map is especially deficient at depicting their internal geographies.

They were mapping a land that was difficult to know and come to grips with. While these surveyors went about mapping space in a mathematical web constructed and maintained by positivism and scientific objectivity, they represented places in their writings according to an interior landscape consisting of discursive formations that both enabled and constrained their relationship to their environment. While these surveyors were measuring winding rivers, jagged mountain peaks, and plotting nature into the coordinates of a Cartesian, geometrical space, they also represented what Jefferson called the "height of our mountains," often according to the eighteenth- and nineteenth-century aesthetics of the sublime.

In this first section of my introduction, I discuss the ways cartographers' maps are useful and the ways they are not, and probe the assumptions that underlie them. After dispensing with some first principles of maps and their authored nature, I examine how they have functioned in practice, sketching a brief history of surveying in America. Using the early maps of John Smith, Thomas Jefferson, and Lewis and Clark, I show how surveying in America has always proceeded from a subjective notion of place, even if a blank one. From there, I discuss a specific incident where the place is anticipated in the writing of a surveyor for the Pacific Railroad, John Lambert. Following Lambert, I discuss the aesthetic category used to preview such places, the sublime, and the sense of place that it communicates, as the Lambert incident forecasts events to come.

Because the sublime is concerned with an aesthetic and emotional response, and surveying with a scientific one, it would seem that the two would be in conflict with one another. The sublime deals with measureless emotion, whereas surveying precisely measures. So how did the two come together in an American literary cartography, and what are the consequences of the sublime as the aesthetic that defined Americans' interior landscape? The sublime, I shall argue, marks an important passage from blank space to place. The sense of place embodied in the sublime, with its imaginative and phenomenological feel for landscape, is an important counterbalance to the land as either private property or resource bank (or blank)—which the surveyor/map locates and validates. Though also a cultural import (like the grid), the sublime bears comparison with native stories that communicated a "spirit of place," a land charged with *numina*.

THE AUTHORED NATURE OF MAPS

Organizing space is a fundamental human activity. We draw our state lines to defend and demarcate their resources; we plot cities so that economic, residential, recreational, and spiritual activities can have their places. Says geographer Yi-Fu Tuan, place differs from space in that "what begins as undifferentiated space becomes place as we get to know it better and endow it with value" (6). That value can be objective and empirical, defined by a border or survey marker, but it can also be imaginative and phenomenological, if writers of place can be believed, defined by memory and affection. If we experience space as an idea, we experience places through sensory impressions—the seen, heard, felt, smelled, tasted.

Maps have historically been the most efficient form of representing a place. They are one of the most "densely packed communications media of any sort," providing a detailed summary of the physical and cultural features of an area as accurately but abstractly as possible, given the limitations of technology and scale (Ryden 20). Through contour lines, a topographical map can indicate the rise and fall of the terrain. And with its system of scale, a map can show spatial relationships and distances between natural and cultural features. Yet, though the modern topographical map is a "marvel of efficient geographical communication" relating much we need to know about places, "in other important ways it does not tell us very much at all" (Ryden 20). The lines on a map draw "all the minor and major divisions by which we separate this green whirling planet to fit our human imagination," notes Appalachian writer Wilma Dykeman in *Explorations* (1984). "Vastness and variety—scenes, smells, sounds, heat, and cold—reduced to a dry, stiff bit of cardboard" (1-2). Maps provide spatial and visual information, are useful for finding our way or locating our property, but they stop far short of dealing with the sense of a place for the people who live there and experience those represented spaces (Ryden 36). A map can no more capture the essence of a place "than a photograph can depict a person's soul," expresses nature writer Jan DeBlieu (24). Yet, maps fascinate us. We stare at them before starting our journeys and draw and sketch them in a multiplicity of forms to show others our worlds.

But whereas knowing places requires an intersection of geography and imagination, cartography's very philosophy, scientific positivism, rejects the notion that knowledge is socially produced. Unlike a verbal description, which may always be suspected of subjectivity, a map would seem to offer a reliable representation of the world. We believe that a map is "innocent," and "a servant of eye that sees things as they really are," write two historians of cartography, Denis Wood and John Fels (64). But creating a map after discovery or exploration was not simply achieved by the transference of objects that are "out there" onto the blank page (Ryan 118). Literary cartographers transfer the "seen,"—already codified according to an aesthetic interior landscape—into what they map or write (Ryan 118).

Though objectivity is the rule, maps have always been subjective. Medieval maps were "more ecclesiastic than cartographic, more symbolic than realistic," writes John Noble Wilford in *The Mapmakers* (34). Early maps reflected a worldview rather than facts. Their style was "symbolic, ornamental, and often beautiful; the geographic content, impoverished and usually misleading; the purposes, a representation of the mind more than of the Earth" (45). Early maps captured more the mythical lands over the horizon than the solid earth at one's feet (Ryden 30).

Historians of cartography describe how such *mappaemundi* (literally, maps of the world) were gradually influenced by regional maps or portolan charts, practical rather than theoretical representations of a particular space. David Woodward writes that the primary function of *mappaemundi* was didactic, "to instruct the faithful about the significant events in Christian history rather than to record their precise locations" (286). If the *mappaemundi* were the cosmographies of landsmen, the portolan charts (or *portolanos,* Italian for "sailing directions"), according to Tony Campbell, "preserve the Mediterranean sailors' firsthand experience of their own sea, as well as their expanding knowledge of the Atlantic Ocean" (372). By means of these practical cruising charts, marine navigators pieced together a more precise outline of the world they came in contact with rather than the one they anticipated. Samuel Champlain's 1607 map of New France, for example, was titled a "description des costs [*sic*]" and was drawn from his own observations, including interviews with Native Americans, and his own calculations ("Samuel"). Such charts were a kind of *periplum* (Greek for "sailing around"), and Pound writes in the *Cantos* about an immediate literary experience: "periplum, not as land looks on a map / but as sea bord [*sic*] seen by men sailing." Thoreau alludes to one of the most famous of these, *The Periplus of Hanno*, at the end of "The Pond in Winter" chapter in *Walden*, where he has constructed his own periplum of the pond (McQuade 9). But that periplum, though constructed "firsthand," serves its particular author's prejudices, purposes, and "worldview."

For the past several decades, cartography has been undergoing a revolution, due in part to the rise of humanistic geography but also because of cartography's intersection with poststructuralist theories. Like the literary work, the map is now being studied as more than just a set of directions and as a cultural text. In "Toward a Cultural History of Cartography," Christian Jacob describes a change in cartographic criticism from the "transparent" view of the map as an "ideal concordance of the world and its image" to an "opaque" view, which takes into account the inescapable contextual influences which shape the transfer of external information into map space (191–92). Historians of cartography such as the late J. B. Harley have explored how maps, rather than an objective representation of the world, are shaped by "social forces" and serve the interests of power and authority. Since the Enlightenment, cartographers have sought the perfectly mimetic map, but Harley and others have helped to break the assumed nonideological link between reality and representation by showing that no matter how much science and technology are used to produce a map, its "facts" are structured by a "specific cultural perspective" (426). Cartographers select their details and "rhetorical styles" from an infinite number of possibilities, using techniques of scale and projection, and must inevitably distort. A map's creator superimposes political, cultural, or other nongeographical features onto a geographical area, and so each map is a product of compromises, omissions, and interpretations, depending on what information a cartographer wishes to show. The Rand McNally road atlases that we keep in our cars and consult before journeys bear this out, privileging the interstate highway system over other routes or natural features. Maps construct, not reproduce, the world, writes Denis Wood: "All maps, inevitably, unavoidably, necessarily embody their author's prejudices, biases, and partialities" (24). Even a good map, says Mark Monmonier in *How to Lie with Maps,* "to present a useful and truthful picture," must tell a multitude of "white lies" (1).

In addition to "post-structuralist agnosticism," Denis Cosgrove cites at least three more reasons for the contemporary revisioning and rethinking of maps. First, globalization and the end of the Cold War have redrawn political maps, rendering boundaries permeable. Second, more and more people fly, seeing the landscape below them "as a map," and the widespread availability of aerial and satellite photography have also made this view a familiar one. And, third, information technology (such as Geographic Information Systems, or GIS) has made it possible to manipulate spatial data at great speed (for example, altering a map of the United States into the electoral map of 2000). This continuous transformation of spatial coordinates produces a kind of "kinetic cartography." This change, along with the "naturalism" of computer-generated images of the earth, has "destabilized the conventional architecture, meanings, and significance of mapping and of maps, helping to expose to scrutiny the 'authored' nature of the latter" (6).

Yet, perhaps there are more "natural," more subtle, kinds of surveying and mapping? Kent Ryden describes how early land surveying in New England (circa 1800) was less an imposition on land than a recording of something more experientially felt. Private property was not yet "surveyed in relation to abstract geometrical points" and "geodetic baselines" (27). "Instead, landhold-ings were outlined through the 'metes-and-bounds' system, a means of meas-urement which depended on the surveyor's immediate and personal contact with the landscape" (27). The surveyor walked a piece of property, measuring straight lines from one landmark to another; when these lines were drawn on paper, "the resulting irregular polygon" established the limits of the property, with landmarks taking the form of "witness trees, durable hardwoods that could be marked by an ax with identifying blazes" (27). Still, surveying in this way superimposed the straight line, which could be measured, over the diver-sity of natural features. By other side measurements, the surveyor "picks up" the "curves of his stream or the wanderings of his roads, or the positions of his hilltops and his houses" (Debenham 5). The resulting landmarks and lines were written on paper to form a deed; however, this map alone did not mean the property was "owned" yet by anyone.

The metes-and-bounds system was a process Thoreau would have been fa-miliar with and one he describes in "Walking," but he worried too that he would see woodlots instead of the woods, polygons instead of organic nature. With the government surveys led by King and Powell in the 1870s, mapmaking was becoming even more scientific and removed from experience. Verplanck

Colvin, who surveyed the Adirondacks beginning in 1872, writes about "improved" methods of surveying and equipment. Theodolites (basically, telescopes pivoted around horizontal and vertical axes) gradually replaced compasses because they could measure angles more accurately. Starting from a baseline, a series of triangles could cover vast distances:

> Thus gradually the region is covered with a [projected] net-work of triangles, great and small, the sides of these triangles being exact distances, as accurately known as though they were nicely graduated ribbons of steel, stretched taut. These triangle sides have also, in every instance, their true astronomical bearings determined from observations of circumpolar stars; and the *termini* under the signals being marked by indestructible monuments of stone. (emphasis added, 20)

The termini thus produced an astronomically accurate map. Colvin adds that the "*true places* of lakes, mountains, or passes, are exactly determined, *so that the actual areas are known*. Should all the old land-lines marked on trees be destroyed by fire, they could be replaced and restored by reference to monuments marking the triangulation" (emphasis added, 20). Surveying signals a kind of triumph over space for Colvin, in which "steel" geometric patterns contain the wilderness.

John Charles Frémont, "The Pathfinder," describes the thrill of mapmaking from his expeditions in the West in the 1840s:

> Mapmaking is an interesting process. It must be exact. First, the foundations must be laid in observations made in the field; then the reduction of these observations to latitude and longitude; afterward the projection of the map, and the laying down upon it of positions fixed by the observations; then the tracing from the sketchbooks of the lines of the rivers, the forms of the lakes, the contours of the hills. Specially is it interesting to those who have laid in the field these various foundations to see them all brought *into the final shape*—fixing on a small sheet the results of laborious travel over the waste regions, and giving to them an *enduring place on the world's surface*. (emphasis added, 75)

For Frémont, space hardly exists until it is brought within the two-dimensional surface of the map, "the final shape." For both Colvin and Frémont, space has no "enduring place" on the "world's surface" until mapped.

Mapping, for them, is the way "true places" are known, but, as Melville knew, they must also be written and explained.

The data Frémont and other surveyors gather comes together into a compressed expression of geographic knowledge: the map. For surveyors, maps summarize a storm of mathematical data into a whorl of contour lines, turning chaos into cosmos. They provide the final depiction of the space the mapmakers travel through, observe, measure, and describe, reframing observed information into a scale model of a geographic reality. In making the unknown known, maps are useful for other explorers, for locating resources, for travelers enjoying the "sights," or for settlers. An enduring version of Western history has it that independent pioneers pushed westward with little idea of the course ahead. In reality they were aided in their journey by the U.S. Government's Army Corps of Topographical Engineers, with surveyed passages and detailed maps.

We can all read and understand maps with little training. Surface features of the earth are keyed to symbolic and conventional characters on the map so that information may be instantaneously and easily extracted. But what do maps imply about how we understand the space viewed within their frame? For Carolyn Merchant, drawing on the ideas of Michel Foucault, mapping and surveying are aspects of domination: "Through the scrutiny of the surveyor, the land is seen as bounded object. A spatial perspective leads to its management and control" (51). One important epistemological consequence of maps is that the representation of land in spatial terms flattens out the land and halts it in time, implying "a static understanding of the environment" (Bryson 14). The spatial narrative of the map freezes the events on the map, devaluing them from sites of power to inert, planar surfaces. The names on the map fix positions and serve as starting points for future exploration, bearers of little more than their own individual names, side by side. Without its history, the map space is "open" to new visions of its potential uses.

Frémont's first draft of a map had such an effect. His father-in-law, Senator Thomas Hart Benton, who "had expected to find the map in progress, was disappointed to see only the blank projection. But his disappointment gave way to interest of another kind when he saw spread out on the tables the evidences of the material first to be digested" (75). The map-in-progress begins to create a desire: Benton "dwelled on the unoccupied country beyond the Missouri and the existing uncertain and incomplete knowledge concerning it" (76). Frémont then remarks, "The thought of penetrating into the recesses of that wilderness filled me with enthusiasm—I saw visions" (76). The blank space on the map effectively creates a static, passive space the explorer may "discover" and supplement with "visions," though it is also a force pulling him in.

A second epistemological consequence of mapmaking is its reliance upon the "visual perspective" (Bryson 14). In constructing maps, surveyors assume a position where the landscape can be viewed. This map view provides an omniscient perspective—what we might call the "master of all I survey" viewpoint.[2] The surveyor looks down and sees all when looking at the map or when gaining a summit to survey the view. From this perspective, the land is a bounded object, within his control, seen but not yet possessing the "sense of place." There is a "lack," which in many cases must by complemented by the written text, by language, to transform map space to human place.

In *Mapping It Out*, geographer Mark Monmonier describes how maps can complement an author's writing: "By helping readers visualize regions and comprehend relative distances and other geographic relationships, maps amplify an author's sentences and paragraphs" (3). Visual information can be processed more easily and quickly than text, and it can be more specific, showing rather than telling. But all too often maps frustrate literary cartographers rather than aid them. An early textbook, *Map Making* (1936), sums up their growing feeling of the artificiality of imposing straight lines on nature: "The detail of nature, such as we wish to record on maps, is woefully disorderly and haphazard. Rivers never run straight, hilltops dot the country without any apparent pattern, and lakes are shapeless things, while contours meander dubiously round the hillsides" (Debenham 4). Thoreau pierces through maps in the woods of Maine and in *Walden* into something more metaphysical; Clarence King transforms the maps he travels with of the Great Basin into a different visual phenomena, a mirage; and John Wesley Powell left a map out of his *Explorations of the Colorado River and Its Canyons* because he feared one would not adequately represent the Grand Canyon or the story of his experiences there. Although maps can perform an expository function in service to writing, as an accompaniment to the literature of place their status is often dubious, conferring a spurious authority over the land, competing with rather than complementing the felt life of the written word.

THE BEGINNINGS OF A
LITERARY CARTOGRAPHY IN AMERICA

From its beginnings, American literature was closely intertwined with American surveying. The new nation's writers took very seriously the practice of delimiting boundaries. Smith's *A Map of Virginia* (1610) begins, "Virginia is a Country in America that lyeth betweene the degrees of 34 and 44 of the north latitude. The bounds thereof on the East side are the great Ocean. On the South lyeth Florida: on the North *nova Francia*. As for the West thereof, the limits are unknowne" (1). Smith gives the coordinate dimensions of latitude to apportion the "New" World into a universal system the Old World could recognize and assimilate. He assigns the new place a structure and location, within the definite and apparently coherent framework of a map.

Thomas Jefferson's *Notes on the State of Virginia* (1785) begins much the same way, revising and filling in Smith's verbal map:

> Virginia is bounded on the East by the Atlantic: on the North by a line of latitude, crossing the Eastern Shore through Watkin's point, being about 37°.57.' North latitude; from thence by a streight line to Cinquac, near the mouth of the Patowmac; thence by the Patowmac, which is common to Virginia and Maryland, to the first fountain of its northern branch; thence by a meridian line, passing through that fountain till it intersects a line running East and West, in latitude 39°.43.'42.4" which divides Maryland from Pennsylvania, and which was marked by Messrs. Mason and Dixon; thence by that line, and a continuation of it westwardly to the completion of five degrees of longitude from the eastern boundary of Pennsylvania, in the same latitude, and thence by a meridian line to the Ohio: On the West by the Ohio and Missisipi [rivers], to latitude 36°.30'. (emphasis added, 3)

Jefferson's dimensions are more precise and refined than Smith's, giving measurements in degrees and minutes, and he also provides more place names. The "great Ocean" is now the Atlantic, and more is known about those western limits. He mentions that the north line crosses through "Watkin's point," a site more locally defined than the territories of "nova Francia" or Florida. Then the description follows the Potomac River, common to two states, until "the first fountain of its northern branch." There are at least three levels of geographical definition in the passage: the coordinate system, local place-names, and dividing lines or boundaries. Like any linguistic sign, "a place-name requires a community of speakers who will agree that a name should be attached to a certain piece of the landscape," and natural boundaries are features of the landscape that predated the signs (D'Abate 65). Jefferson's nomenclature stems from a living local community, there on the ground, whereas Smith's names, in a sense, belong only to maps. Natural boundaries denote in plain sight to human cultures where one locality stops and another begins. From abstract coordinate system through humanly designated place-names to natural features of the landscape, geographic knowledge becomes more tangible and closer to our experience of places and geographical boundaries, to the "cognitive maps" we draw of them inside our minds.[3] In Jefferson's description, the marks on the map make sense less to a remote audience than to the one living within or near those boundaries. Jefferson's boundaries are humanized, made familiar, known locally and on a smaller scale.

And yet, Jefferson was also responsible for developing the system used to divide western townships into rectilinear plots. Congress passed a modified version of Jefferson's system in 1785, and it became a template for defining the American hinterland in the West, mirroring the system that had worked in the East. The Land Ordinance of 1785 established that everything west of the Alleghenies would be surveyed into six-square-mile townships, regardless of topography. It provided for the scientific surveying and systematic subdivision of the northwest territory's lands. The system was an efficient, democratic way to identify parcels, reduce border disputes, and keep records, but not everyone ended up with a fair share, nor were parcels of equal value, especially for farming. Speculators moved in quickly to divide up the parcels for profit, without ever settling. The system provided abstraction and speculation rather than a humanistic experience of place.

Jefferson's gridding survives. It is the basis of township borders, cut at right angles across the land, carving up America into "remorseless rectangularity," as geographer Wilbur Zelinsky describes it, "and with the greatest possible disregard for the sphericity of the earth" (47). When flying over the Midwest, one sees the striking geometry of these shapes, a quilt of square brown patches framing irrigated green circles, inscribed by technology, the pattern only occasionally disturbed by a jagged set of hills or the veins of a watershed. The lines are not landmarks that could be committed to memory, as could, perhaps, the meandering Potomac or its "first fountain." In *Common Landscape of America* (1982), John Stilgoe calls the grid an expression of Enlightenment abstraction: "the grid objectified national, not regional, order, and [by the 1860s] no one wondered at rural space marked by urban rectilinearity" (106–7).

Stilgoe, however, paints a complex picture of the grid. The land was laid out in such strict linear patterns that corrections had to be made for the curvature of the earth, producing irregularities in areas and zones supposed to be equivalent. Legislators revised the 1785 law and its neat, geometrical pattern so the grid could catch up with curved and converging meridians (99–107). According to Hildegard Binder Johnson in *Order Upon the Land* (1976), at every fourth township (or twenty-four miles) surveyors established a new baseline or "correction line" from which they shifted meridian lines farther west, often creating a dogleg in north-south running section roads (57). Before this Enlightenment system, "natural" topographical features determined how areas in the West would be laid out. When "squareness" arrived, it left a mixture of cartographic systems written upon the land from different surveyor-authors in different historical periods.

Still, for early American cartographers, the landscape beyond the known was "blank," even its extent and ending obscure, therefore needing some system with features to fill it in. Their desire to know and thereby possess those landscapes is well encapsulated by Marlow in Conrad's *Heart of Darkness* (1902): "Now when I was a little chap I had a passion for maps.... At that time there were many blank spaces on the earth, and when I saw one that looked particularly inviting on a map (but they all look that) I would put my finger on it and say, When I grow up I will go there" (20–21). Conrad's passage is often invoked by postcolonial critics to discuss the map's dual role in colonization, of both opening up space and then closing it in (by erasing existing names and then replacing them with their own). The blank spots on the map, those exciting spaces of white paper, entice the explorer and his imagination; they provide him with his initial motivation. These blank areas on maps are places where the explorer's—and the writer's—imagination may have free rein. The creation of blankness constructs a beginning tabula rasa where the writer's fantasies originate.

Beginning with Smith's description of "limits unknowne," the conception of western America as space and not yet place, as a blank spot on the map (or terra incognita), was a notion that was deeply embedded in the national consciousness. In *Errand into the Wilderness* (1956), Perry Miller called it a "vacant wilderness" (vii), and Roderick Nash in *Wilderness and the American Mind* has shown that wilderness was intensely feared outside man-shaped structures, where formlessness reigned (26–30). Nathaniel Hawthorne describes a forest chaos in "Young Goodman Brown" that is "heathen," "dark," "benighted," and "unconverted," the "moral wilderness" Hester Prynne must also travel through. Therefore, those spaces needed to be contained, even "redeemed" by early explorers. Yet, the blank spaces on maps, in the West and elsewhere, took on a different symbolic value for ecologist Aldo Leopold, writing in the 1940s (294). For him, they were still the locations of wilderness and of original mysteries, but now also sites of vital biological life. They could be valued not for their invitation to be filled in and possessed, but for their representation of fecundity and freedom. Leopold wrote about the need, not to chart a course through the unknown, but to discern landmarks and natural signs to achieve a sense of place.

Though surveyors such as King and Powell went to map blank spaces, to fill them in with features of landscape, as writers their purpose often became somewhat different. Even as they were mapping places and giving them visual substance, they projected some ambivalence about the institutional project in which they were participating, as mapping the places took away their allure, their attraction to the explorer. When a portion of the globe was mapped, Marlow says, "It had ceased to be a blank space of delightful mystery" (22). If the role of the surveyor was to present an abstract topography by drawing it into the grids of the map, the writer was often engaged in a reverse process, creating a substantive place in the reader's imagination, unmeasurable and volatile, the "true" places Melville noted as impossible to map (59).

Reading these American literary cartographers, we enter a dialogue through which a community has evolved and made a place out of space. They have imposed an abstract plan on nature, but have also "discovered" how the places they surveyed retain a qualitative, unmapped value. Jefferson writes in the *Notes* that "the height of our mountains has not yet been estimated with any degree of exactness," and adds, "the mountains of the Blue ridge, and of these the Peaks of Otter, are thought to be of a greater height . . . than any others in our country" (20). Today, we know that the Peaks of Otter are not as high as their Blue Ridge counterparts to the south (Mount Mitchell, part of the Black Mountain chain of the Blue Ridge, rises to 6,684 feet), but to Jefferson, whose Monticello looked out on their peaks, the Blue Ridge Mountains rose the "highest."[4] Of course, Jefferson was speaking both literally and figuratively, as editors Michael Branch and Dan Philippon suggest in a recent collection of regional nature writing titled *The Height of Our Mountains* (1998) (1–2). Just as the mountains had yet to be accurately surveyed, the new nation had also yet to discover its potential.

Beginning with Jefferson, the scientific enterprise of surveying the mountains has had a strong connection to the literary project of coordinating the height of our mountains to the depth of our character. The voyage of discovery to what lay over those mountains was Jefferson's dream. As Frank Bergon has written, Jefferson sought for some twenty years to find the personnel and funds to do what Lewis and Clark finally achieved in 1804 when they launched from St. Louis ("Wilderness" 131). Prior to their journey, that vast terrain was the site of political and territorial battles, subject to murky claims by Great Britain, Spain, France, and Russia. Jefferson tried to assure the minister of Spain, the Marqués de Case Yujo, that the proposed expedition was a "literary pursuit," that is, an aesthetic quest, but he told Congress something else—that he was primarily interested in the voyage for its possible trade routes and commerce (*Journals*, De Voto xxv).

Although the commercial and political ramifications of Lewis and Clark's trek are well known, they should not completely overshadow the literary pursuit. In fact, as Bergon notes, the trip may have succeeded more as a literary pursuit than as a commercial one: The expedition failed to find the hoped-for practical water route across the continent—there was no Northwest Passage. Lewis and Clark also failed to find workable routes to capture the Canadian fur trade and failed to make a lasting peace with native peoples, both elements of Jefferson's instructions ("Wilderness" 133). But as a "literary pursuit," a description and narration of the lands, animals, and people of the American West, the "expedition succeeded in ways that are more appreciable after 200 years" ("Wilderness" 134). Judging by the popular success of Stephen Ambrose's *Undaunted Courage* (one million copies sold as of August 2001), the expedition still maintains its hold on American imaginations, equivalent to a national epic. In line with the heroes of the *Epic of Gilgamesh* and the *Odyssey*, Bergon observes, Lewis and Clark adventured into unfamiliar and frightening wilderness, and came home to tell the story (129).

When they returned in 1806, Jefferson greeted Lewis and Clark with "unspeakable joy," noting that even the "humblest" of American citizens looked forward to the publication of the journals (qtd. in "Wilderness" 134). Jefferson envisioned a "revised, polished version of the raw journals," similar to the literate accounts of Bartram's *Travels* (134). From his instructions, the men were to observe with "great pains and accuracy, to be entered distinctly, & intelligibly for others as well as yourself . . . to fix the latitude and longitude of the places at which they were taken" (482). These mathematical observations that "fixed" the unshaped spaces were to be reproduced in duplicate and triplicate to guard from "accidental losses"—they were the most important product of the expedition.

Yet, Jefferson had also wanted the men to acquaint themselves with the "people inhabiting the line you will pursue" (482). He could hardly speak about the interior of the continent without referring to geometry. Explorers would map lines that inhabitants would live on. Lewis and Clark were to not only know the people, "their language, traditions, monuments . . . food, clothing, & domestic accommodations," but also the "face of the country" (483). What animals, minerals, volcanoes, and climate were there? In their journals Lewis and Clark were to put a face on an otherwise unknown "body."

However, in the actual journals, we find the men coming up short against their Enlightenment expectations of harmony and order in the wilderness. Instead of perfectly measurable and symmetrical rivers that led quietly to the ocean, they encountered floods, storms, grizzlies, "feet torn and bleeding," "incessant rain, fleas, and mosquitoes" (Bergon, "Wilderness" 147). One region Lewis found to be "dark and gloomy": "The tow[er]ing and projecting rocks in many places seem ready to tumble on us." On their map, this region looked to Jefferson like a labyrinth of lines "scattered confusedly" (qtd. in Bergon, "Wilderness" 147).

The experience proved difficult to "map." This "new" territory necessitated a new vocabulary as, pursuing their instructions from Jefferson, Lewis and Clark sought to record everything they saw. Their prose struggles to give expression to the new country and the native inhabitants. According to Bergon, the words they coined, twisted, and adapted for the occasion produced the addition of over fifteen hundred new English words, "many of them adapted from Native American languages and frontier French, others jammed into new linguistic hybrids, like 'mule deer' and 'prairie dog'" ("The Journals" 142–43). Not only were their maps inadequate to this experience, so was the language they brought with them. Surveyors' maps would seem to proffer authority and control over a particular space, but the writing in their journals registers a different experience: confusion, anxiety, wonder, elation.

SURVEYING AND ITS "PLEASURES OF HOPE"

Later in the nineteenth century, the debate between measureless emotion and scientific and realistic measurement played out in the influential literary periodicals of the day. In 1848 Thoreau sent his "Ktaadn" to Horace Greeley ("Go west, young man, go west"), who published parts of it in his New York *Tribune,* and then sent it on to the *Union Magazine,* edited by Caroline Kirkland. Ten years later Thoreau published "Chesuncook" in *The Atlantic Monthly,* under editor James Russell Lowell. King also published in *The Atlantic Monthly*; the first chapter from *Mountaineering in the Sierra Nevada* appeared in 1871, taking editorial direction from William Dean Howells. And John Wesley Powell, who perhaps had the least amount of literary background of the three, published excerpts of his *The Exploration of the Colorado River and Its Canyons* in *Scribner's Monthly* in 1874, then under the direction of Richard Watson Gilder. Powell published the more scientific "Physical Features of the Valley of the Colorado" in *The Popular Science Monthly,* which counted William James and John Dewey among its contributors.

John Charles Frémont also had literary ambitions, possibly aided by his wife Jessie Benton Frémont, who was a far more prolific and accomplished writer than he was.[5] With the journals of Lewis and Clark as his model, Frémont made a concerted effort to include data as frequently and as accurately possible. However, similar to the works of both Powell and King, Frémont's work is part scientific exploration and part adventure narrative. He constructs scenes less interesting for their scientific precision than for their use of metaphor. In one "rather picturesque spot," Frémont blends a dispassionate scientific voice in the poetic description of the parts of a spring, describing it "in form like a jet," as "a steamboat in motion," and with "urn-mouthed form" (221). The theoretician of the picturesque, William Gilpin, warned in *Essays on Picturesque Beauty* (1794) that "it is not from this *scientific* employment, that we derive our chief pleasure." Instead, we gain an *impression* of the scene: "We rather *feel* than *survey* it" (50). Aesthetic codes and scientific ones collide here: The whimsy of a subjective impressionism, allied to an individual mind's conception of place and the subjectivities of metaphor, belies the uniformity of maps, and the detached, objective writing common to scientific exploration narratives. Beneath the figuration of objectivity, surveyors' places can change at will, and the "real" mapped world begins dissolving into a world of the imagination.

Of course, mappers and explorers have always had strong imaginations. From Coronado to de Soto to Ponce De Leon, fantasy has often driven cartography. As geographer John L. Allen writes, the imagination has had a powerful influence on exploration, providing explorers with what Allen calls the "lands of myth and waters of wonder."

> Imagination becomes a behavioral factor in geographical discovery as courses of action are laid out according to preconceived images; later decisions based on field observations may be distorted by these images. The results of exploration are modified by reports written and interpreted in the light of persistent illusions and by attempts made to fit new information into partly erroneous systems and frameworks of geographical understanding. (43)

The first modern world atlas, Abraham Ortelius's *Theatrum Orbis Terrarum* (1570), has no Alaska and no Great Lakes, but only a vast Arctic sea that presses down on the top of the American continent. This continent struggles toward definition, and may still contain a Northwest Passage or other "waters of wonder." On John Speed's *America* (1626), California appears as an island. Even after the exterior boundaries began to be fixed, the interior was still guesswork. And so, early explorers relied on "the best authorities" to record what they had not seen and charted for themselves. These early maps are projections of a wish, drawn and interpreted according to not only what was verifiable but what explorers *hoped* to find before they encountered it.

In 1539 Spanish explorer Fray Marcos de Niza spoke of what he and his fellows conceived as the "gold in the Seven Cities of Cibola." The interior landscape for the Spanish spoke of boundless gold, and it pulled them farther and farther into the continent searching for productive mines (Poulsen 28). Subsequently, tales of lost Spanish mines spoke to the westerner, as the inhabitant of this visionary landscape, up through the Gold Rush. Another mythic image that dominated in the minds of many was of a great river that flowed west to San Francisco Bay from the inland desert of Utah or Nevada. According to

Bernard De Voto, Jefferson spoke of it in his instructions to Lewis and Clark (DeVoto xlvii). This river was imagined to be a major drainage system from the interior of the American West to California. Its source was repeatedly searched for but not found. In the words of Richard Poulsen, author of *Landscape of the Mind*, "[The river's] existence was so real, so culturally felt, that it was mapped" (32). Jed Smith dispelled the myth in his 1826 exploration, but maps kept the legend of the Rio Buenaventura (literally, good fortune) alive, until, finally, John Charles Frémont eliminated it from his map in 1843. Geographically, of course, the river did not exist, but culturally, it was a reality. This cultural dream was transformed into the fixity of a map for decades, a mythical frontier etched onto paper and into thought and memory. These cultural and personal expectations can influence and define geography more than meticulous surveying, anticipating it before *contact* is made.

The Seven Cities of Cibola had a counterpart in the northeast. Both England and France found a rival, if only in the imagination, in the myth of Norumbega, the name sixteenth-century explorers gave to the territory known today as New England. In his *Cape Cod*, Thoreau writes of how Champlain is convinced that those who speak of the great city have never seen it, "but repeat mere rumor" (189). In *American Beginnings: Exploration, Culture, and Cartography in the Land of Norumbega* (1994), Richard D'Abate writes that the puzzle of how this place gets written down on maps and then disappears, how it migrates through many degrees in latitude and can at once name a city, region, and river, illustrates "how deeply human knowledge may be, at any point, constructed in its own self-reflecting imagery" (69).

Neither Columbus nor John Smith nor Lewis and Clark "discovered" the lands they explored or surveyed. One of the powerful myths of exploration is that knowledge gathering, especially objective surveying or mapping, takes place through the explorer's seeing "new" land for the first time. According to this myth, as Simon Ryan has shown in *The Cartographic Eye*, the explorer accurately and disinterestedly describes the "new land that he sees" (54). But far from being a "fresh and innocent transcription" of the natural world, the writing of surveyors is generated by existing personal and "cultural formations" (54). One of their fundamental assumptions is that they will "discover" places, but while "discovery" produces an "initial disturbance to a particular set of expectations," what is found through an examination of these literary cartographers is that discovery has also been anticipated (10). Exploration and even surveying proceeds through a combination of real and imagined geographies. Empirical experiences in the field are understood, interpreted, and influenced by expectations, desires, and preconceptions.

To illustrate the place as predicted, I turn to an example from John R. Lambert, one of the surveyors for the *Reports of the Explorations and Surveys, to Ascertain the Most Practical Route for a Railroad from the Mississippi River to the Pacific Ocean* (1853–54), made under the direction of the War Department. Lambert enters the valley of the Clark Fork River in Montana and a cultivable intermontane valley, calling it an "an aggregate of everything that is sublime and beautiful in scenery" (172). In other words, the valley is a total of familiar aesthetic categories, the sublime and the beautiful, to which might be added the picturesque.[6] Standing on the riverbank and looking up the same valley, Lambert is drawn into the scene and its resemblance to these aesthetic "maps": "the view embraces all the elements of grandeur and beauty that can be imagined in mountain scenery, and in an extent which an artist would choose for a single picture" (173). The scene is as beautiful as a painting—nature is imitating art in Lambert's figuration:

> It is late in the morning when the sun overtops the crowded mountains and lights their deep recesses, gilding the autumnal foliage of the little islands, which derive additional beauty from their clear reflection in the still black water created by the meeting of rivers; the massive outlines of the foreground are still enveloped in shade, while the mighty opening, rocks and trees, pool and torrent, are glowing in a blaze of light. Such are the scenes that reward the way-worn tourist throughout this great region, and it is almost sorrowful to reflect that very purpose of our explorations will soon dispel the "enchantment that distance lends," when it will no longer be an event in life to have crossed the mountains. (173)

When he reflects on the place's beauty, he realizes he is at cross-purposes with the institutional endeavor of the report—to locate a suitable site for the railroad. The mapping of the area and its potential consequences could harm the "enchantment" of it, as if measuring and surveying would make it less a work of art (in a curious conflation of nature and art) or a spellbound dream. The railroad will make the mountain crossings easier and the place more known, and therefore, Lambert worries, less sublime. Instead, he wants to keep this space at such a distance that it can be held up in a "glowing blaze of light," numinous, full of supernatural glory. The sublime presented nature as a symbol of omnipotent perfection, a sign of God's presence. To order, alter, or disrupt that nature was to violate that sublimity, and cause it to disappear.

The phrase the "enchantment that distance lends" is adapted from Scottish poet Thomas Campbell (1771–1844) in *The Pleasures of Hope* (1799):[7]

> Why do those cliffs of shadowy tint appear
> More sweet than all the landscape near?—
> 'Tis distance lends enchantment to the view,
> And robes the mountain in its azure hue.
> Thus with delight we linger to survey
> The promised joys of life's unmeasured way. (1–2)

Campbell refers to the effect produced in the viewer by remote landscapes, ideal scenes of "delight" that the imagination revels in contemplating. He continues, in the next few lines, that what is "dim-discovered" is more pleasing than what is already known, as it resides in anticipation and hope, an interior landscape projected in mystery.

Though Lambert most likely joined the railroad survey to explore and map for the purposes of economic expansion and science, he also wished to see the land in an aesthetic way, in the "dim-discovered" light of the imagination, and worried that the scientific report wouldn't represent it adequately. He wrote his scientific report as if it were literary narrative, making recommendations not only on where the railroad route should go, but on how the land should be seen and used—as art. In a sense he wants to leave the space blank, as potential, a place always awaiting further exploration. He faces what John Tallmadge calls the paradox that explorers eventually confront: "their discoveries destroy the very mysteries that allured them" (1178).

This image of a blank and sublime space celebrates two central myths of the American past—the free land to be explored by heroic individuals and the regenerative properties of it that define and enlarge that individual—but each act of exploration and reporting limits the richness of his experience and limits the place. Another problem with Lambert's sense of place is that it is seen only as it resembles previous aesthetic "maps," but they were not imminently portable in the arid West. To really see the place, Lambert needed a more particularized understanding, an "enchantment" that involved a history and experience of the place, not a "lingering" and "unmeasured" one. At the very least, he needed to explore the interior landscape from which he viewed the place.

I have not included surveyors Ferdinand Vandiveer Hayden or Lt. George M. Wheeler of the "Great Surveys" because they never paused, like Lambert, to question the purpose of their endeavor. Also, they wrote for a different audience. Their scientific reports are interesting mostly to scientists, whereas the narratives of Powell and King blur genres, providing both factual information about the views in their transit as well as moments when that view breaks down, adding art to the literal landscape. Too, the narratives of Powell and King attract a wide and durable following, both a century ago and today; like the writing of Thoreau and Stegner, they continue to influence how we think and write about place.

Nor am I interested in places that reside only in the dim-discovered light of the imagination that are famous in our literature, where the literal aspects of place are sacrificed to achieve symbol.[8] I focus on writers who were encountering real places, though they are imagined as they are experienced; on maps with a geographical referent, though the maps can present their author's biases; and on nonfiction writing that provokes reflection about the environment by expanding on a cartographic means to understand a geographical area. I examine how the sense of place, itself with various depths, heights and latitude, gets written into geographical areas through literature.

FROM AN INTERIOR AND
SUBLIME LANDSCAPE TO PLACE

Though Lambert worried about the detrimental effects of his survey, cartographic achievements in America often fueled a self-fulfilling political and economic program.[9] William Byrd writes in the *History of the Dividing Line* (1728) that it is strange that "the Government has never thought it worth the Expense of making an accurate Survey of the Mountains, that we might be Masters of that Natural Fortification before the French" (240). Surveying could have not only political advantages but economic ones: "Another Reason to invite us to Secure this great Ledge of Mountains is the Probability that very Valuable Mines may be discover'd there" (240). Surveying and mapping were useful for finding resources and "claiming" land. According to the *Oxford English Dictionary*, the word *claim* took on a new meaning in Australia and the

United States in the late eighteenth and early nineteenth century: "a piece of land allotted and taken, especially for mining purposes" (261).

In America, cartography was a tool that enabled the beginning nation's leading men to identify resources and control access to those resources. According to a University of Virginia exhibit (1995) and Web site, *Exploring the West from Monticello: A Perspective in Maps from Columbus to Lewis and Clark*, "A knowledge of surveying gave Virginia gentry inside information on the choice of new lands.... George Washington chose surveying as a career, in part to insure that he would have access to the most desirable properties. When laying off the bounty lands received for services in the French and Indian War, Washington reserved the best lands for himself" (III, par. 5). John Noble Wilford writes in *The Mapmakers* that "no one could have been surprised, in the atmosphere of colonial Virginia, when young George Washington decided on surveying as his first profession. Land was the way to affluence and social position, and where there was land to be claimed, parceled, and settled, there had to be surveyors" (178).

If surveying mapped economic resources and political and private property, it also fueled and was concomitant with a desire for self-fulfillment—the height of our mountains. In his essay "Walking," surveyor Henry David Thoreau presented an afternoon ramble as an instance of the migration of European culture, proposing that the character and culture of America would rise in proportion to its environment:

> If the moon looks larger here than in Europe, probably the sun looks larger also. If the heavens of America appear infinitely higher, and the stars brighter, I trust that these facts are symbolical of the height to which the philosophy and poetry and religion of her inhabitants may one day soar.... I trust that we shall be more imaginative, that our thoughts will be clearer, fresher and more ethereal, as our sky—our understanding more comprehensive and broader, like our plains—our intellect generally on a grander scale, like our thunder and lightning, our rivers and mountains and forests—and our hearts shall even correspond in the breadth and depth and grandeur to our inland seas.... Else to what end does the world go on, and why was America discovered? (205)

"The question was rhetorical," writes Wallace Stegner in the essay "The Twilight of Self-Reliance": "[H]e knew the answer" (MSF 190). To Thoreau and many of his generation, the story of peopling the New World, remaking a culture and society into something new and refreshed, was the greatest human opportunity ever. The culture and character of the new nation, the interior landscape, was to grow in response to the external environment. And the external environment would be seen from this country of the mind.

In his "Essay on American Scenery" (1835), painter Thomas Cole addressed those who thought American scenery deficient compared to that of Europe. In gazing on Niagara, where the sublime and the beautiful are brought together, "we feel as though a great void had been filled in our minds—our conceptions expand—We become a part of what we behold!" (105). In his introduction to *The Home Book of the Picturesque* (1852), E. L. Magoon wrote that "we proceed to show that, in the physical universe ... what is most exalted, is most influential on the best minds; and that, for these reasons, national intellect receives a prevailing tone from the peculiar scenery that most abounds" (4). Sublime scenery will produce sublime minds. "Grand natural scenery tends to permanently affect the character of those cradled in its bosom," he continues (25). In the same volume, in "American and European Scenery Compared," James Fenimore Cooper concluded that although Europe has the "noblest scenery," we "claim for America the freshness of a most promising youth, and a species of natural radiance that carries the mind with reverence to the source of all that is glorious around us" (69). Cooper, of course, had never been west, and Thoreau had never gone abroad.

American writers and artists gathered vitality from their landscape. Addressing his remarks to skeptical Europeans, Cole continues, "We have many a spot as umbrageous as Vallombrosa, and as picturesque as the solitudes of Vaucluse, but Milton and Petrarch have not hallowed them by their footsteps and immortal verse" (108). To look down on Mount Albano or Rome, he adds, is to have the mind "peopled with the gigantic associations of the storied past, but he who stands on the mounds of the West, the most venerable remains of American antiquity, may experience the emotion of the sublime, but it is the sublimity of a shoreless ocean unislanded by the recorded deeds of man" (108). The sublime authenticated the new lands. Without previous "maps," Americans would be free from the weight of earlier geographical perceptions to "discover" this noblest of emotions. For vast prairies, immense extensions of space, awesome mountains of an inhuman scale, the varied landscape was called—and perhaps still is—sublime.

The sublime is the response invoked for places that are "unislanded by the recorded deeds of man." Though the sublime, being ineffable, is unmappable, like maps (mostly spatial representations) the sublime locates places outside history. Without previous "maps" to go by, writers and artists could experience the indescribable, although they would then go on to describe it. In the view of many American artists and writers, from such an "unislanded ocean" would come more fertile soils. According to the theories of Edmund Burke, Immanuel Kant, the English aesthetician William Gilpin, and others during the eighteenth century, "sublime landscapes were those rare places on earth where one had a chance to glimpse the face of God" (Cronon, "Wilderness" 475). The literary cartographers in this book were surveying sublime and last things. Clarence King went on to map the highest mountain (Whitney), Powell the deepest canyon, as if it were their teleological duty: Else to what end does the world go on, Thoreau says, and why *was* America discovered?

In nineteenth-century America, Thomas Jefferson was one of the first to enjoy sublime scenery. In *Notes on the State of Virginia,* he writes, "The Natural Bridge is the most sublime of nature's works, [and] though not comprehended under the present head, must not be pretermitted" (24). Though it surprises and disarms, it must not be disregarded or let go. Even though the "rapture of the spectator is indescribable," the bridge itself is not. Jefferson gives a summary description of its measurements: "The fissure, just at the bridge, is, by some admeasurments, 270 feet deep, by others only 205. It is about 45 feet wide at the bottom, and 90 feet at the top . . . Its breadth in the middle is about 60 feet, but more at the ends, and the thickness of the mass of the summit of the arch, about 40 feet" (24). The specificity of the measurements is undermined by their repeated disagreement and the uncertain adjective *about.* Jefferson proceeds to describe its shape: "The arch approaches the Semi-elliptical form; but the larger axis of the ellipsis, which would be the cord of the arch, is many times longer than the semi-axis which gives it it's [*sic*] height" (24). Only after describing its dimensions and geometry does Jefferson describe its effect on the observer:

> You involuntarily fall on your hands and feet, creep to the parapet and peep over it. Looking down from this height about a minute, gave me a violent head ach [*sic*] [but, when the eyes descend] . . . to the valley below, the sensation becomes delightful in the extreme. It is impossible for the

emotions, arising from the sublime, to be felt beyond what they are here: so beautiful an arch, so elevated, so light and springing, as it were, up to heaven, the rapture of the Spectator is really indescribable! (25)

The experience of the arch cannot be described, although its shape and dimensions can be. For Jefferson, the sublime is less an aspect of nature than an effect on the perceiver, and on the interior. Jefferson's sublime is closer to Kant's, for whom the sublime was an effect on the mind: "Sublimity, therefore, does not reside in any of the things of nature, but only in our mind" (504). But for Burke, in his *Philosophical Enquiry Into the Origin of our Ideas of the Sublime and the Beautiful* (1757), nature elicited the sublime; the external stimulus was central: "The passion caused by the great and sublime in *nature,* when those causes operate most powerfully, is Astonishment" (his emphasis, 57). Burke described characteristics of the sublime to include power, vastness, and magnificence, producing two levels of effects in the human observer: first, astonishment, terror, and "horror," and then admiration, reverence, and respect, though these latter are "inferior effects" (57).

Although admiration, reverence, and respect are germane to the passage above, horror and terror are not emphasized, as we shall also see in passages from Thoreau, King, and Powell. Compared to the sublime Burke describes, it seems a characteristic American trait to represent the awe and rapture of such experiences as primary. Repeatedly surveyors will describe from an elevation, a perspective point that is not only scientifically useful but emotionally charged, like Jefferson's description of the natural bridge. When Thoreau gets to a high position in Maine, he sees the "country west and south for a hundred miles. There it was, the State of Maine, which we had seen on the map, but not much like that" (66). Of course, the scene is more glorious than even Thoreau had expected, though it has been anticipated through his "map." Here is Frémont upon seeing his first view of the Great Salt Lake:

We reached the butte without any difficulty, and, ascending to the summit, immediately at our feet beheld the object of our anxious search—the waters of the inland Sea stretching in still and solitary grandeur far beyond the limit of our vision. It was one of the great points of the exploration; and as we looked eagerly over the lake in the first emotions of excited pleasure. . . . It was certainly a magnificent object, and a noble *terminus* to this part of our expedition; and to travelers so long shut up among moun-

tain ranges a sudden view over the expanse of silent waters had in it
something sublime. (243)

Whereas the "terminus" for the surveyor (from Adirondacks surveyor Colvin)
was the map, for the explorer it was the sublime.

Gaining a summit position has obvious benefits for Euro-American scientists, for it allows them to gain a "survey" (or surveillance) of a particular space.
To see the landscape unfolded before one from an elevated view is to see as one
views a map, omnisciently and remotely. Atop Mount Shasta, "from a com-
manding foothold in the sky," John Muir gazed "on the glorious landscapes
spread maplike around the immense horizon," himself at the center (62). Muir
saw the landscape as a map in other instances as well. From "Summer Days at
Mount Shasta," "The view from the summit in clear weather extends to an immense distance in every direction. Southeastward, the low volcanic portion of
the Sierra is seen like a map" (53). From "The San Gabriel Mountains," "I
reached the summit and I had time to make only a hasty survey of the topography of the wild basin now outspread maplike beneath" (50). From the high
falcon's perch, the earth looks orderly and patterned. But to move from the
map to the landscape, or even from the summit to the more sheltered forest or
canyon, is to undergo an interpretive or "hermeneutic shift" (Ihde 67). Shifting
from reading the landscape through a map to reading the landscape as place
requires a different mode of perception; one is no longer above that landscape
but in it, and so the perceiver has to adjust his vision. The surveyor must shift
from the scale of the map and the activity of mapping to something outside
the interpretive system he has been using. Though also an abstraction, the
sublime marks a perceptual shift from experiencing space as static, contained,
and seen, to space more active, less limited, and felt. The map reduces what is
immense to a scale the mind can understand. Similar to the map, the sublime
is a way of apportioning what humans see within a system of representation.
Though indescribable, it occupies a position in a stable, recognizable code, but
it carries with it different assumptions than the map.

Though Burke found them to be inferior effects, the sublime evokes reverence and respect. And in the process of sublimation, "we become part of what
we behold." The sublime attempts to describe the paradoxical sense of joy and
pain one senses in the presence of something that lies outside our powers of
representation. In her introduction to *The American Sublime,* Mary Arensberg

describes the sublime as it arrives from Longinus. The sublime, she states, is the "realm of things beyond ourselves, the dimension of otherness we can never know" (1). The sublime consists of an emotional response, to some power or authority, which causes a disruption of normal consciousness. Then, equilibrium is restored through an identification with that power or authority and a "sublimation" of that power. The sublimation takes the form of a defense, usually a mimesis, where the object is not mastered or known (or mapped), but is at least described (3-4). For Thomas Weiskel, author of *The Romantic Sublime*, equilibrium is restored through the mind's "constituting a fresh relation between itself and the object such that the very indeterminacy ... is taken as symbolizing the mind's relation to a transcendent order" (105).

The sublime is no less than a participation in the infinite, and it descends from animism, the belief that there was a "spirit of place." Author of several books on the topic of "place," Edward Relph writes that it was believed, and in some cultures still is, that localities were occupied by "spirits or gods who served both as their guardians and as a source of their identity. Mount Olympus was the home of Zeus, and every mountaintop, grove and spring was the home of some lesser deity who had to be acknowledged" (909). This spirit of place (or genius loci) "has its origins in this polytheistic sense of environments as diverse sites, each with a guardian spirit" or activity (Relph 909; also White, Jr., 10).

Of course, to those already living there, the landscape was not sublime in Burke's sense; it was their home, site of historical events and rich with spirits and with narrative. Leslie Marmon Silko maintains that the word *landscape* as we use it is misleading, assuming as it does that the viewer necessarily stands "*outside* or *separate from* the territory he or she surveys" (84). The truth is, we live inside our "maps." We use the word *landscape* as if we could escape, stand far enough back to see it clear, instead of looking at the ground beneath our feet. For Silko and her people, the Pueblo Indians, stories are firmly attached to the land, always told as people pass the relevant place. Such stories commemorate events, but they also provide crucial geographical information and thus function as maps: "stories described key landmarks and locations of fresh water. Thus a deer-hunt story might also serve as a 'map'" (88). These narratives serve as the central means through which oral cultures organize space, as a means of keeping "track" of animals or places. Such "story maps" hold an intimacy with landscape that modern visual maps do not. The map becomes a "mnemonic device," recording a sense of the land with such topographical specificity that the landscape is "suffused with memories" and meaning: The sacred, profane events that have taken place there survive, increasing the likelihood of stewardship (Lopez 278, 297).

In Australian aboriginal belief, the gods entered an empty landscape and made the natural features. The pathways they left tell the stories of their adventures. Deborah Tall observes that "the repeated, ritualistic walking of these sacred pathways by generations of aborigines, and the singing of their associated stories, has made this symbolic landscape more 'real' than the visible one" (23). The paths are called "songlines," a spiritual link to when the ancestors wandered the continent "singing the world into existence," as Bruce Chatwin describes it. "Each totemic ancestor, while traveling through the country, was thought to have scattered a trail of words and musical notes along the line of his footprints" (13). The songs serve as a "map" to their sacred sites (Tall 23).

Ever since people began interacting with their environment, they have sacralized natural terrain. According to Yi-Fu Tuan, "The ancient landscape was full of *numina* or local powers. One could hardly move about in the countryside without meeting a shrine, a sacred enclosure, an image, a sacred stone, a sacred tree" ("Geopiety" 18). In such symbol making, the landscape ceases to be a bounded, separate object, but numinous, imposing, alive, and real. To those who are *in-habit* with it, the landscape is a language, one many of us have lost the ability to read.

David Abram, author of *Spell of the Sensuous*, writes that among aboriginal cultures we find the most "intimate possible relation between land and human language. Language here is inseparable from human song and story, and the songs and stories, in turn, are inseparable from the shapes and features of the land" (172). For Abram, maps and writing further abstracted places, made them separable from the actual events where they occurred: "*[T]he visible text becomes the primary mnemonic activator of the spoken stories*" and not the places themselves. (183). In *Native American Testimony*, Peter Nabokov writes that "Indians generally viewed themselves as the earth's occupiers and custodians, not as its surveyors and engineers" (70). For native peoples, there was no need to make the perceptual shift from map to landscape. The land was already codified according to the web of stories they possessed in their minds, not a map they had in their hands.

The awareness of this different kind of knowing shocks surveyors. It shocks

Thoreau in the woods of Maine, King at the base of Mount Whitney, and Powell in the Grand Canyon. These writers operate from the stance of the map reader, the bird's-eye view, which orients in terms of vast distances. Indians usually do not "survey" the space from above, nor do they need a map to find their way. The clash of these different kinds of mapping represents a conceptual crux that European-American writers have had to confront as they worked over the centuries to form an American culture and literature, as they wrote about the American place and themselves as Americans.

In invoking the sublime, literary cartographers draw on a different interior landscape than the one they create in their scientific duties. If the map values the land for its pathways and resources, the sublime values it for its emotional richness. And though sublimity still draws something "useful" from the landscape, it is certainly an extraction that is less destructive to its source. When these surveyors come up against something they can't easily map, they invoke the sublime. Thoreau experiences the sense of awe in the "Burnt Lands" region of Mount Katahdin, a place that is, importantly, off the map he uses to get there. King finds the whole experience of mountaineering sublime, and Powell says the Grand Canyon is "the most sublime spectacle on earth" (390). For certain landscapes such as the Grand Canyon, or the Yosemite Valley that King mapped, the sublime is the "map" for the surveyors encountering it and for those who came after. Says John Elder, "Such repeated [sublime] responses [need not be seen as] a failure of imagination but rather a gathering of vision and energy around particular natural objects and phenomena" (xix).

As William Cronon has written in "The Trouble with Wilderness" (1995), the experience of the sublime and its representation by literary cartographers in the late nineteenth century led to preservation of America's first national parks: Yellowstone in 1872 (Ferdinand V. Hayden[10]), Yosemite in 1890 (King and Muir), and the Grand Canyon in 1919 (Powell and Dutton).[11] However, for Cronon the sublime was a formulaic and overused word, a stock response to unmapped wilderness, and an enticing "flight from history," society, and responsibility (484). Furthermore, Cronon finds that the sublime reinforces the notion that humans and nature are separate. But sublimity has had many faces from Thoreau to Powell, and it was not the only response these surveyors brought to and took from these landscapes.

They were also changed by their experiences, shaped by the places they encountered as they went about mapping them. These writers remind us that geologic developments are not static forms in the landscape; they have been "projected upon as they have been encountered, created as they were perceived, and reinterpreted as they were represented in literary texts" (Branch and Phillipon 2). What lies at the heart of their changing experiences of landscape is that it may not be measured, mapped, or molded in any single, replicable way. In their duties as surveyor they divide and subdivide, cordon off space, and regulate it. They frame the boundaries into an indisputable system for farms, parks, lots for sale, state capitals, and even nations. But as writers they also allow for a space evolving, perceptually unsecured, from which shifting, even conflicting, profiles of place emerge. Is it a geography of hope or one of broken dreams, a fertile garden or barren desert, a place of Manifest Destiny or one to be left alone?

If the map produces a static landscape that can be managed from above, the sublime produces an active, resistant space and promotes humility; the sublime space is larger than the writer though he is a part of it.[12] According to the aesthetic of the sublime, humans are not the masters of landscape but are, instead, included in the web of its mystery. Rather than produce knowledge, as the map does, the sublime beggars it. Though it was indeed a cultural expression and the fashion of the time, Donald Worster offers a different interpretation from Cronon's of the sublime's widespread currency as a token for what surpasses the ordinary in human experience:

> [the sublime] may be understood as an effort to recover and express those deeper feelings which in all sorts of cultures have linked the beauty of the natural world to a sense of wholeness and spirituality. The enthusiasm for [sublime] wilderness in America was undeniably a cultural fashion, but it also drew on that other-than-cultural hunger for the natural world that persists across time and space. ("Wilderness" 11)

Perhaps the sublime also drew on or even created a reverence for the land. It manifests itself at the moments when these surveyors are relying more on immediate sensory experience and orienting themselves less on the basis of an abstract, mapped reality based on quantitative measurement, instrumentation, or other exclusively human involvement, when they participate in what Abram calls the "more-than-human life-world" (217). In a sense, the sublime marks a shift away from a purely human set of signs to the animate earth. By assigning a positive even if immeasurable value, the sublime marks a transition from space to place. These writers couldn't have the same intimacy with place as did Indians already living there for generations, but the sublime allows for the possibility of that relationship. It was a way of letting the landscape in, rather than bound and set off.

Even after the sublime is tamed, as cartographic methods progress (along with other innovations in science and technology), late-nineteenth-century writers can be seen to shift the focus of sublime from the feelings existing only in the perceiver to an aspect of the landscape itself, constructing something closer to the "spirit" of the place than a personal sense of it. It is not the map's (or the mapper's) fault that the land cannot be adequately represented, but the land's resistance to being mapped. The land is seen less as blank potential, to be enchanted through distance ("a pleasure of hope" for Lambert), but more a place, revealed through close inspection. Especially for John Wesley Powell—who couldn't get the "grand view" while constantly traveling through the Grand Canyon—current maps, both aesthetic and cartographic, were inadequate to represent the kaleidoscopic forms in the arid West. The sublime for him came less from an unmapped wilderness than from a terrain with both human and geological marks all over it; his sublime required time and patience to cultivate an understanding, from several vantage points and perspectives, to interpret the sublime in nature rather than the one in the perceiver. Following Powell, Wallace Stegner recognized the mystery and wonder of nature, but he turned away from the supernal, wanting to locate our spiritual and intellectual "home" in where we live now, finding our place more on the ground than in the sky. For him, both maps and the sublime were not "termini" but points of entrance.

MAPPING WHAT IS TO COME

The following chapters examine the writing of four American surveyors and literary cartographers. In each chapter, I examine selected texts in detail, asking what is the stance in regard to place that emerges from these texts: Is it a desire to map objectively and scientifically, or a more sublime and subjective attitude toward landscape? How are the two impulses articulated within the texts?

In chapter 2, I examine the work of Henry David Thoreau, a surveyor by trade who found maps useful for navigating in the Maine woods, but who also found that too often a map failed to represent the place as he experienced it; that it was necessary to discard "maps," both cultural and topographic, to experience "contact." Thoreau attempted to look not *at* the landscape or maps but *through* them, to penetrate higher lessons and higher truths. He wanted to unmap the landscape to make way for fresh perception, a notion that left the landscape as blank wilderness, less of a human place and more a transcendental space. In *Walden* (1854), I demonstrate that Thoreau found maps useful for the unity that they revealed, the creative metaphysical force of nature that the map could express. Thoreau was ever less interested in the physical aspects of landscape than in the metaphysical presences, an interior landscape of his mind. Then, I examine "Walking," where, in a sequence of events through space and time, Thoreau attempts to unify interior and exterior landscapes. However, Thoreau ultimately remained interested in an imaginative and unfamiliar landscape that he could enter on his walks, a place unsurveyable and that could only be mapped inside the mind.

Chapters 3 and 4 examine the work of two nineteenth-century surveyors, explorers less of metaphysical landscapes than of ones that could be mapped objectively, but who nevertheless imported cultural "maps" to view their the respective places. If Thoreau wanted to clear the map or see through it, Clarence King wanted to add to or revise existing maps to create an impressionist scene or mirage, to describe landscapes as he perceived them. King was the first director of the USGS, Yale educated, and a friend of Henry Adams. He "painted" his verbal landscapes according to his reading of the English aesthetician John Ruskin, not only by describing their physical characteristics but also the sublime impressions they made on him. Though King sought a language and discourse of belonging to, and imaginative possessing of, landscape, toward the end of *Mountaineering in the Sierra Nevada* (1872), after an embarrassing mistake of climbing the wrong mountain, King jettisoned his impressionist stance toward the Sierra Nevadas and reverted to a desire to see Mount Whitney "as it really is," scientifically determined and mapped.

Whereas for King nature was an object to be perceived and described from an individual perspective, for John Wesley Powell, who explored the canyons of the Colorado and Green Rivers, there was no one perspective from which to paint, possess, or map the landscape he traveled through. In his *Exploration of the Colorado River and Its Canyons* (1874), Powell struggled to represent the multifarious forms and colors of the canyon, and like Thoreau and King, he too relied on the sublime, but a decentered one. If the sublime for Thoreau and King was mostly a literary representation, for Powell the sublime could aid in scientific representation and understanding. The canyon country could not be represented from one perspective: a map, a painting, a text. I argue that Powell's radical proposals in his *Report on the Arid Region of the United States* (1878)—that Americans revise the system of rectangular survey to have them conform to natural conditions—evolved from his earlier representations of the nature he had encountered: His gradual understanding of the difficulty of representation led to a destabilization of his trust in the map and its fixed identity. Though Powell *proposed* a system for organizing nature into a coherent text rather than *imposing* on it an incoherent and alien system, the landscape was already culturally "mapped" in the minds of the public and the U.S. government, a phenomenon for which Powell must also bear some responsibility because of the images of heroism and sublimity he wrote into his *Exploration*.

Finally, I discuss some of the nonfiction work of Wallace Stegner. Stegner was not a surveyor, but, fascinated with the "mapping" of the American landscape, he wrote about Thoreau, King, and Powell, and about geographical perception and the sense of place. Stegner provides a crucial "middle ground" between a set of familiar responses for literary surveyors: a subjective loss of self and "contact" on the one hand and a more objective mapping on the other; the desire to locate an unmediated sublime or blank spot in the nonhuman environment—the Romantic stance—and a commitment to a detached, scientific discourse common to exploration narratives, arising out of the Enlightenment and corresponding to American realism and naturalism. Stegner abjures both a depersonalized attention to place and the sense of it that is infused with ecstatic reverie and epiphany. In the former view, place fails to be individuated; in the latter, the writer loses a critical context from which to evaluate his view of the place and his position in it. I examine Stegner's *Wolf Willow* and his essays about surveyors and place, where place itself becomes a process rather than a spot fixed on the map or existing only in the mind. In this middle ground, Stegner recognized, more self-consciously than his predecessors, the responsibility that ensues when we project language onto nature, the ethical obligations generated by a writing about place—a writing that helps us to know it better.

CHAPTER TWO

....

Surveying the Strange
Henry David Thoreau's Intelligence of Place

How little there is on an ordinary map! How little, I mean, that concerns
the walker and lover of nature. Between those lines indicating roads is
a plain blank space in the form of a square or triangle or polygon or
segment of a circle, and there is naught to distinguish this from
another area of similar size and form . . . The waving woods, the dells
and glades and green banks and smiling fields, the huge boulders, *etc.*,
etc., are not on the map, nor to be inferred from the map.
—Thoreau's *Journal*, November 10, 1860

After deciding that his father's pencil factory wasn't a satisfactory "place" to
earn a living, Thoreau became a surveyor and cartographer by trade.[1] Lawrence
Buell writes that Thoreau was "very likely the most skillful cartographer who
ever penned a literary classic" (276). Surveying suited Thoreau because he
could be outside, he could set his own hours, and he was a stickler for accuracy
and detail. He could walk around the perimeters of clearings and delineate the
contours of the boundaries between clearing and wilderness, exploring edges.
Yet, as Thoreau wrote in his journal on New Year's Day, 1858, he feared that the
schematic view of the earth afforded by surveying might distort his vision of
nature:

I have lately been surveying the Walden woods so extensively and minutely that I now see it mapped in my mind's eye—as indeed, on paper—
as so many men's wood-lots . . . I fear this particular dry knowledge may
affect my imagination and fancy, that it will not be easy to see so much
wildness and native vigor there as formerly. No thicket will seem so unex-

plored now that I know that a stake and stones may be found in it. (*Journal*, x, 233)

Thoreau worried that he would confuse the map for the territory,[2] that he would see *lots* (real estate) instead of the plenty (lots) of "wildness and native vigor." He worried that the measured-off physical presences of place would prevent him from "mapping in [his] mind's eye" as he does in *Walden*, investing places with symbolism and spirit, rather than representing them on paper as "men's wood–lots." As Robert Stowell and William Howarth have shown in *A Thoreau Gazetteer*, Thoreau was both attracted to and repulsed by maps (x). On one level maps were important artifacts of experience. Though he never published it, Thoreau drew a map depicting his first long journey in 1839, a voyage up the Concord and Merrimack rivers with his brother John. While working on his essays for *Cape Cod* (1855), he studied early maps of the region, determining that the French charts were the best: "They went measuring and sounding, and when they got home they had something to show for their voyages and explorations" (184). Thoreau inserted nearly ten pages in the "Provinceton" chapter of *Cape Cod* on the history of exploration and cartography of the region.

Of course, maps also frustrated Thoreau. He longed for a map that would be not just a guide for physical navigation but also an iconic sign for spiritual navigation. He felt that too often people accepted the static geometrical surface of the map without recognizing the active and "waving woods, the dells and glades and green banks and smiling fields," and expressed his frustration that maps could not "bring back the sights and smells of the forest, seacoast, or mountain" (Stowell and Howarth x). Despite his interest and research into early explorations and mapping, he concluded that maps didn't tell people what he wanted them to know.

This chapter explores Thoreau's attitudes toward mapping, surveying, and walking as they relate to his aesthetics of place.[3] It is broken down into three main sections. In the first section, I examine *The Maine Woods*, in which the strangeness and unfamiliarity of the Maine wilderness forces Thoreau to be attentive to maps and to signs of where and who he is. And yet, Thoreau also insists that the wilderness not be mapped, and effectively clears it of prior perceptions to make way for his own. In his Indian guide Joe Polis he sees a model for perception based on the particular and direct rather than the abstract and vicarious, a person who "relies on himself in the moment" and doesn't need a map to know the territory but has "intelligence with the earth" (Walden 138). In the next section I focus on the map Thoreau drew of Walden Pond in 1846, the same year he climbed Mount Katahdin in Maine and discovered a place strange, sublime, and not on the map. In *Walden* he returns to the map as a representational model for cognitive abstraction. He gives the particular dimensions of the pond but extends the map's reach, extrapolating the map to reveal universal truths, as if he were mapping the spiritual rather than physical place. If the Maine woods made him aware of the physical presences of places, in *Walden* he uses a map to project himself beyond physical place to an interior landscape, a place in the mind. In the final section I examine Thoreau's "Walking," in which he seems to abandon surveying—and mapping—as a way of experiencing landscape in favor of the walk. During his walks, rather than impose a system ("a square or triangle or polygon or segment of a circle") on the landscape, he responds to the contours of the land in the moment, creating a fluid and intimate relationship between walker and land, mind and body, maps and place. Walking allows him to lose himself and to reperceive the familiar as strange and infinite, so that places recover a meaning that is more than "men's wood-lots." "Walking" unifies the physical aspects of place so important in *The Maine Woods* with the metaphysical presences of *Walden*.

MAPPING AND UNMAPPING
IN *THE MAINE WOODS*

Thoreau made three trips into the Maine wilderness: in 1846, 1853, and 1857. These trips are broken down into the three chapters of *The Maine Woods,* "Ktaadn," "Chesuncook," and "The Allegash and East Branch." The first two chapters were published during his lifetime—"Ktaadn" in the *Union Magazine,* 1848; "Chesuncook" in *The Atlantic Monthly* in 1858—but the final text, *The Maine Woods,* appeared in 1864, two years after his death.

The first, "Ktaadn," is clearly related to the themes of *Walden*; Thoreau took his first journey during his two-year period at the pond ("I never fastened my door night or day . . . not even when the next fall I spent a fortnight in the woods of Maine" (*Walden* 172). "Ktaadn" records the climbing of the mountain as a symbolic episode, and it chronicles his attempts to extend his experiment at the tame pond to the actual wilderness, to explore more extreme boundaries. The next chapter, "Chesuncook," is less philosophical than Ktaadn, and focuses more on narrating the trip and describing the scenery. And "The Allegash and East Branch" is even more journalistic; its descriptions of wilderness are less poetic and more scientific than the two previous chapters. Typical of his empirical and journalistic approach is his act of finding a "bottom" (Schneider 78). An act invested with symbolic resonance in *Walden,* which I will discuss in more detail later, it receives little attention in *The Maine Woods*: "the stream, though narrow and swift, was still deep, as I proved by diving to it" (208–9).

The subject of maps appears frequently in *The Maine Woods.* By my count, the word "map" is used forty times in the text (ten in "Ktaadn," six in "Chesuncook," and twenty-four in "The Allegash and East Branch"). In some respects, Thoreau's references to maps bring up themes he developed in the first few chapters of *Walden,* such as the discrepancy between appearances and reality. In "Where I Lived and What I Lived For" Thoreau would announce his purpose: the need to "see" fully and to "front the facts of life," not the mirage of Concord's business district and its materialism, but "only the reality" (96). The crucial question of vision that he poses of his audience is "Will you be a reader, a student merely, or a seer?" (111). Thoreau challenges readers to see natural facts more accurately, but also urges us to "see" in the mystical sense, as someone who perceives the spiritual truth contained within nature's facts: "I perceive that we inhabitants of New England live this mean life that we do because our vision does not penetrate the surface of things" (96).

Consulting his map in the woods of Maine, Thoreau finds it does not represent accurately what he *sees.* From the very beginning, he says that one particular town, Passadumkeag—the Indian translation Thoreau gives in the Appendix: "where the water falls into the Penobscot above the falls" (323)—"did not look [as it did] on the map" (8). Instead, he finds anything but what the name implies and the wilderness he expects and anticipates. He finds "earnest politicians" talking about an election, as if he hadn't left Concord square. In another instance, surveying the view on the way up Mount Katahdin, he writes about the reality of what he sees and the false appearance and inadequate preparation the map gave him: "From this elevation, just on the skirts of the clouds, we could overlook the country west and south for a hundred miles. There it was, the State of Maine, which we had seen on the map, but not much like that" (66). The map has prepared him for a State and not a state, and he has to remind himself and his readers that "we are concerned now, however, about natural, not political limits" (66). The "we" that comprises Thoreau and his companions is concerned with the natural limits they must overcome to climb. The "we" made up of Thoreau and his readers is concerned about other kinds of natural limits, namely perception. Maps designate boundaries and provide an initial orientation, and provide data for property and political limits, but can distort what is *really* there. The moment marks a perceptual shift— from one scale and reduced version of reality, the map, to the "map" of the transcendental seer, who uses an entirely different scale or scheme.

If all maps can present a false appearance of reality, at times the maps Thoreau carries are just plain wrong, and he expresses his frustration with them. For example, they confound names and geography: "we rowed a mile across the foot of Pamadumcook Lake, which is the name given on the map to this whole chain of lakes, as if there was but one, though they are, in each instance, distinctly separated by a reach of the river, with its narrow and rocky channel and its rapids" (41). And they get distances wrong: "The distance is nearly twice too great on the map of the Public Lands, and on Colton's Map of Maine" (94). According to the scale of one map, a lake is one length, but according to someone who knows the place, it is much longer: "Measured on the map, Moosehead Lake is twelve miles wide at the widest place, and thirty miles long as it lies. The captain of the steamer called it thirty-eight miles as he steered" (165). At times, the places he travels through aren't even on the map: "We could not find much more than half of the day's journey on our maps" (280). This can cause frustration, but sometimes he manages to joke about the inaccuracies: "we went . . . through more than a dozen flourishing towns, with almost every one its academy; not one of which, however, is on my General Atlas . . . The earth must have been considerably lighter to the shoulders of General Atlas then" (86).

In another early instance, before his departure for Mount Katahdin, Thoreau perpetuates the errors created by maps, and seems good-humored about his mistake:

> The last edition of Greenleaf's Map of Maine hung on the wall here, and, as we had no pocket map, we resolved to trace a map of the lake country: so dipping a wad of tow into the lamp, we oiled a sheet of paper on the oiled table-cloth, and, in good faith, traced what we afterwards ascer-

tained to be a labyrinth of errors, carefully following the outlines of the imaginary lakes which that map contains. (15)

Greenleaf's Map of Maine is a "labyrinth of errors," with "imaginary lakes" filled in because Greenleaf seems to have based it on one of the original plot maps. Those maps were not intended as guides, but as brochures or advertisements for selling off the land. The details on the blank squares were to be filled in later. Greenleaf probably used one of these plot maps and filled in some lakes to construct his image of "Maine."[4] When Thoreau traces Greenleaf's map from the wall of a cabin in Mattawamkeag, he perpetuates the mistakes and creates an even more perplexing "labyrinth of error," scaling down an already reduced version of *the place*. His trip through the woods of Maine lets him fill in the details of what was not on Greenleaf's map, or any other map, as he gets to know the trees and lakes as living presences, and adjusts his map-based version of reality.

After this incident, Thoreau seems to want to correct and provide a map, giving readers his own verbal maps in the meantime: "I am particular to give the names of the settlers and the distances, since every log hut in these woods is a public house, and such information is of no little consequence to those who may have occasion to travel this way" (18). He later writes in the same chapter, rather sardonically, "I will give the names and distances, for the benefit of future tourists," and does (45–46). If the book is to be useful, it must be accurate. But this produces a conflict of genre: Although Thoreau provides geographical facts, focusing on accuracy and detail of description, and in doing so delivers "useful" information to the traveler, this kind of detail is undermined by the narrative of the transcendental explorer. This exploration narrative charts a different path, of places not so easy to access or map, of "natural limits" to overcome.

Though early on Thoreau is engaged in paying attention to coordinates and precisely locating himself and "political limits," toward the end of the "Ktaadn" chapter something happens to seriously shake Thoreau's trust in maps, so he would have us believe. During the summer of 1846, the writer/explorer tried to "scale" Mount Katahdin, but the mountain resisted his plan. He lost his way many times, and a storm prevented him from reaching the summit. His descent, however, led to a discovery, for the slope that his map called "Burnt Lands" was actually a young forest with patches of blueberries.

"Burnt by lighting" Thoreau speculates about the cartographer's choice for a name, "though [the area] showed no recent marks of fire" (70). Thoreau's map may have been outdated, as the lands may have burned prior to the mapping and later recovered, or the alpine tundra may have had a "burnt" appearance to the namer and mapper. Whatever the case, Thoreau isn't prepared for what he sees, and he begins to distrust his map as a guide to the natural world.

Thoreau is trailing some moose when he comes across this "dense thicket" and "small meadow," home to the moose and *perhaps never seen by a white man before, where one would think that the moose might browse and bathe, and rest in peace*" (emphasis added, 69). Though there is no threat of danger here, suddenly a "full realization" comes to him: "this was primeval, untamed, and forever untamable *Nature*, or whatever else men call it" (68). This "realization" occurs not on the wild, inhospitable summit, but in an almost tame meadow (i.e., *Nature* is untamable though this piece of it may be tamed). His passage was blocked previously by "non-human" nature, as if to assure us that there is no human "proprietor" there (70). But the absence of humanity that he perceives is just that—a matter of perception more than a fact of the landscape. Just a page earlier he is "startled" to see the imprint of a man's foot, and feels "how Robinson Crusoe felt in a similar case," then remembers that the group had come that way before. He seems to savor the idea that he and his companions are first, and wants to "unmap" the landscape of previous footprints and perception so he may provide his own.

Thoreau writes about a space, though *called* "Burnt Lands," that is somehow off the map. "It is difficult to conceive of a region uninhabited by man. We habitually presume his presence and influence everywhere." Thoreau is referring not only to humans' physical presence, but the presence of our signs. He calls our attention to naming—"*Nature*, or whatever else men call it"—and seems to want things to be other than what they are called or "mapped." The space is blank: "not even the surface had been scarred by man" (71). Thoreau is "discovering" something unmapped: "Here was no man's garden, but the unhandselled globe"—and "globe" itself is a representational term. "It was not lawn, nor pasture, nor mead, nor woodland, nor lea, nor arable, nor wasteland,"—all words to describe human places. This place was something different: "the fresh and natural surface of the planet earth, as it was made forever and ever." "Man was not to be associated with it," he says, his tone changing from surprise to something like awe. It was not a "dwelling" place, not "Mother

Earth" but "vast," "terrific," "not for [humans] to tread on, or be buried in."
This was something "not bound to be kind to man," "a place for heathenism
and superstitious rites," not for human-centered religions. "Talk of mysteries!"
he continues, both excited and anxious about this natural world that seems
devoid of human meaning and that doesn't need us: "Think of our life in nature,—rocks, trees, wind on our cheeks! the *solid* earth! the *actual* world! the
common sense! Contact! Contact! Who are we? *where* are we?" (70–71).

No map prepared him for this "solid earth" that he touches and experiences, as opposed to the virtual one he anticipated through a two-dimensional
simulacrum. On Katahdin he "discovers" the "inadequacy of maps and plans
in the face of wilderness" (Howarth 56), and a world that is almost pre-
linguistic—one that excludes human categories, a notion he emphasizes
through negations in the passage: "not lawn nor pasture, nor mead, nor woodland, nor arable, nor waste-land." The punctuation, broken syntax, and repeated
exclamations culminating in questions mirror his sense of separation from himself and nature. He seems to doubt his foothold on reality at this moment,
screaming for *contact* with it. The "Burnt Lands" gave him a momentary sense of
the strangeness of the earth, before perception was mediated by the presence of
human "maps." His disorienting cry entails a "violent subversion" to prior shapes
of the world as a "prelude to fresh discovery" (Abrams 257). Thoreau seeks to
empty the landscape of its pre-existing structures to experience "contact" with a
world not of his own making, not seen through mediating filters.

The signs are everywhere, but Thoreau wants to "unmap" them. He fears
"bodies, I tremble to meet them," because he fears the introduction of human
assumptions into the scene. Though he fears human signs, he can't help but
invoke them. In pages leading up to the climax on Katahdin, Thoreau calls our
attention to Aeschlyus, "It reminded me of the creations of the old dramatic
poets . . . Such was Caucasus and the rock where Prometheus was bound.
Aeschlyus had no doubt visited such scenery" (64), to Milton's *Paradise Lost*
(64), to *Robinson Crusoe* (68), and to state surveyor Jackson, who measured
Ktaadn to be 5,300 feet (65). Thoreau says that this is "that Earth of which we
have heard," have previous knowledge of (70). A dialectic emerges in the passage between "mapping" and "unmapping"—or, as Lawrence Buell observes,
between emptying and filling—clearing the landscape but importing the sublime (71). The map for Thoreau serves as a metaphor of previous perceptions
of the landscape, but it is also the means for imagining new cartographies.

Thoreau effectively clears the space and map, even the linguistic signs, to make way for a new "discovery." Once he has no "map," he can experience the sublime.[5]

In a college essay on the sublime, Thoreau quotes from Edmund Burke: "terror is in all cases whatsoever, either more openly or latently, the ruling principle of the sublime" (*Early Essays* 93). He continues to discuss Burke's other elements of the sublime—mystery, power, and silence—only to "reject terror as the basic element of the sublime in favor of 'reverence'" (Schneider 85). "I would make an inherent respect or reverence, which certain objects are fitted to demand, that ruling principle; which reverence, as it is altogether distinct from, shall it outlive, that terror to which [Burke] refers, and operate to exalt and distinguish us, when fear shall be no more" (96). "The infinite, the sublime, seize upon the soul and disarm it," he goes on to say, but do not "terrorize" it. There is reverence in Thoreau's "contact" passage, as the gods demand. "What is this Titan that has possession of me?" he says, referring to the landscape as evidence of God's presence: "it was a specimen of what God saw fit to make."

Readings of the "Burnt Lands" passage often focus on two extremes: the one that elevates terror—Katahdin genuinely frightened him and he beat a path back to Walden Pond (Lebeaux 56)—or the ecocritical one that elevates awe (Marshall 230–31, O'Grady 39). Thoreau's early essay would seem to support the latter reading, but the occasion for the sublime experience has occurred because the place is supposedly unmapped or "unhandselled." According to the *Oxford English Dictionary* (OED), "unhandselled" was first used by Emerson in his 1837 "The American Scholar" (addressed to Thoreau's graduating class) to describe where artists come from, "out of unhandselled savage nature...come at last...Shakespeare" (2170). According to the OED, "to handsel" is "to inaugurate the use of; use for the first time," as in a ceremony (735). Thoreau's "handselling" is a different kind of initiation: a ritualistic un-mapping.

At the end of "Ktaadn" he marvels that there are still more "unhandselled" places, "the virgin forest of the New World," "unmapped and unexplored" (83). Eleven years after his first trip to Maine, Thoreau gives an account in his journal of a recurring dream, "for the twentieth time at least," of his way up a mountain. On October 29, 1857, he attempts to describe his dream:

My way up used to lie through a dark and unfrequented wood at its base,—I cannot now tell exactly, it was so long ago, under what circum-

stances I first ascended, only that I shuddered as I went along . . . and then
I steadily ascended along a rocky ridge half clad with stinted trees, where
the beasts haunted, till I lost myself quite in the upper air and clouds,
seeming to pass an imaginary line which separates a hill, mere earth
heaped up, from a mountain, into subterranean grandeur and sublimity.
What distinguishes that summit above the earthy line, is that it is unhandselled, awful, grand. It can never become familiar; you are lost the
moment you set foot there. You know the path, but wander, thrilled, over
the bare and pathless rock, as if it were solidified air and cloud. That
rocky, misty summit, secreted in the clouds, was far more thrillingly awful
and sublime than the center of a volcano sprouting fire. (*Journal* X, 142)

The passage bears comparison to the one from "Ktaadn"; he infuses it with the
same sense of awe and uses the same unusual word, "unhandselled" (O'Grady
41). This landscape is the antithesis of the pastoral, humanized one near Concord. Though there is fear in the passage, as he "shuddered" along and was
"haunted" by beasts, he is also "thrilled." He knows the path, but has lost his
way, has crossed some border or "imaginary line," and is off the "map" (the
"pathless rock"). But, from the clearing of the "map," new shapes evolve: "solidified air and cloud."

When places aren't on the map, he expresses the liberating effects of this
lack, in the passage above and in one from a later chapter in *The Maine Woods*,
"Chesuncook":

Those Maine woods differ essentially from ours. There you are never reminded that the wilderness which you are treading is, after all, some villager's familiar wood-lot, some widow's thirds, from which her ancestors
have sledded fuel for generations, minutely described in some old deed
which is recorded, of which the owner has got a plan too, and old bound-
marks may be found every forty rods, if you will search. 'Tis true, the map
may inform you that you stand on land granted by the State to some academy, or on Bingham's purchase; but these names do not impose on you, for
you see nothing to remind you of the academy or of Bingham. [6] (152)

The map may tell him where he is, but these names do not "impose" on him,
for there are no visible signs connecting what he sees to what is on his map.

Earlier, this absence of signs called for a celebration of sublime rock and sky, but a few pages later in the chapter he writes that "it was a relief to get back to our smooth, but still varied landscape. For a permanent residence, it seemed to me that there could be no comparison between this and the wilderness, necessary as the latter is for a resource and a background" (155). The wilderness is "resource and a background," but not a dwelling place—in both senses of the word "dwelling"—like the one at Walden Pond.[7] If the landscape *there* is smooth and varied, wilderness must be impenetrable, rough, and unvaried, hence difficult to differentiate and locate oneself in, a much different version of *there*.

> When the place is not on the map, he gets close to something sublime. Maps would therefore seem to be an impediment to the spiritual; they structure and fix what is otherwise volatile and unstable. But if the earlier instance of being off the map caused sublime reverence, later instances in *The Maine Woods* arouse the very fear that he characterizes in his early essay as unsublime. There is fear in his "Burnt Lands" passage on Katahdin but mostly reverence. In later instances in the book Thoreau experiences a fear that cannot be mistaken for awe; he experiences not mystery but a very practical (and unspiritual) concern for physical and bodily safety. Thoreau expresses this anxiety when he loses his companion in the unvaried wilderness: "For half an hour I anticipated only the worst. I thought what I should do the next day, if I did not find him, what I *could* do in such a wilderness, and how his relatives would feel, if I should return without him." (259)

While descending a stream, Thoreau and Joe Polis were separated from Thoreau's cousin and companion, Edward Hoar. A near frantic Thoreau shouted through the woods, but Polis remained calm: "The Indian showed some unwillingness to exert himself" (259). At the first glimmer of morning, Thoreau wanted to renew the search, but Polis wanted breakfast. Thoreau "reminded him that my companion had had neither breakfast nor supper" (261). Later in the morning, they spotted Hoar. "Before I saw him I naturally shouted again and again, but the Indian curtly remarked, 'He hears you,' as if once was enough" (262). Thoreau's opposing reaction is in part due to his relationship with Hoar; Thoreau doesn't want his relative to die. But more important, what accounts for Thoreau's anxiety is his relationship to the wilderness. To Polis, a man spending a night alone in the wilderness has nothing to fear. What seemed a trackless wilderness to Thoreau was for Polis a "mapped" terrain (Lynch 41).

When he was lost, Hoar left signs, a scrap of his shirt to which he added a note: "[Hoar] had already stuck up the remnant of a lumberer's shirt, found on the point, on a pole by the water-side, for a signal, and attached a note to it, to inform us that he had gone on to the lake, and that if he did not find us there, he would be back in a couple of hours" (263). Thoreau thinks about how with one wrong turn he could lose his friend forever, "like looking for a needle in a hay-mow" (263). Thoreau and Joe substitute for his note "a card containing our names and destination, and the date of our visit, which Polis neatly closed in a piece of birch-bark to keep it dry" (263). The next morning, Thoreau "hallooed in a high key from time to time, though [he] had little expectation that [he] could be heard over the roar of the rapids" (261–62). Finally though, Hoar hears the human sounds above the wild ones and he and Thoreau are rejoined.

Being lost in the woods generates some special circumstances. In a place so vast and indefinite, Thoreau needs to shout to create some contours of location (Garber 58). Also, both men need to write. Hoar leaves his note on the shirt, informing them of where he would be and when. Thoreau responds that he and Polis had been there and at a specific time and date, the only statements they can be certain of. As if to stress the tenuousness of the message, they wrap it in birch bark to protect it, a gesture that seems symbolic: nature covers over the human-made signs. The humans assert themselves by leaving signs. Clothing and writing (and with them shelter), are basic signs that define the human in the presence of a vast, chaotic space. In this wilderness, they can at least be sure of their names and the date (Garber 59), which Polis will later carve into a tree as a "gazette" (271).

In the woods, writing notes and reading them are acts of stabilizing space; they are cartographic. Shouting to each other and leaving notes are the beginnings of a map (though only for the moment), of fixing places in an otherwise unmapped wilderness. Frederick Garber, who pays close attention to Thoreau's sign making in *Thoreau's Fable of Inscribing*, writes that "writing and reading" in this way, "are acts through which we locate ourselves, their purpose to settle ourselves more surely into the world" (60). Through this process, we begin to see why there are forty references to maps in *The Maine*

Woods, twenty-four of them in this last chapter. The woods themselves have put maps and writing on shaky ground, so the humans there constantly need to be "re-inscribed" (Garber 60–61). Writing the notes—or making a map—clarifies *who* Thoreau and his companions are as well as *where* they are. These were questions he asked on Katahdin (*"Who* are we? *Where* are we?"), though in the presence of so much vastness, who and where he is while "lost" in the woods needs more attention than does who and where he is in the universe. On Katahdin Thoreau dispenses with maps so he can have his thrilling wilderness experience, but writing becomes a special kind of cartography when trying to find his cousin in the woods. In the forest signs are fragile and need protection from the elements, but they create contours of location, and shape the vast space into a place. Though Thoreau wants to locate outside the stable schemata of maps, the world without them is lost.

The references to maps can be seen as more than signs of Thoreau's fussiness with a field he knew something about; they provide crucial information about where one is and perhaps even who one is. On the top of Katahdin, Thoreau doesn't recognize himself: "I stand in awe of my body, this matter to which I am bound has become strange to me" (71). In a strange and nonhuman place, he loses track of himself. Maps may prevent our chances for "discovery," but they help to distinguish among things. After his metaphysical questions at the end of the "contact" passage, Thoreau writes in the very next sentence: "Ere long we recognized some rocks and other features of landscape which we had purposely impressed on our memories, and quickening our pace, by two o'clock we reached the batteau [*sic*]" (71). The physical signs "impressed on [his] memor[y]" bring him back to a human-made presence and material object: the bateau that will take him home through a well-navigated and familiar river. He has "unmapped" to make way for unmediated perception, but he "maps" again when he sees some things in relation to others. He has assembled the landscape into a recognizable pattern, not the authoritative (but defective) one of Greenleaf, but a cognitive map "impressed" in his mind.

Thoreau pays particular interest to human signs in *The Maine Woods,* especially to the marks loggers make on their logs: "It requires considerable ingenuity to invent new and simple marks where there are so many owners. They have an alphabet of their own, which only the practiced can read. One of my companions read off from his memorandum book some marks of his own logs, among which there were crosses, belts, crow's feet, girdles, &c., as Y-girdle-crowfoot, and various other devices" (42). Such signs set off the logs from each other; through all the jostling and colliding of the drive down the river, the logs maintain their identity (*who* are we?), and do not get "lost" (Garber 65–66). Several pages later, Thoreau describes a brick "in the midst of dense underwood," brought to the woods for purposes of "tamping." The brick is like any other, "clean and red," but he regrets that "we had not carried [the brick] on with us to the top of the mountain, to be left for our mark" (45). One companion notes that crosses are still found on trees, set there by the first Catholic missionaries (45). In the wilds of Maine, Thoreau pays particular attention to these signs and how they are used: for commerce (marks on the logs), as tools (bricks), and, lastly, as religious symbols. They are all left behind as records, traces of the travelers' passage, encoding the landscape like a map.

Within the vastness of the woods, there are the beginnings of a human system, a way of ordering and mapping. Thoreau's brick, had he placed it, would have been not only a cairn but his jar on a hill in Tennessee (Garber 67). However, like Stevens, Thoreau resisted those schemes of order, which ultimately leave things "gray and bare" (Stevens 76). The trees, he felt, contained better "poetry and mythology" than humans could produce, and he distrusted maps even as he was fascinated by them. We can detect his uneasiness about many signs of humans' presence, such as when he was "strangely affected by the sight of a ring-bolt well drilled into a rock" (42). Thoreau seems startled to discover so plain a trail of humans in the woods. Possibly, the ring-bolt was placed there by a previous surveyor. Surveyor of the Adirondacks Verplanck Colvin describes these bolts as "astronomical stations, and so connected by measurement with other copper bolts set in the summits of mountain peaks that, were these monuments destroyed, new ones could be reset with accuracy in the same locations" (27). These bolts represented an improvement over old methods, where lines were marked on trees ("after the fashion of the Indians" 26). Whatever its purpose, the ring-bolt affected Thoreau differently than the other signs of industry and commerce, such as the marks on logs or trees.

Perhaps because he realized how dependent he was on signs, he at times distrusted them. Thoreau scholar Richard Schneider says that if Thoreau fears the wilderness, he realizes "how completely the wilderness can throw one back on physical necessity; in preserving physical safety, it is easy to forget one's spiritual goals" (87). While constantly paying attention to signs, features of rock, or other presences to find his way, he is not afforded the luxury of "finding" himself in any metaphysical sense, which seems to require an "unmapping" of the physical landscape, making way for other versions of reality. Most likely, the ring-bolts signify that the wilderness was now mapped according to modern methods of surveying, the victory of system over nature, making it impossible to be truly lost and experience *contact.*

INDIAN NAVIGATION:

JOE POLIS'S INTELLIGENCE OF PLACE[8]

Maps were necessary in the vast Maine woods for Thoreau to figure out where he was and where he had gone. And yet, when he is constantly looking at the map, he is not able to pay attention to the "wildness and native vigor," the waving woods. Perception is mediated through the map, rather than through the capacity for seeing the world itself.

However, Thoreau observes a different way of navigating and ordering in the Indians he travels with as guides. In general, he concludes that Indians did not rely much on distance or markers in the way he did. He writes of his first guide, Joe Aitteon, in "Chesuncook":

> I was surprised by Joe's asking me how far it was to the Moosehorn. He was pretty well acquainted with this stream, but he had noticed that I was curious about distances, and had several maps. He, and Indians generally, with whom I have talked, are not able to describe dimensions or distances in our measures with any accuracy. He could tell perhaps, at what time we should arrive, but not how far it was. (131)

In one instance, Thoreau listens to a group of Abenaki Indians and tries to guess at their subject by their gestures or their use of proper place-names, "but [he] could not understand a syllable of it" (136). Then, in the midst of their conversation, Joe Aitteon suddenly appeals to Thoreau, as if to underscore the differences in their respective languages of place, "to know how long Moosehead Lake was" (137).

Studying Indians' names for places, Thoreau "observed their inability, often described, to convey an abstract idea" (140). Instead, he sees immediate perception of the particular while traveling with Joe Polis in "The Allegash and East Branch":

Often, when an Indian says, "I don't know," in regard to the route he is to take, he does not mean what a white man would by those words, for his Indian instinct may tell him still as much as the most confident white man knows. He does not carry things in his head, nor remember the route exactly, like a white man, but relies on himself at the moment. Not having experienced the need of the other sort of knowledge, all labeled and arranged, he has not acquired it. (185)

What stuns him is that, even without this knowledge, all labeled and arranged, his guide is better than he at wayfinding. After Thoreau is separated from Joe for a time, the guide reappears from out of the wilderness:

This surprised me, for without a compass, or the sight or noise of the river to guide us, we could not have kept our course for many minutes, and could have retraced our steps but a short distance, with a great deal of pains and very slowly, using a laborious circumspection. But it was evident that he could go back through the forests wherever he had been during the day. (251)

Joe appears to absorb "all the intelligence of forest and stream into himself" (253), an idea with echoes from *Walden*: "Shall I not have intelligence with the earth? Am I not partly leaves and vegetable mould myself?" (138). Intelligence of the earth requires knowing its secrets and language. For the most part, Thoreau travels through a landscape that gives little useful information; there is little that corresponds to the map, little to navigate by, save for an occasional river or path. The Indian, however, is able to "rely on himself in the moment," by imprinting the steps he takes in his mind. He creates a track where there had been none, "absorbing the intelligence of the forest." The pattern he creates seems more closely based on the pattern of the forest than that of the map. The Indian, in other words, makes *contact*.

The Maine Woods is concerned with these tracks and with the problem of locating oneself in the world, through maps and other ways of writing and "intelligencing" place. As he did with the logger's hieroglyphics, Thoreau makes a special point about a pictograph that Joe Polis draws. They return to one of the Indian's camping grounds, "one of his homes," and find a charcoal drawing on the trunk of a fir tree: "It was surmounted by a drawing of a bear

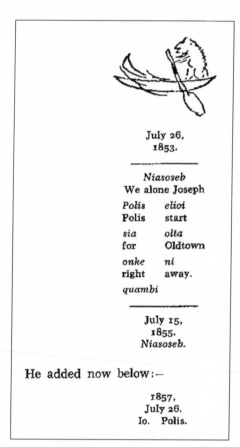

Fig. 2.1. Joe Polis's "map" celebrating the anniversary of his
visits. The pictograph is the
"sign of his family always." *The
Maine Woods* (1972), 199.

paddling a canoe, which he said was the sign which had been used by
his family always. The drawing, though rude, could not be mistaken for anything but a bear, and he doubted my ability to copy it" (199). Thoreau reproduced the copy of the image with the Indian words "interlined" in English. The
column is interspersed with dates: July 26, 1853; July 15, 1855; and his addition
for that excursion, July 26, 1857, as shown in Figure 2.1. Polis gives the dates, his
name and his destination: "We alone Joseph Polis start for Oldtown right
away" (Thoreau's translation 199). Apparently, Polis did this kind of recording
quite often. Thoreau tells how they set off from another camp, "the Indian as

usual having left his gazette on a tree" (271). The event has obvious similarities to the earlier one with the name card: name, time, and destination. But there are key differences. For one, Polis is not lost: He is recording a history instead of a particular pass-through. From the closeness of the dates, we can see that his visit to the campsite is something ceremonial, an anniversary, like a visit to a sacred place. The bear is the totemic image of his "family always," as he says, and is timeless. Polis's "map" is not only a physical mark of a place but something more eternal. His map is not only a representation of place, but a ritual of return. Unlike early explorer's maps, which offered a *mappaemundi* (map of the world), Polis's map concentrates on a small fraction of space, the local, the details.

Polis made quite an impression on Thoreau. Emerson counted Polis along with Whitman and John Brown as the three contemporaries whom Thoreau most admired (Schneider 83). On his return to Concord, Thoreau writes in a letter to H. G. O. Blake on August 28, 1857:

> I have made a short excursion into the new world which the Indian dwells in, or is. He begins where we leave off. It is worth the while to detect new faculties in man—he is so much more the divine,—and anything that fairly excites our admiration expands us. The Indian who can find his way so wonderfully in the woods possesses so much intelligence which the white man does not, and it increases my own capacity, as well as faith, to observe it. I rejoice to find that intelligence flows in other channels than I knew. (qtd. in Moldenhauer 134)

Thoreau made a bargain with Polis to "tell him all I knew," in the course of their journey, and he in turn "should tell me all he knew" (168). Joe shared knowledge about plants, crafts, cookery, and other survival skills, but about one issue they couldn't communicate. About locating oneself from an arbitrary wilderness location, Joe says, "O, I can't tell *you*. . . . Great difference between me and white man" (185).

Joe seems to prove that there is no epistemological consensus, that there are different ways of knowing, modes more direct and immediate. The dilemma that Joe presents is one Thoreau will work through in *Walden:* how to write a map (or a text) that is both a representation of a place but also embodies the place, a scheme but also something more active and alive. And yet, Joe is adopting from Thoreau and others' white ways, becoming a Christian and learning to calculate, for in no other way can he learn to keep his property—that is, to understand the white system of private property and deeds (293). Joe must learn the more abstract system of calculations, to correspond boundary markers on the land with the boundaries on the map. Thoreau, on the other hand, wants to know more about Joe's particular "intelligence" of place, how to impress places on his memory so he won't need a map and "can rely on himself in the moment," and be closer to reverence and further from fear.

In this last chapter of *The Maine Woods*, "The Allegash and the East Branch," Thoreau writes that much has changed since he was there eleven years earlier: "Where there were but one or two houses, I now found quite a village, with saw-mills and a store" (287). Progress and time marched on, and now the maps weren't accurate, not because they couldn't express the primeval forest but for another reason. Whereas earlier he noticed that his "physical atlas" gave "no adequate account of a primitive pine-forest," that it didn't accurately represent the wilderness he experienced, in 1857 that wilderness was disappearing (153). On the last page of the book, he describes his visit to Joe's home and one last map: "A large new map of Oldtown and the Indian Island hung on the wall and a clock opposite to it" (297). Joe probably put it there because he was learning to read it and to locate himself and his property on it, as he was no doubt learning the Euro-American way of measuring time. But for Thoreau the clock and the new map signify the passing of time; this is his last visit to the woods and his last look at the changing face of the landscape as captured in the map. Maps have served as necessary guides during his Maine excursions, but they possess two polar flaws: They can't represent the intelligence and sense of place on the one hand, and can't capture the sense of time and change on the other.

THE METAPHYSICAL MAP: SOUNDING THE POND IN *WALDEN*

Thoreau's knowledge of surveying and cartography, along with his strong interest in geography, inspired the map of Walden Pond that he inserted in "The Pond in Winter" chapter of *Walden*. As "the sole illustration in the main body of the text," the map stands out as a "bizarre interruption" (Buell 276). It accompanies Thoreau's sounding of the pond, where he suspends the poetic dimension of *Walden* to give us geometry and statistics (Buell 276). The narrative, like the map, shows Thoreau at his most "deliberate": "I fathomed it easily with a cod-line and a stone weighing about a pound and a half" (285–86). Then he writes about the map itself:

> When I had mapped the pond by the scale of ten rods to an inch, and put down the soundings, more than a hundred in all, I observed this remarkable coincidence. Having noticed that the number indicating the greatest depth was apparently in the centre of the map, I laid a rule on the map lengthwise, and then breadthwise, and found, to my surprise, that the line of greatest length intersected the line of greatest breadth exactly at the point of greatest depth, notwithstanding that the middle is so nearly level, the outline of the pond far from regular, and the extreme length and breadth were got by measuring into the coves; and I said to myself, Who knows but this hint would conduct to the deepest part of the ocean as well as of a pond or puddle. (289)

The survey map of Walden Pond (Figure 2.2) is crucial to understand Thoreau's overall meaning in *Walden,* for in "recording the depths of the various parts of the pond, it verifies that humans are capable of fronting the facts of the natural world regardless of how difficult the task is thought to be" (Schneider 64). Furthermore, the map suggests the possibility of deducing the pattern underneath. Thoreau speculates about whether "this hint would conduct to the deepest part of the ocean as well as of a pond or puddle" and that it may be "the rule also for the height of mountains" (289). He proceeds to project this observation to human behavior: "draw lines through the length and breadth of the aggregate of a man's particular daily behaviors and waves of life into his coves and inlets, and where they intersect will be the height or depth of his character" (291).

The map is a guide not only to the physical but also the metaphysical. In converting the natural facts to universal laws, Thoreau seems to conform to Emerson's dictum in *Nature*: "Particular natural facts are symbols of particular spiritual facts" (565). Significantly, in the original survey map, the one housed in the Concord Free Library from his survey of 1846, Thoreau inserted arrows pointing north, south, east, and west (Stowell and Howarth 6). But on

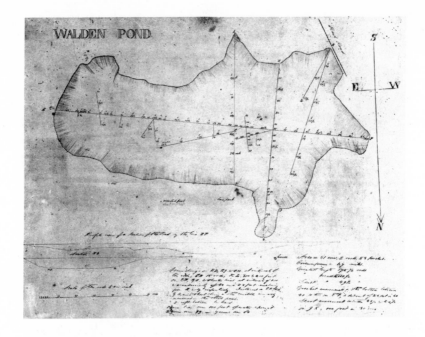

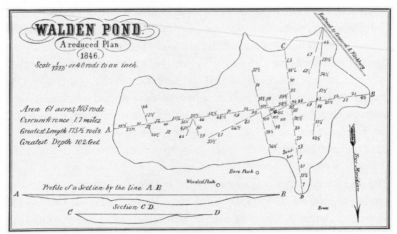

Fig. 2.2. The original made in 1846, with survey notes at the bottom, and Thoreau's final map of Walden Pond, pointing toward "True Meridian." *A Thoreau Gazetter,* 8; *Walden,* 286.

the printed and final version, the one in the final text of *Walden,* he drew only an arrow pointing toward "True Meridian." Thoreau is indeed searching for the truth: "Meridian" comes from *dies,* which is Latin for "day" (*medius* and *dies signifying* midday), but is also closely related to deity (both from *dei-,* to gleam or shine). "Meridian" used to signify the highest point of a heavenly body, though it also referred to the distinctive character of a particular place (OED 631). Note also that the subtitle is called "A reduced Plan," capital "P," as if to remind us that this is a map not only reduced in the cartographic sense of scale, but a reduced version of some larger Plan.[9]

Early readers misunderstood its purpose. Emerson told Thoreau of a friend who admired *Walden,* "but relished it merely as a capital satire and joke, and even thought that the survey map of the pond was not real, but a caricature of the Coast Surveys" (*Journal,* vii, 102–3). But the map is part of Thoreau's dream of synthesizing things poetical and spiritual with things scientific and physical, and the passage ends by lamenting the split between the two (Buell 276). "It is true, Thoreau says, that "we are such poor navigators that our thoughts, for the most part, stand off and on upon a harborless coast, are conversant only with the bright bays of poesy, or steer for the public ports of entry, and go into the dry docks of science, where they merely refit for this world, and no natural currents concur to individualize them" (292). Thoreau's aim in *Walden,* and with the map, is to "navigate" these harbors of unmapped thoughts, poetic bays and scientific docks, so that they might join into the same body of fluid water. Without the aid of poetry, natural facts are "dry," but without science, there can be no harbor in which to anchor poetry. In *A Week on the Concord and Merrimack Rivers* he says, about the union of poetry and science afforded by the map: "As we thus rested in the shade, or rowed leisurely along, we had recourse, from time to time, to the Gazetteer, which was our Navigator, and from its bald natural facts extracted the pleasure of poetry" (107). A map anchors natural facts, but one can extract from them the "bays of poesy."

Paradoxically, in "The Pond in Winter" Thoreau maps a frozen pond, but the ice moves. He sounds the bottom by cutting a hole in the ice, which causes its depth to fluctuate, "though [it] appeared firmly attached to the shore" (293). As water runs into the holes, "it raised and floated the ice" (292). From his observations, he deduces something at the same time scientific and poetic: "ice rosettes" form in the holes, "produced by the water flowing from all sides to a centre" (293). But if the ice flows in, Thoreau himself refracts out: "Sometimes, also, when the ice was covered with the shallow puddles, I saw a double shadow of myself, one standing on the head of the other, on the ice, the other in the trees or hillside" (292). As the ice constricts and freezes into a pattern, Thoreau's image as it is reflected in the ice also divides into a symmetrical pattern, one joined to the head of the other, another moving out into the surrounding trees and hills. The map, too, as it is drawn, is a perfect counterpart to the hole, its lines moving inward toward the center, but its "truths" radiating out into the surrounding hills.

Thoreau introduces his pattern of radiating marks even earlier. The image of the lines covering a hole in space first appears earlier in the chapter in his discussion of branches that a fisherman placed on the ice. He

> placed alder branches over the narrow holes in the ice, which were four or five rods apart and an equal distance from the shore, and having fastened the end of the line to a stick to prevent its being pulled through, passed the slack line over a twig of the alder, a foot or more above the ice, and tied a dry oak leaf to it, which, being pulled down, would show when he had a bite. These alders loomed through the mist at regular intervals as you walked halfway around the pond. (284)

The branches cover the space symmetrically, and are also spread out evenly, in length from each other and from the shore of the pond, and have an even height. They convey more than two dimensions, and seem to prime us for and parallel a map that will also have a symmetrical length, width, and depth (and from above present the same image, lines crossing in the center with a line to the bottom—Thoreau's attached to a stone to sound the bottom), and will "fish" more than one hole. As the fisherman's art covers several deep holes, so Thoreau's cover more holes (wholes) than Walden Pond.

Far-reaching implications of the fisherman's and Thoreau's respective maps are evident in the work that is performed in the chapter, work that is conducted both near and far. The map is a piece of professional work, completed by a skilled surveyor and functioning alongside the narratives of others who work at the pond that Thoreau relates for the rest of the chapter. Thoreau tells of those who came not to farm the land, thus adding something to it, but to cut away the peat: "I was looking sharp to see what kind of seed they dropped into the furrow, [when] a gang of fellows by my side suddenly began to hook up the virgin mould itself" (295). These men also come "to and from some point of the polar regions, as it seemed to me, like a flock of arctic snow-birds" (295). The ice cutters have the same initial impression, of those who plan to work the land, but who take from it, and in doing so, carry the water outward and distant: "Thus it appears that the sweltering inhabitants of Charleston and New Orleans, of Madras and Bombay and Calcutta, drink at my well" (297–98). The water of Walden, Thoreau wants to believe, "is mingled with the sacred water of the Ganges" (298). Of course, Thoreau is being fanciful, but he wants the particular natural facts to be universal. In doing their professional work, those who make a living at the pond are also doing so in service to the larger community, as is Thoreau. In one sense, Thoreau undercuts the image the maps gives, a fixed and stable outline, with the image of workers taking away both the pond's surface and its shore; but likewise in carving up the pond, Thoreau is mapping places both near and far, movable and fixed. That the pond has a bottom, and can be known, "maps" the way for further explorations of waters thought to be bottomless and infinite.

Until the pond-sounding episode, Thoreau has represented the pond without much surveyor's geometry (Buell 277). In "The Ponds," he briefly says of Walden Pond that "some think it is bottomless" (178) and describes its water as "seemingly bottomless" (189). In this chapter, his representations of the pond are persistently metaphoric. Rather than a picture of the visible, natural pond, we are presented with Thoreau's interior landscape. He says the shores are anthropomorphic lips "on which no beard grows." As water touches these lips, "it licks the chaps from time to time" (181–82). And, of course, he says it is an eye, describing the color as he would the eye's iris (176), writing that "it is earth's eye" (186), and implying that it looks at us. The trees are the "slender eyelashes which fringe [the pond], and the wooded hills and cliffs around are its overhanging brows" (186). From the dreamy imagery of the chapter ("It is a soothing employment, on one of these fine days in the fall when all the warmth of the sun is fully appreciated, to sit on a stump on such a height as this, overlooking the pond, and study the dimpling circles which are incessantly inscribed on its otherwise invisible surface." [187–88]), and the personification of the features of the pond, an interior sense of place begins to build: "inviting, mystical, leafy," and soothing (Buell 277). The pond is an old friend whose parts of the face we can recognize, even the "dimpling circles" on its surface. Some of Thoreau's meticulousness appears in this chapter, for instance where he describes lake levels during the summer of 1852 (180), but it continually dissolves into fanciful figures, such as the licking of chaps (181). The lake levels provide particular measurements in place and time, but the figures Thoreau uses express notions of eternity and infinity (earth's eye). The measurements help him study the pond in an empirical sense, but sitting on his stump on a fall day, he can also study the circles "inscribed on its otherwise invisible surface." He detects what isn't readily empirical or "mappable," but, rather, takes shape in the imagination.

The map of Walden Pond would seem to provide more system to the lake and less affect, but it doesn't necessarily individualize any more than does Thoreau's lyricizing in "The Ponds." The map, remember, is not just a map of the physical pond but the essence of metaphysical proofs. The map is therefore consistent with his symbolizing in "The Ponds," acknowledging the temporal but also an emblem of the eternal. "The Pond in Winter" begins on a specific morning when Thoreau proceeds with his "morning work," which consists of his physical and spiritual chores. The surveying also takes place during a specific time, "early in '46." But Thoreau ends the chapter telling us that in the morning, he "bathe[s] [his] intellect in the stupendous and cosmological philosophy" of a sacred Hindu text, Bhagvat Geeta, "since whose composition years of the gods have elapsed" (298). The metaphoric map represents something not only spatial but eternal, as it reaches out but also down through time and human history, sounding the deep bottom of human thought. He says in the "Conclusion" that "there is a solid bottom every where," if we are willing to explore beneath surfaces (330).

The problem with surveying is that it doesn't penetrate surfaces, but is concerned with the view from above. When not denoting Thoreau's occupation, "surveying" in *Walden* is associated with birds, the hawk: "aerial brother of the wave which he sails over and surveys" (159), the phoebe, "who surveyed the premises" of Thoreau's house at the end of "Spring," and also the loon, who "coolly surveyed the water and the land"(234). But such bird surveying helps revise the traditional kind of land surveying that Thoureau engages in to make a living. Notice that that the surveyor-hawk's wings correspond to waves of water, and even the phoebe is surveying a threshold, to see if the shelter is deep and "cavern-like enough," and the loon—Thoreau's playful counterpart—can, through surveying, quickly make up his mind and "put his resolve into execution" (234–35), diving deep into the pond and coming up some unexpected elsewhere. And in their game of checkers, Thoreau attempts to divine "[the loon's] thought in mine" (mind) (235). As a surveyor, Thoreau is indeed a loon, divining and mining through surfaces, from vast heights and perches, "survey[ing] the country on every side within a dozen miles" of where he lives, to purchase them in his imagination and emerge in some different place (82).

The surveying and specific map of Walden Pond is a call to further "mapping." "Is not our own interior white on the chart?" he says in the "Conclusion," "black though it may prove, like the coast, when discovered" (321). The map of our interior may be blank at the moment, inviting further exploration, even though what we find may be "black." But we need not travel anywhere to conduct this exploration. Thoreau quotes some verse from one of the metaphysical poets influenced by John Donne, William Habington (1605–54): "Direct your eye sight inward, and you'll find / A thousand regions in your mind / Yet undiscovered. Travel them, and be / Expert in home cosmography" (321). Habington pairs internal and external through his rhyming of "mind" and "find," and the state of "be"-ing with the paradox of exploring near home, "home cosmography." Thoreau adds to the idea of internal exploration: "Is it the source of the Nile, or the Niger, or the Mississippi, or a North-West passage that we would find?" He continues, "Be rather the Mungo Park, the Lewis and Clarke [sic] and Frobisher, of your own streams and oceans; explore your own higher latitudes" (321). Maps can be guides to such exploration, inviting the mind to settle in other latitudes, but the mind itself is the thing to be mapped: the latitude and longitude of our own streams and oceans.

What Thoreau seeks through exploration of his own interior is new knowledge and new ways of seeing. When he writes in cartographic metaphors, directions, and frontiers, he refers to the frontiers of perception and experience. In his earlier work, *A Week on the Concord and Merrimack Rivers,* the one he actually wrote at the pond, Thoreau links the physical frontier with one more epistemological:

> The frontiers are not east or west, north or south, but wherever a man
> fronts a fact, though that fact be his neighbor, there is an unsettled wilder-
> ness between him and Canada, between him and the setting sun, or, fur-
> ther still, between him and *it.* (304)

The challenge is to "map" that wilderness between him and reality—a border that is always receding and advancing. When he does find a route, it's time to discard it: "It is remarkable how easily and insensibly we fall back into a particular route, and make a beaten track for ourselves" (*Walden* 323). The path between him and the pond has become worn. In essence, his map has "become" the territory: The tropes and figures he has used to represent the place have lost their freshness and immediacy, the vitality between word and thing or text and place. He needs a new way to "map" his landscape, since a pattern has taken over instead of what it is new and immediate. Only by encountering something "not on the map, not previously charted," do we confront "IT" (Bickman 119) .

"Lostness" leads to a fresh discovery in the Burnt Lands passage from *The Maine Woods,* something he also emphasizes in the "The Village" chapter of *Walden*:

> In our most trivial walks, we are constantly, though unconsciously, steering like pilots by certain well-known beacons and headlands, and if we go beyond our usual course we still carry in our minds the bearing of some neighboring cape; and not until we are completely lost, or turned around,—for a man needs only to be turned around once with his eyes shut in this world to be lost,—do we appreciate the vastness and strangeness of nature. Every man has to learn the points of the compass again as often as he awakes, whether from sleep or any abstraction. Not till we are lost, in other words, not till we have lost the world, do we begin to find ourselves and realize *where we are* and the infinite extent of our relations. (emphasis added, 170–71)

When he loses track of where he is, he has to map the world all over again and see it in a fresh and unfamiliar way. Being lost takes us out of familiar, coherent structures into what "flickers and waves" at the edges of perception (Abrams 254). As Robert Abrams has written, "Where we are" then becomes the state of "blurred categorical boundaries" and shifting relations, a kind of "phenomenological theater" (254–55). At the same time Thoreau wants to become familiar with the place, to know its geometry and seasons, he also wants to keep it strange and unmapped. "In our most trivial walks," he writes, we can "appreciate the vastness and strangeness of nature"—what he found on Katahdin. But we need to recognize that a map or any pattern *in here* falsifies and distorts what remains ambiguously *out there.* He has mapped the pond in *Walden* and sounded its bottom, but he also wants to keep the place infinite and strange.

BEING IN STEP: THOREAU'S WALKING

I turn now to walking, because, from the passage just quoted, this everyday physical action is the way to get "lost" and reperceive familiar places. And, from the epigraph of this chapter, we learn that maps are of little use to the "walker and lover of nature." Thoreau searches in *Walden* for the form that can capture the essential flux of the place and time. In some respects, his map approaches this ideal—his is a poetic map that moves—but the leaf on the thawing railroad bank in "Spring" even more closely approaches some unification of internal and external, form and flux. The streams of sand, he says, take "the forms of sappy leaves or vines." Seeing this sand foliage while walking on a single spring day, Thoreau is "affected as if in a peculiar sense I stood in the laboratory of the Artist who made the world and me,—had come to where he was still at work, sporting on this bank, and with the excess of energy strewing his fresh designs about" (306). The design he finds there is an expression of the internal design: "No wonder that the earth expresses itself outwardly in leaves, it so labors with the idea inwardly" (306).

Though he wants the map to move, the problem with maps is that they can't represent the life of the things they depict. Thoreau's map of the pond is mostly symbolic of the correlation between his mind's eye and the earth's, but he loses the physical connection between the "map" and landscape that he gained in *The Maine Woods.* The map in *Walden* is too mental, representing mostly an interior landscape, and thus loses its *contact.* The surveying and mapmaking he reports in *Walden* are also too static and fixed, often leaving him with just a map or path rather than the earth itself. Thoreau says early in *Walden* that he'd rather be a "surveyor, if not of highways, then of forest paths and all across-lot routes, keeping them open" (18). By creating boundaries, surveyors close routes, but his kind of verbal surveying will be "across-lot" and will keep routes unobstructed and unbarred. Thoreau's opposing desires are brought together on the walk: to fix and map landscape, but also to keep it wild and alive. While walking, he covers ground and creates a path, but each step is new, and the path is never the same.

Thoreau put together "Walking" on his deathbed in 1862. It appeared one month later in the June issue of *The Atlantic Monthly.* Thoreau writes in this, his last essay, that "some do not walk at all; others walk in the highways [made by surveyors]; a few walk across lots" (199). Thoreau writes about a vision in which surveying boundaries, those fixed lines on paper and imposed on landscape, catch fire: "I saw the fences half consumed, their ends lost in the middle of the prairie, and some worldly miser with a surveyor looking for an old post-hole in the midst of paradise" (198). The miser is "worldly" as he is concerned with dead, physical things, post-holes and survey stakes, symbolizing abstract "possession." Thoreau continues with an image of hell: "I looked again, and saw him standing in the middle of a boggy, stygian field, surrounded by devils, and he had found his bounds without a doubt, and looking nearer, I saw that the Prince of Darkness was his surveyor" (198). Surveying had been a means of employment; it enabled him to produce maps, but Thoreau implies here that in surveying he has done the devil's work. Later in the essay, while describing surveying a straight line through a swamp, Thoreau writes that the words Dante read over the entrance to the infernal regions—"Leave all hope, ye that enter"—might have been written there. In "Walking," surveying, death, and hell are grouped together and opposed to walking, the wild (and things alive: "in wildness is the preservation of the world"), and heaven.

Maps have provided a useful representation of the world, useful for way-finding in Maine and symbolizing symmetries of the pond in *Walden,* but they are less useful as a way of apprehending actual environments in a spiritual way. If surveying is a way of fixing and possessing (the devil's work), walking in this essay is a way of opening or freeing, a relational and exploratory approach to surroundings, a way of keeping things alive, where one is lost in the moment. To be lost is to "appreciate the vastness and strangeness of nature" (*Walden* 170).

Walking brings him to the edge where mind and nature meet, beyond boundaries: "For my own part I feel with regard to Nature I live a sort of border life, on the confines of a world into which I make occasional and transient forays only" ("Walking" 217). In his walking he breaks out of what has been surveyed and mapped, for the problem with maps is that they reinforce the gap between human signs and the world: Maps are not the territory. While walking, Thoreau can experience the immediacy and intimacy of place, see it as familiar but also as unmapped and strange, therefore "open" to receive revelation from it. Though he walks in familiar places, walking carries him into the unknown. In our devotion to the walk he tells us, we must be able to "leave father and mother, brother and sister, and wife and child and friends, and never see them again" (195).[10] Once we've experienced the "subtile [*sic*] magnetism"—described as being like the needle of a compass (201)—of nature and the walk, we will never "see" friends, family or familiar surroundings in quite the same way. As Thoreau practices it, the walk allows him to reperceive the familiar in new ways: "Two or three hours' walking will carry me to as strange a country as I expect ever to see." Each time we walk, even if over the same terrain, we are a different person, changed by our experience. "There is a subtile [*sic*] harmony," Thoreau says, between the dimension of an afternoon walk and the years of human life. Neither will "become quite familiar to you" (198).

To walk is to be engaged in a process always taking *place* in the present. "The Gospel according to the moment" celebrated in "Walking" involves immediate responsiveness to changing phenomena, a constant attentiveness and alertness (219). The key to this devotion is that it comes from the natural rhythms picked up on the walk and not from a map that gives an *a priori* view of landscape. Thoreau traces walking back to the saunterer, which he derives etymologically from one going to Sainte Terre, a Sainte-Terrer or Holy Lander. But his Holy Land is all around him, while for the medieval pilgrim the Holy Land is a particular hallowed place. Thoreau delights in the "old, meandering, dry, uninhabited roads . . . along which you may travel like a pilgrim, going nowhither," for the secret of successful sauntering is being "equally at home everywhere" ("Walking," 194).

In a passage in his journal closely related to the later essay, Thoreau insists that the goal of the walk is not to "exercise—the legs or body merely—nor barely to recruit the spirits but positively to exercise both body and spirit, and to succeed to the highest & worthiest ends by an abandonment of all specific ends" (3: 176). Surveying is an end- (or boundary-) directed activity, imposing a system from without. But he is concerned with the correspondence between mind and body, with "facts which the mind perceived—thoughts which the body thought," and these facts and thoughts are brought together by walking (4: 170). Walking unifies the physical facts of place that struck him in the woods of Maine with the imaginative and mental exploration he does in *Walden*—both the "contact" with the earth and the imaginative and figurative representation of it. Indeed, walking is both symbol and activity: symbolic of a way of perceiving and living but also an activity that touches the solid ground.

Though walking has symbolic ramifications, the physical activity of walking is crucial. When his legs are still his thoughts are stagnant, but "the moment [his] legs begin to move, [his] thoughts begin to flow" (2: 404). When he walks, the "rills" themselves "which have their rise in the sources of thought— burst forth & fertilise [his] brain" (3: 378). Walking on various terrain, the elements of weather and landscape informing his consciousness, Thoreau adapts to the ground under his feet, and the topography of the place frames the topics of his thoughts (Simpson 18). Thoreau's walking is driven by this creative, nonimposing adaptation to the land, so different from surveying. While walking, Thoreau remains concerned with "whatever things [he] perceives," not with those things that lead to clear and distinct ideas. This is the sort of immediate perception he saw in the Maine Indian guide, Joe Polis. In "Walking," Thoreau tells us that "the highest thing we can attain to is not Knowledge, but Sympathy with Intelligence" (216). "Knowledge" is "labeled and arranged," mapped, but "sympathy with intelligence" involves a more spiritual knowledge, an entering into another mental or physical state—and not State. And Joe, remember, absorbs the "intelligence" of the "forest and stream into himself" (253).

Walking enables him to go beyond map-knowledge, as Thoreau describes a walk in "Walking" where map and surveyor knowledge give way: "The walker in the familiar fields which stretch around my native town sometimes finds himself in another land than is described in their owners' deeds" (217). In *The Maine Woods*, Thoreau found himself in a real wilderness: "Those Maine woods differ essentially from ours. There you are never reminded that the wilderness which you are treading is, after all, some villager's familiar wood-lot" (152). He was liberated by lack of familiarity with the place, but the wilderness also necessitated his paying attention to maps and signs of where he was. Near home he transforms the "map" so that the farms that Thoreau has himself surveyed, the bounds which he has set up, disappear, and "fade from the surface of the glass," giving way to the actual world: "the picture which the painter painted stands out dimly from beneath" (217).

The actual world he finds on Katahdin is the physical one, the "*solid* earth! the *actual* world!" he makes contact with, but in "Walking" the "actual world" is beyond surfaces and more like an ideal world. "The world with which we are commonly acquainted leaves no trace, and it will have no anniversary" (217). The signs or traces of owners' deeds disappear, and the (actual) "world" will have no anniversary because it will not happen again exactly the same way, but continues to happen, in the present, "forever and ever an infinite number of evenings" (220). The experience is both temporal and atemporal, in a specific place and everywhere. "For the leisurely afternoon walker, the 'idea' of Concord—indeed, the whole landscape as named, conceived, and organized through the lens of a map—seems to vanish into 'another land'" (Abrams 249). Thoreau advertised in his handbill (Figure 2.3) that he could "accurately describe boundaries," lot off woods "distinctly and according to a regular plan." However, in his writing and on his walks, these static areas transform into shifting profiles and perspectives, and topographical features that would seem to have been located within the stable boundaries of a map or deed remain in flux (Abrams 261). The "regular plan" gives way to a more "incongruous sense of the real" (Abrams 261). "Fresh, unsuspected reality" can develop immediately in what he appears to see, when apparently tangible scenery gives way to "other versions of *there*" (Abrams 249). Robert Abrams has written about Thoreau's "anti-geography," that he "traffics in the crumbling of rigidified versions of 'here'" (249–50).

In such an activity, his "sense of immediacy deepens" (Abrams 250), as Thoreau's writing about his walks consistently reflects an intense present awareness: "now" and "new" are consistently repeated (Simpson 27). "Above all, we cannot afford not to live in the present," he says, in "Walking." (219). Thoreau is ever responsive to what *presents* itself, and through the use of the second-person pronoun, engages the reader in that process of discovery—as if taking them on a walk. Indeed, to some readers' lament, Thoreau's style can resemble one of his morning rambles, but exploration, not explanation, is precisely the goal.

When we walk, all energy flows into the activity itself, in a sort of "rhythmical cadence," as Thoreau says in "A Walk to Wachussett," stimulating an "inner walk" of the mind free and fully open to future and to the surrounding landscape (Robinson, *Walk,* 65). Thoreau picks up the idea of the "inner walk," that mental and physical states parallel each other, in "Walking."

> We would fain take that walk, never yet taken by us through this actual world, which is perfectly symbolical of the path which we love to travel in the interior and ideal world; and sometimes, no doubt, we find it difficult to choose our direction, because it does not yet exist distinctly in our idea. (201)

Once we have the "idea" that the actual world corresponds to the ideal one, that

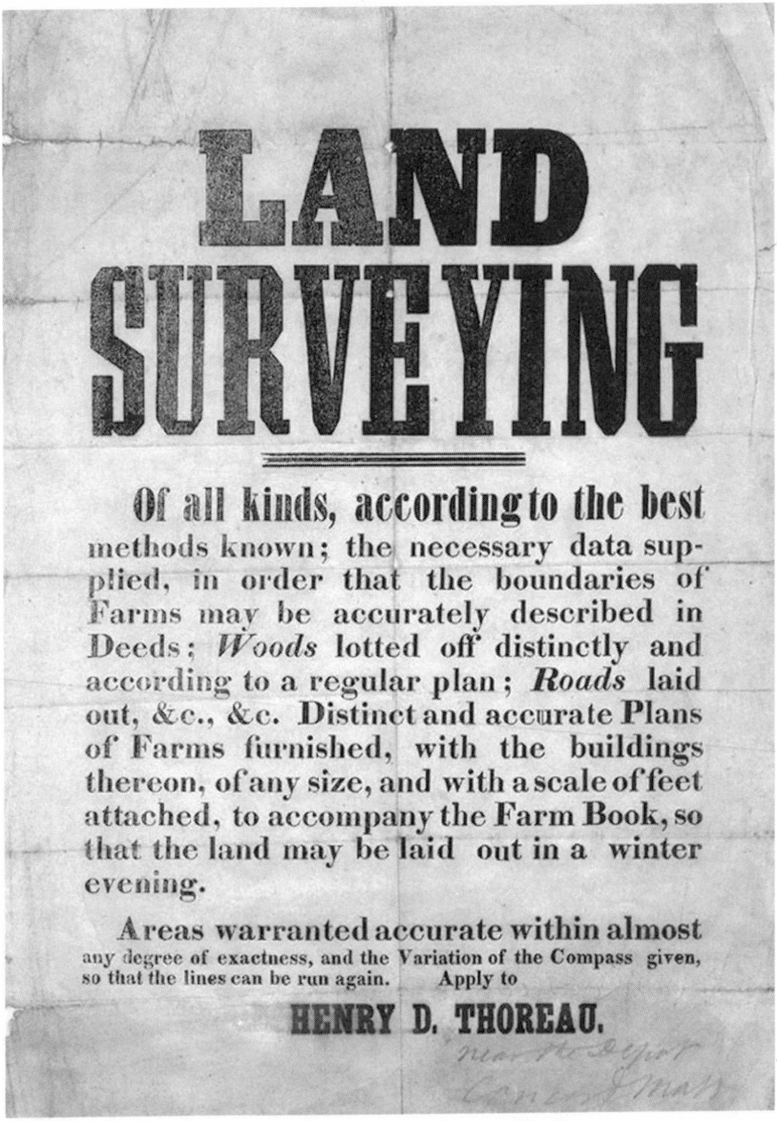

LAND
SURVEYING

Of all kinds, according to the best methods known; the necessary data supplied, in order that the boundaries of Farms may be accurately described in Deeds; *Woods* lotted off distinctly and according to a regular plan; ***Roads*** laid out, &c., &c. Distinct and accurate Plans of Farms furnished, with the buildings thereon, of any size, and with a scale of feet attached, to accompany the Farm Book, so that the land may be laid out in a winter evening.

Areas warranted accurate within almost any degree of exactness, and the Variation of the Compass given, so that the lines can be run again. Apply to

HENRY D. THOREAU.

near the Depot
Concord Mass

Fig. 2.3. Thoreau's handbill to survey. Surveying was a way to earn a living, but not a way *of* living: He worried that he would see nature as "men's wood-lots." *A Catalog of Thoreau's Surveys* (1976), 4.

the external walk is "symbolic" of the "inner walk," we know our direction. As metaphor for a way of experiencing the world, "walking" here is not a conscious choice, but rather a state of being open to what presents itself in the moment, with each becoming step. Once we have this "idea," our response to the moment is intensified and becomes the "great awakening light" ("Walking" 220). We walk toward the symbolic West ("the West of which I speak is but another name for the Wild" 206)—not the geographic referent, but the place of the imagination, where the sun goes down.

Walking is an approach that involves discovering what is ahead but also forgetting what is behind. For Emerson, this forgetting is crucial: "The one thing which we seek with insatiable desire is to forget ourselves . . . to do something without knowing how or why, to draw a new circle" ("Circles" 288). For both Thoreau and Emerson, walking is an experience that with each step jars and loosens the old and helps stimulate and bring on the creative and new. Walking becomes a central metaphor to "draw a new circle," or should I say a new map, literally on the walk and figuratively in the mind, with each step. Thoreau says he actually prefers the parabola to the circle to describe his walks: "The outline which would bound my walks, would be, not a circle, but a parabola, or rather like one of those cometary orbits, which have been thought to be non-returning curves, in this case opening westward, in which my house occupies the place of the sun" (202). The "parable" that "Walking" teaches is that his walks must be open, like parabolas, and not closed, like circles or maps. He wants a form, such as a parabola, but a form that will remain open, and parabolic walking fulfills this desire. You don't really come back to where you started, but begin again from a new, if nearby, position.

At the end of this essay, Thoreau imagines a new mental map of a place he is familiar with: "I took a walk on Spaulding's Farm the other afternoon" (217). He knows the place, but he imagines that another family (or gods, perhaps) have settled there: "as if some ancient and altogether admirable and shining family had settled there in that part of land called Concord, unknown to me" (217). In his mind the place is new to him, but the vision is transient, "but I find it difficult to remember them. They fade irrevocably out of my mind even now while I speak and endeavor to recall them, and recollect myself" (217). Although he finds it difficult to remember who they are, and who he is, if it weren't for such liberating moments and families, Thoreau writes, "I think I should move out of Concord" (217). Thoreau's place-sense requires that the familiar be made strange, that places be invested with a glow of transcendence.

Right after the vision at Spaulding farm, he writes about climbing a tree and being afforded the view a map would give, from above, but he directs his eyes to something smaller, "a few minute and delicate red cone-like blossoms" on the bark—a new aspect of the place previously undiscovered (219). Whereas the earlier excursion to the Maine woods taught him the necessity of knowing the place, of making the strange familiar through writing and mapping, the sense of place that emerges from "Walking," both the essay and the activity, is like a dream or vision, a kind of imaginative journeying that requires making the familiar strange. Thomas Cole would write about the magnificence of American skies in his "Essay on American Scenery": "sunsets are filled with the alchemy that transmutes mountains, and streams, and temples into living gold" (108). Thoreau describes such an alchemic, "awakening light" in the closing passages, a "golden flood" that made things "gleam like the boundary of Elysium, and the sun on our backs seemed like a gentle herdsman driving us home at evening" (220). If surveying led him to the gates of hell, walking takes him to the boundaries of the Holy Land, though he never really leaves Concord.

Scholars such as Lawrence Buell and Joseph Moldenhauer have observed that the arc of Thoreau's writing is toward the scientific and empirical, though I have argued that he was moving away from the geometry and calculus of the surveyor's map (Buell 117).[11] While Thoreau was becoming more particular in his study of natural history, he was less interested in maps as ways of knowing place. His scientific studies were ways of filling in the maps and better locating himself in the world. Such a progression (toward the scientific) would, however, reflect changes in the culture at large over those same years. I discuss those changes and how they affected surveying and writing about landscape in the next chapter, with Clarence King.

CHAPTER THREE

Mapping the Mirage
Clarence King's Impressions of Place

> The search for the mountain springs laid down upon our maps was probably to find them dry, and afforded us little more inducement than to chase the mirages.
> —Clarence King, *Mountaineering in the Sierra Nevada*

Leaving Thoreau, who, after his climb of Mount Katahdin, still marveled at the "wav[ing] virgin forest of the New World . . . unmapped and unexplored," I turn now to one who explored and mapped that "new" territory, Clarence King. After graduating from the Sheffield Scientific School at Yale University in 1862 (the year Thoreau died) and serving as a field geologist (1863–66) with Josiah D. Whitney's California Geological Survey (cgs), King sought federal funding to conduct a geological survey of the Great Basin region. With the backing of the War Department, King obtained Congressional approval to create detailed maps and chart the resources for an area one hundred miles wide (through which the Transcontinental Railroad would run) along the 40th parallel between the Sierra Nevada and Rocky Mountains. According to his friend Henry Adams, when the bill passed on March 2, 1867, King "had managed to induce Congress to adopt its first modern act of legislation" (*Education* 312)

King's *Mountaineering in the Sierra Nevada* was published as a complete text in 1872 (though serialized in the *Atlantic Monthly* in 1871 with William Dean Howells serving as its editor). The book describes King's life and impressions during his years as official surveyor on both the California and U.S. surveys (covering the period between 1864 and 1874), yet accounts for little of his duties as scientist or cartographer. The book conveys the sense that those years were filled with much adventure yet little scientific enterprise. The highs of the text, literally and figuratively, often occur during moments of adventure, such as when King daringly ascends Mount Tyndall. The lows occur when King spends time on the duties of science, "the more prosaic labor of running the boundary line" that he uses to map the valley of Yosemite, though a perceptual breakthrough—insight into King's concern not with conquering peaks as mountaineer or mapping them as scientist—occurs somewhere in-between (157). King's experiences in the mountains reveal the desire not to conquer but to inhabit. High mountain peaks, with their extreme horizontal and vertical distances and "indistinguishable" (hence unsurveyable) topography reveal to him and to us (through his characterizations of them) the tenuousness of his balance and "place" in the world (248). They are wilderness, the antithesis of home, but they teach him the value of home. What becomes apparent as *Mountaineering* progresses is that as his maps and the activity of mapping begin to fail him as ways of comprehending space, an impressionistic sense of place begins to emerge.

After the Civil War, Americans turned to the West to locate its geography and character, and they turned to sublime places to describe a national pride in landscape. Explorers incorporated the rugged peaks of the Rockies and the Sierra Nevadas, the deep chasms and rainbow vistas of the Grand Canyon, into this new sense of geography and place. King was at the vanguard of that movement. In 1871, when he wrote most of *Mountaineering,* George Wheeler was exploring eastern Nevada and Arizona south of the Central Pacific; Ferdinand Hayden was in Wyoming exploring the Yellowstone and convincing Congress to set it aside as a national park, and John Wesley Powell was beginning his second descent of the Green and Colorado Rivers. In the minds of these surveyors, they were mapping the national treasure, heroically laying out the paths for white settlement.

But if the maps from these surveys were useful to grid the unfamiliar and disorienting landscape, especially for purposes of military reconnaissance or mineral extraction, they didn't help the mappers (or the nation) feel settled or placed in these landscapes. Through examining primarily King's major work, *Mountaineering in the Sierra Nevada,* I will show how maps function in this important example of the literature of exploration during the late nineteenth century in America. Maps are a textual expression of empirical measurement (latitude and longitude, altitude), though they also show political boundaries. Maps for the explorer signal victory over the chaotic or amorphous space of the wilderness, but for the writer maps can't represent place as *it really is*. Maps summarize observed information into a static, spatial representation, and they make sense only within a visual framework—especially the bird's-eye view—at the expense of ground-level perspectives and the way landscape is both felt and experienced, as we have seen in Thoreau.

The crucial first chapter of *Mountaineering in the Sierra Nevada,* however, begins as a kind of map. "The Range" demarcates the boundaries of the adventures to come as the first sentence plots the western edge in figures of textual space, construction, and sea: "The western margin of this continent is built of a succession of mountain chains folded in broad corrugations, like waves of stone upon whose seaward base beat the mild small breakers of the Pacific" (21).

The word "margin" makes us aware of a map, and the "succession of mountain chains" that King refers to were still among the last unknown places on European-American maps, though he demystifies these locations through narration of his adventures over rocks and crags and description of their physical processes and topography. "Unknown to science" was the mantra at this time, and King and other explorers felt they were assembling an "inventory of earth" (Vesilind 43). But King's discoveries aren't always of geological or scientific significance; he also discovers that every ascent and mapped place diminishes the quantity of available mysteries. What begins to mystify him happens at lower altitudes, when King comes back down from the mountain and reflects on his discoveries. This man of science, first Chief of the USGS and in charge of naming and mapping open space for his government, discovers that his subject shapes and influences his personal thoughts and character as he begins to form an affection for place that is other than scientific. In *Systematic Geology* (1878), the scientific report published from his Fortieth Parallel Survey, King writes that "unmapped, unstudied, [the area covered by the survey] was *terra incognita*" (4). What King finally mapped was the unknown territory of his mind.

King continues his opening *mise en scène*, extending his "margins" to draw and animate the mountains and linking old-world peaks with the new nation's time and space: "its crest [is] a line of sharp, snowy peaks springing into the sky and catching the alpenglow long after the sun has set for all the rest of America" (21). Sunsets form the boundaries of the first chapter of *Mountain-*

eering and capture the tone of the rest of the text. King hints at the cultural significance of his sunset (like Thoreau in "Walking"), which has progressed along with the march of the nation from east to west and lingers in the Sierra, as if they hold some vital quality that Frederick Jackson Turner would soon attribute to the frontier (Lukens 35). But while the first sunset catches a prophetic light, the one that concludes the chapter "cast[s] a gloom over foot-hill and pine, until at last only the snow summits, reflecting the evening light, glowed like red lamps along the mountain for hundreds of miles. The rest of the Sierra became invisible. The snow burned for a moment in the violet sky, and at last went out" (44). These mountains have none of the exuberant energy ("springing into the sky") of the earlier ones. Between the first and the last description, King crosses the range from the east, relaying its geological history along the way. In doing so he also crosses into the realm of the interior landscape, since the mountains reflect his own mental state and the movement of the book as a whole: from activity to repose, daring adventure to quiet reflection. King is at his most wistful in his preface to the 1874 edition of *Mountaineering,* an edition that added maps and corrected an earlier scientific mistake. Looking back over his experiences, King writes reflectively, generalizing his first-person experience to third-person:

> There are turning points in all men's lives which must give them both pause and retrospect. In long Sierra journeys the mountaineer looks forward eagerly, gladly, till pass or ridge-crest is gained, and then, turning with a fonder interest, *surveys* the scene of his march; letting the eye wander over each crag and valley . . . discerning perchance some *gentle reminder of himself* in yon thin blue curl of smoke floating dimly upward from the smouldering embers of his last camp-fire. With a lingering look he starts forward, and the closing pass-gate with its granite walls shuts away the retrospect, *yet the delightful picture forever hangs on the gallery wall of his memory.* (emphasis added, iv–v)

The verb "surveys" in this context refers to looking over the "scene of his march," the tracks he has left behind, but also to looking for himself in the "picture" he sees. The Sierra Nevadas are the "scene of his march" and the site where his sense of place and self are formed. He writes soon after the above-quoted passage that "the serious services of science must hereafter claim me," but the sobering tone of that claim only heightens the "delightful" appeal of the place and the past, which are hung in his memory like a painting. Ostensibly, "the serious services of science" are what brought him to the Sierra in the first place, but King must have had some doubts about his legacy, doubts that arose from his embarrassment over climbing a neighboring peak instead of Mount Whitney (which he named for the chief of the CGS), an incident King blamed on his map and about which I will have more to say later. First, I want to chart the progression of King's "mapping" through *Mountaineering*.

YOUNG MAN GOING WEST: THE INTERIOR LANDSCAPE IN THE EARLY CHAPTERS OF *MOUNTAINEERING IN THE SIERRA NEVADA*

King left the banks of the Colorado River with his friend John Gardiner in May of 1866 to join Whitney's survey party in California. In his narrative King describes a mock-heroic tale of the pair heading west through the Great Basin on mules not fit for their excursion. He also begins to question his route and guide maps. As Gardiner lags behind, King begins to worry about their lack of water when places he had planned to drink from are not there: "springs which looked cool and seductive on our maps prov[ed] to be dried up and obsolete upon the ground" (34). Thirst and heat begin to distort his perception, producing a transformative vision of a human paradise:

> As we sat there *surveying* this unusual scene, the *white* expanse [of desert] became suddenly transformed into a placid *blue* sea, along whose rippling shores were the *white* blocks of roofs, groups of spire-crowned villages, and cool stretches of *green* grove. A soft, vapory atmosphere hung over this sea; shadows *purple* and *blue*, floated slowly across it, producing the most *enchanting effect of light and color.* The dreamy richness of the tropics, the serene *sapphire* sky of the desert, and the cool, *purple* distance of the mountains, were grouped as by a miracle. It was if Nature were about to repay us an hundred-fold for the lie she had given the topographers and their maps. (emphasis added, 35)

What the map presents is not what the eye sees, but the eye also transforms what it sees into a delicious "miracle" and mirage. King's vision of a "placid blue sea" metamorphoses into a pastoral village through the act of interpretation. The desert beguiles with these "ever changing illusions" as well as with the "phantom lakes" pictured on maps, nowhere to be seen but everywhere to be "seen" (35). King's "sea" is perhaps a product of his geological knowledge that the area was once a vast sea, but the rhetoric seems designed to re-create the place, to "enchant" what was an otherwise blank desert (a "white expanse" akin to a blank map) with a "miracle," to color his canvas. Rather than a surveyor's representation of topographical features, King writes an impressionist's picture of landscape, less stable and more ephemeral than a map, yet for that moment, a narrative also more "true."

Scholars do not seem to know what map King used to navigate across the desert. According to a historian of Western exploration, William Goetzmann, the Central Pacific Railroad's map of 1864 was apparently unknown to King or was considered inadequate (439). The atlas of General G. K. Warren was one of the best, according to King biographer Thurman Wilkins, but useful mostly for military purposes; the map's large scale was useful for gaining an initial reconnaissance (100). The incident described seems close to Thoreau's predicament in *The Maine Woods*, where Greenleaf's Map of Maine was made on a large scale, the grid laid, and "imaginary lakes" filled in.[1] King would write in *Systematic Geology* that when his survey corps took to the field, "there was no authentic map which displayed the continuous topography from California to the Great Plains" (1). He says that the labors of some military explorers, Frémont among them, lifted knowledge "out of the condition of myths," but gaps in topographical knowledge still existed (1). Yet he creates in his narrative his own myth of man as recipient of nature's color, the heir of its benevolence, rather than active painter of its forms. In his own experience with the inaccuracy of maps, Thoreau gets lost, empties the landscape of all familiar associations but awe, so he can experience "contact." King aims not to empty the map but to revise it, to differentiate the surface of the earth with more color, light and form, so he can experience his impressionistic mirage—something more human-made than sublime. "To search for the mountain springs laid down upon our maps was probably to find them dry," King writes (quoted as my epigraph), though one wonders if the pronoun "them" refers to springs or maps. These "maps" may indeed be dry, and "afforded [him] little more inducement than to chase the mirages" (36). Any geographical order that may be subsequently "found" in the landscape must be taken as a visual impression, and not from the map's precise relationships of length, height, and space.

King did eventually get to water, the real thing and not a mirage, an oasis that is probably now Palm Springs. King says that "we lay down in the grass, drank, bathed our faces, and played in the water like children." After straining westward over one hundred and fifty miles of desert, "it was a deep pleasure to lie under the palms and look up at their slow-moving green fans" (38–39). During that desert crossing and oasis experience, King developed his idea to make a better map (that is, to conduct the Fortieth Parallel Survey). According to Historian Richard A. Bartlett (*Great Surveys of the American West*), King and Gardiner felt that "their previous activities in Arizona and California had made it clear that a true comprehension of the geology of the West could be mastered only through studying 'the structure, topographical and geological, of the whole mountain system from the plains to the Pacific'" (141). The idea for a better map may have been born after this desert crossing, where King expressed his frustration over the inaccuracy of the existing maps, but in this first chapter King was also building credibility for the rest of his narrative that will tell about mapping the region and will do so better than the inadequate map that came before.[2] By invoking the blank spot on maps, King, like Thoreau, creates a space to fill with his own interior landscape.

Interestingly, the descriptions of the oasis incident and the mirage that preceded it demonstrate how much King was dependent not on earlier maps but on earlier myths and narratives. The maps may be wrong, but King says he has heard "information" about the location of the oasis. This information must come not from government science but from early explorers in the area and from local lore. The Spanish knew the place as *Agua Caliente* (because of its hot springs) as early as 1774, and no doubt the Indians before them. The description of the mirage evolves from his geographical knowledge, that the Great Basin was once a vast sea, as well as from his hopes of seeing the oasis and the optical phenomenon of mirages. He sees what he expects to see and draws from his "mental map" of the area.

This "map" is in fact the one that dominates the first chapter of *Mountaineering*. By his own faith in Western science, King should be representative of the trajectory in the later half of the nineteenth century toward a more "objective" science. The "Great Surveys" took advantage of the improvements in technology and standardized methods of data collection, supposedly removing the subjective observer's fallibility. But the impressionism King paints makes a mockery of the precision of scientific surveying, so that King's places can change shape and color and dissolve into a mirage.

KING'S CATASTROPHISM
TO CHARACTERIZE GEOLOGY

Nineteenth-century geology was a discipline filled with disagreements. Clarence King endorsed the "catastrophic" theory of geological change, called so because of its emphasis on violent, vigorous change. The catastrophic theory competed with that of Charles Lyell, who in *Principles of Geology* (1830) set forth the theory of uniformitarianism, which saw change happening over gradual increments and long periods of time (Brush 56–58). Catastrophism still held ties to theology, as if a god had intervened with catastrophic events to bring about change, whereas uniformitarianism was allied with the research of Darwin, whose *Origin of Species* appeared in 1859. William Goetzmann faults King for endorsing catastrophism, seeing it as a kind of aberration in an otherwise brilliant career (465). Francis Farquhar, editor of a 1935 Norton edition of *Mountaineering*, calls the theory "misleading" and completely "disproved" in his footnotes (27, 53). Ironically, catastrophism as an explanation for geologic change may be the version closer to the truth. If reexamined in light of the recent resurrection of "catastrophism" by Stephen Jay Gould, whose theory of "punctuated equilibrium" has revised Darwin and Lyell, King's theories seem "prescient" and "perceptive" (Burich 235).[3]

When King made his stand against uniformitarianism in an 1877 address to his alma mater, he proclaimed that catastrophism was more than just a scientific theory. Rather, it was a belief that "has its roots in the actual experiences of man, who himself has been witness to certain terrible and destructive exhibitions of sudden, unusual telluric [terrestrial] energy ... has felt the solid earth shudder beneath its feet, and the very continent change its configuration" (450). Though King says he has witnessed this energy, speaking about glaciation and "hardly conceivable floods," his information is more than evidentiary; it is also something he senses and conceives. "Catastrophism is therefore the survival of a terrible impression burned in upon the very substance of human memory" (450). King later charges that uniformitarians refuse "to look further than the present, or to conceive conditions which the senses have never reported. They lack the very mechanism of imagination" (451).

However accurate as a scientific explanation, "catastrophism makes for more compelling literature" (Tallmadge 1176). It implies that nature offers stories not readily available to the untrained eye, and that the hero/geologist "looks further than the present" to interpret them. Through inference and the "mechanism of imagination," he will relate these temporal narratives to the reader. In the first chapter of *Mountaineering*, "The Range," King begins his creation story "in the beginning," reaching as far back in geologic time as possible: "The ancient history of the Sierra goes back to a period when the Atlantic and Pacific were once one ocean, in whose depths great accumulations of sand and powdered stone were gathering and being spread out in level strata" (2). Boundless stretches of geologic time are condensed into these opening paragraphs. As he describes the passing of time, King's sentences evoke violence and havoc on a huge scale. He presents the history of the Sierra as unfolding in a five-part drama:

> First, the slow gathering of marine sediment within the early ocean, during which incalculable ages were consumed. Second, in the early Jurassic period, this level sea-floor came suddenly to be lifted into the air and crumpled in folds, through whose yawning fissures and ruptured axes outpoured wide zones of granite. Third, the volcanic age of fire and steam. Fourth, the glacial period ... with huge dragons of ice crawling down its slopes, and wearing their armor into the rocks. Fifth, the present condition, which the following chapters will describe. (25)

King's language, "yawning fissures and ruptured axes," seems intended to meet his audience with the same force he describes. Even the slow work of glaciers is presented as fiery-hot "dragons of ice," "wearing their armor into the rocks." This kind of "catastrophic" theory allows for descriptive, metaphorical language rather than static taxonomy.

Yet, after providing the figure for glaciers and the five-act drama, in the very next sentence, King relates the cartographic coordinates of the range ("From latitude 35° to latitude 39° 39'"), and he proceeds to give the view north, south, east, and west, along with distances. In addition to using "margin" to describe the edge of the continent, he uses the word four other times in the chapter, to describe the edges of mountains, the Great Basin, an oasis, and rivers (31, 35, 37, 43). He describes the "limit" of an alpine meadow, a "strip of actual desert," and a "belt of pines," demarcating where one natural feature ends and another begins as if charting them on the map (31, 32, 29). But he describes the same mountains as "sea-waves," compares the trees to the "slender spars" of ships, and tells us the oasis is a "disk of delicate green" (27, 30, 38). Today, we often separate word and image, but in King's day, with so few existing maps or images of the region, he "mapped" the range through verbal description, fusing images and words. Trained in a rich metaphorical tradition, his narrative is a fusion of literature and cartography.

The writing in "The Range" relies on King's ability to blend facts with figurative language, scientific geology with portraits of a temporal narrative. John McPhee has observed that geology is a "descriptive, interpretive science," not only classifying what the eye sees, but also evoking change that it cannot (379). Surveyors look at surfaces, but geologists can detect the traces of earth's forces in that topography, scars of geological time, producing something like a "deep map" (to use William Least Heat-Moon's term) rather than a superficial one.

Consider a passage where King relates "a chapter of very remarkable events" that occurred in the late Tertiary period. King says the beds of the sea bottom "were crumpled" by the shrinking earth. From these folded rocks, caused by the "fierce dynamical action," there "poured out a general deluge" of molten rock.

> From the bottom of the sea sprang up those fountains of lava . . . and all along the coast of America, like a system of answering beacons, blazed up volcanic chimneys. . . . At intervals along the crest of the range, great cones arose, blackening the sky with their plumes of mineral smoke. At length, having exhausted themselves, the volcanoes burned lower and lower. (23–24)

King provides a violent and even erotic rendition of geologic change, all of which is based on his interpretation of the evidence or "signals" remaining in the rocks and topography. Again, he is focused on visual images of light and color, red "beacons" that blaze. The evidence he looks on is immobile, but King provides the dynamism, his description conveying excitement and atmospheric tension: the sense of cataclysm that he believes characterizes the processes of change. He writes in a later chapter, "The Descent of Mount Tyndall," that the scene "impresses me as the ruins of some bygone geological period, and no part of the present order, like a specimen of chaos which had defied the finishing hand of Time" (98).

RUSKIN'S IMPRESSIONISM
TO CHARACTERIZE LANDSCAPES

King describes a set of contrasts ("What contrasts, what opposed sentiments, the two views awakened!") in "The Range" between East and West, mountain and desert. The desert is "stark and glaring, its rigid hill-chains lying in disordered grouping, in attitudes of the dead" (41). Meanwhile, to the west are farmsteads stitched together and full of life: "checkered fields of grass and grain" (41). On the one hand, King sees in nature a chaotic collection of debris; on the other, he sees a struggle for meaning and order (Tallmadge 1174). (Or, as his friend Henry Adams later observed: "Chaos was the law of nature; Order was the dream of man" (451). Although the surveyor/geologist role demands the former view as its starting point, because of his sensibilities he engaged the "dream" much more readily. Before heading west in 1864 to the California survey, King and several friends joined up with some "practical Ruskinites" in New York and formed a "Pre-Raphaelite" brotherhood that proclaimed its fidelity to nature in art (Wilkins 43). During that time King read Ruskin's *Modern Painters,* especially the mountain chapters, and adopted Ruskin's aesthetic valuing of mountains over the lowlands. Ruskin saw an "increase in the calculable sum of elements of beauty to be steadily in proportion to the increase of mountainous character" (*Modern Painters,* Volume IV, 337). King describes lowlands, especially the desert, as being a "meaningless disk," whereas the mountains have an inspiring grandeur. King's narratives fit into this Ruskinian scheme: The lowlands are the site of the local color stories, such as "The Newtys of Pike" chapter, or of pure science, such as "Merced Ramblings" where King discovers a fossil; the chapters that take place in the mountains involve triumph and beauty (Lukens 25–26).

Seeing through the interpretive filters of his geographical theory and his reading of (European) alpine literature, King projects his own interior landscape upon his surroundings. For example, after the descent of Mount Tyndall (which he named for the writer known for his glacier essays on the Alps), King says he "allows" himself to be impressed by the "Dantesque surroundings," with dangers overpowering to the soul. After the ascent, through "impassable" crests, crevasses, precipices, and steep ice and snow, King and his companion Cotter name the peak, only to find that there is a higher one (which they name Mount Whitney) to the east, separated by an apparently impassable gulf.

Naming is a crucial act of geographical "discovery," because it establishes proprietary claims through linguistic association. In his history of the exploration of Australia, *The Road to Botany Bay*, Paul Carter distinguishes between exploration and discovery: Discovery rests upon an assumption of a world of unknown fact, whereas exploration is a "spatial discourse" in which traveling itself is knowledge. Seen in this light, Australia wasn't really discovered, but had to be made, and this "spatial history" begins and ends with language, where space is given a history and transformed into place (xxiii–iv). King doesn't really "discover" these peaks either, because they were already known to exist in a general sense, but he "possesses" them through exploration and naming, and most of all, writing.

The "impenetrable gulf" that King claims exists between the peaks is an example of how he transforms space and makes it his own. When King reached the summit of Tyndall he "look[ed] back over *our* new Alps" (emphasis added, 111). Vast distances do not faze him: They provide the testing ground for feats of manhood and bravado and summon an energy commensurate with the landscape itself. After "fatiguing exercises" to gain a resting place, King says that "the mind has an almost abnormal clearness: whether this is wholly from within, or due to the intensely vitalizing mountain air, I am not sure; probably both contribute to the state of exaltation in which alpine climbers find themselves" (78). As King explores the boundaries between internal and external landscape, lying under the stars that evening on a shelf of granite—like Thoreau on Katahdin—he feels his "bones seeming to approach actual *contact* with the chilled rock" (emphasis added, 79). Rather than interpret its physical processes or map its exterior (which depend on a visual paradigm), King is feeling the rock, his bones seeming to approach the same temperature as surfaces external to them. After all, to "feel in one's bones" is to have intuition and sense of something. However, King's "contact" is mediated through how it *seemed*.

Though King's contact is more Realist-impressionist than Romantic-intuitive, he displays an allegiance to the transcendental strain in American literature, depicting his landscapes in terms of the Romantic sublime, with its fiery colors, waterfalls, "contrasts of light and shade," "heaps of ruins," "abrupt forms," and sense of the indescribable (Tallmadge 1177), all highlighted below. It is a stimulating environment that exalts but humbles:

A few fleecy clouds, dyed *fiery orange,* drifted slowly eastward across the narrow zone of sky which stretched from summit to summit like a roof. At times the sound of *waterfalls,* faint and mingled with echoes, floated up through the still air. The snow near by lay in cold ghastly *shade,* warmed here and there in strange flashes by *light* reflected downward from drifting clouds. The sombre *waste* about us; the deep violet *vault* overhead; those far summits, glowing with reflected rose; the deep *impenetrable gloom* which filled the gorge, and slowly and with vapor-like stealth climbed the mountain wall extinguishing the red light, combined to produce an effect which *may not be described;* nor can I more than hint at the contrast between the brilliancy of the scene under full light, and the cold, deathlike repose which followed when the wan cliffs and pallid snow were all overshadowed with ghostly gray. (emphasis added, 78–79)

Such vistas confirm the sense of nature that King has brought with him into the mountains from his reading of Ruskin. The scene is "ghastly" and "ghostly," "wan," "pallid," and "deathlike"; it takes on kind of cadaverous personification and King succumbs to the pathetic fallacy (a term coined by Ruskin in *Modern Painters*), describing its "feeling" as being "sombre." Though denying the possibility of true description, King is deft at word painting, and he employs not only Ruskin's sense of the Gothic and sublime, but also Ruskin's argument to freely improve on the topographical view to give a place's "true impression" (Lukens 26). If a painter has "inventive power" when painting a subject, Ruskin says he should give more than the "actual facts of it, but the impression it made on his mind" (IV: 19) Artists should not be bound "so much by the image of the place itself, as the spirit of the place" (IV: 22). Ruskin calls such a representation "useless" to engineers, surveyors, and geographers, yet capable of producing on the "far-away beholder's mind precisely the impression which the reality would have produced" (IV: 22). A topographical delineation of facts alone would fail to produce the sublime, for the mountains "speak quite another language."

The sublime is a way of comprehending what one sees by including it within a system of aesthetics. The sublime is a recognizable other, and though "quite another language," it occupies a position in familiar *topos.* To say that the effect "may not be described" is to invoke the "topography" of the sublime,

already familiar to readers of travel literature, and to excuse oneself of any defi-
ciency in descriptive powers. Of course, designating something as "beyond
description" does not avoid the problem of a clichéd vocabulary, since the
phrase or its variation can become a cliché in itself (Ryan 85). King will say it
cannot be described but go on to do just that. This paradoxical process works
in favor of the writer's authority. Indicating the difficulty of describing a scene
and then describing it constructs the explorer as "surmounter of linguistic, as
well as geographical, obstacles" (Ryan 85). The declaration of ineffability is followed by description in terms of absence: wan, pallid, ghostly gray. It is not the
describer at fault, but the land's failure to provide the recognizable differences
from which the writer's language can operate. Still, the land is within his system of representation and not a blank. The scene's absence is only viewed
against the brilliant light, and even its blankness is a presence, a "ghostly gray."
It isn't a symbolic wilderness he wishes to describe, but the spectrum of an
atmospheric effect. Thoreau dispensed with "maps" to get to contact, but King
is dependent on them: his contact is described through his impressionist
"map."

If the land resisted verbal description, it hardly ever resisted King's ability
to see it. In description, the writer's subjectivity could be called into question,
which is part of the reason he shrinks from describing it. But a map offers a
"seemingly indisputable representation of the world." In reproducing the
land's features as it does, a topographical map positions the observer above the
earth, leaving it open to scrutiny and inspection. Perspective is absent, since
the land is not seen from any focalized direction but in an omniscient view
(Ryan 97). But as we have already seen, while King was involved in mapping
the place, he was simultaneously (and contrastingly) engaged in representing
its *genius loci,* its impressionistic spirit.

This dual endeavor is most apparent in "Around Yosemite Walls," where
King and Gardiner were producing information for the official map of the
Yosemite Valley.[4] Yet this is also one of King's most "impressionistic" chapters,
as King generalizes about "perspective effects":

Perspective effects are marvelously brought out by the stern, powerful reality of such rock bodies as El Capitan. Across their terrible blade-like
precipice edges you look on and down over vistas of cañon and green
hill-swells, the dark color of pine and fir broken by bare spots of harmoni-

ous red or brown, and changing with distance into purple, then blue, which reaches on farther into the brown monotonous plains. (158)

Here again we see King's Ruskinian devaluation of the plains. We also see the many hues on his palette: the "dark color of pine," red, brown, purple, and blue. Perhaps the most noteworthy aspect of the passage is the generalization about "perspective effects." For the purposes of making a map, El Capitan is a one-of-a-kind place; it will exist on only one section of the CGS quadrangle. But the impact of this singular place reaches beyond the atlas to other places with rock outcroppings, providing a model or strategy for the word-painter. King is taking in not only a specific geologic phenomenon, but the impression and "perspective effects" such rock outcroppings make, as if he has been thinking about how they might be reproduced in a painting. Rock outcroppings provide a foreground against which we can judge and arrange the background. Paintings are, after all, concerned with such perspectives, whereas maps are concerned with the view from above that flattens the real into the scheme. "Perspective" is also the central means through which art attempts to achieve a lifelike and truthful representation.

In the verbal landscape painting by which King was tempted, it is easy to see the influence of some of the painters who traveled with the surveys of the West, Bierstadt and Moran being the most famous.[5] Both infused their subjects with a romantic and exciting aura, and the big, spectacular, colorful scenes they liked to paint King would describe in writing. More like a painter than a surveyor, King would veer from the meticulous to the metaphorical, the mythic.

King liked to sit and stare over such vistas, but finding places from which to view a country was not simply a means of locating a vantage point for the artist, but an essential element in scientific surveying and measuring of land. However, his predilection for gaining those views earned King some contempt from his scientific fellows. The paleontologist on the survey, William Gabb, especially criticized King for his preference for daydreaming and frivolous pleasure seeking over fossil hunting. "Can it be," King muses, "has a student of geology so far forgotten his devotion to science? Am I really fallen to the level of a mere nature lover?" (193). When King comes to Inspiration Point later in the same chapter, he says he "always go[es] swiftly by that point of view now, feeling somehow that I don't belong to that army of literary travelers who have planted themselves and burst into rhetoric" (165). Such rhetoric would sound "too amusing among these dry-enough chapters." King says "point of view" and not just point, as if the nineteenth-century traveler's "point of view," with his or her throbbing capacity for wonder, is the one he is bypassing and not just the physical point. Not the "point of view" of the surveyor/scientist, it suggests King has indeed become a nature lover, attracted to the beauty of nature and the ways that it might be replicated in all its glory for his audience. Ironically, King's share of the map for the Yosemite Valley would have mistakes in it, causing Whitney to declare it a "complete sham" (qtd. in Wilkins 80). Was King too occupied with his impressionist "point of view" to produce a meticulous map?

In at least one instance, King's impressionistic sense of the place was more useful to him than the exact data he was able to produce with his surveyor's instruments. In "A Sierra Storm," when King wakes to a foot and a half of snow, he says that he had "taken a precaution to make a little sketch-map in my notebook, with compass directions of our march" (175). He then proceeds to tell us that "but for the regular form of the moraine, with whose curve we were already familiar, I fear we must have lost our way" (175). Is it the map of the place or the impression of the landscape's curves that he is familiar with? When he comes back to Inspiration Point, the famous "point of view," he says that "had it not been for the extreme frequency of our journeys I should never have been able to follow [the trail]" (185). Although the trail was made unfamiliar by snow, King wayfinds through the familiarity of the route, the imprint it has made on his memory. Significantly, he can't *see* the blazes (markings) on trees because of the snow, but has to feel for them: "we were ordinarily rewarded after searching upon a few trees, and the blaze once found reanimated us with new courage" (186). Two years later (1866), while hunting in the Yosemite Valley for fossils, King revisits "all our old points," not to verify them on the map, but "to complete within our minds the conception of this place" (198)

The imaginative picture, "the impression it has made on his mind," is the one more relevant for King, the one that later "hangs on the gallery wall of his memory," and is the picture that King must have known would interest his audience. This picture is not a diagrammatic (or mapped) one, but a synthesized version composed of its look and feel as he experienced it. The landscape makes an impression on him that his scientific tools can't measure, and these tools become less useful as his rhetorical tools become stronger. In one of the later chapters of *Mountaineering,* during extreme wind and cold on Mount Shasta in 1870, King shows his disenchantment with scientific tools and thinking, writing: "I abominate thermometers at such times. Not one of my set ever *owned up to the real state of things"* (emphasis added, 251). The comment is one Thoreau might have made. In "Shasta Flanks" King scrambles around the first active glacier discovered in North America, "steadying [my] ascent by the tripod legs used as an alpenstock" (265). If the scientific tools fail him, or at least begin to have other uses, a different impulse seems to emerge—not of finding scientific wealth, or even aesthetic wealth, but of finding a home.

MISSING THE MARK: FINDING A HOME

The later half of the nineteenth century was a period of frenetic activity in the West: The rush was on to extract minerals and to explore and map the national treasure. King's survey party was often one step ahead—or behind—the race for mineral extraction. Surveying was being lifted beyond the realm of military reconnaissance into what King calls the more "professional work of the country" (qtd. in Wilkins 118). One of his greatest successes was his inspection of the Comstock Lode in 1868. Whitney and other experts had declared it exhausted of minerals, but King's optimism proved the better "claim," since a second bonanza was be found in 1876. King verified that ore existed there, but an even greater success was his verification that diamonds didn't exist where they were reported to be in 1872. Financiers in San Francisco were caught in a craze of speculation over reports of precious stones. Thurman Wilkins has called this craze "the most urgent thing since Coronado's quest for Cibola" (171). Although the location of the place was kept a secret, King deduced "from a knowledge of the country" that "there was only one place ... which answered to the description" that he read from reports by respected mineralogist Henry Janin,[6] and it lay within the limits of the Fortieth Parallel Survey (qtd. in Wilkins 175). King and several men from the survey found the spot and exposed the fury as a hoax. Gems were found in crevices and anthills marred by small scratches: the old trick of "salting" the field (O'Toole 35–36). "We have escaped, thanks to GOD and CLARENCE KING, a great financial calamity," wrote an editorial in the *San Francisco Chronicle* on November 28, 1872. The *San Francisco Morning Bulletin* reported on November 27, 1982, that "In thirty more days, but for the timely exposé of Clarence King, no less than twelve million dollars of stock would have been put upon the market." King exposed the swindle through a combination of detective work and knowledge of place, sleuthing the exact location from descriptions of it and his own prior knowledge, and became a hero.

However, King wasn't always comfortable with the mining aspects of his job, since the beauty of the mountains was also priceless to him. After the incident in which he was accused of nature loving, King "re-dedicates" himself to geology but is distracted by a "gateway of rolling gold and red cloud," where "summits seemed infinitely high and far, their stone and snow hung in the sky with lucent delicacy of hue, brilliant as gems yet soft as air—a mosaic of amethyst and opal transfigured with passionate light, as gloriously above words as beyond art" (193). In what seems a conversion to Thoreauvian thinking, King asserts that the value of the Sierra lies in its gem-like beauty rather than its mineral deposits. Although King thrust himself into the middle of this frenetic chase for wealth and the Big Bonanza—and would indeed die penniless after chasing minerals in Mexico—a countermovement ran in King's mind: that of inhabiting a place. Part of the wistful recollection that "hangs in gallery wall of his memory" involves the "thin blue curl of smoke floating upward from the smoldering embers of his last camp-fire" (iv). The image of this hearth, if fleeting, looms over *Mountaineering in the Sierra Nevada*. Even after the climactic summit of Mount Tyndall, Cotter and King come happily back down to camp: "with a feeling of relaxation and repose we threw ourselves down to rest by the log, which still continued blazing" (102).

King reflects on this domesticity at the base of the Obelisk (Mount Clark) in 1864: "One of the great charms of high mountain camps is their very domestic nature. Your animals are picketed close by the kitchen, your beds are between the two, the water and wood are always in most comfortable apposition" (173). The *opposition* of human home and inhuman, sublime space appealed to King as well. The cold, craggy summits, though the site of some of the most glorious moments in his career, also bring about a sense of anticlimax and repose, something again he can barely account for:

I always feel a strange renewal of life when I come down from one of these climbs; they are with me *points of departure* more marked and powerful than I can account for upon any *reasonable ground*. In spite of any scientific labor or presence of fatigue, the lifeless region, with its savage elements of sky, ice, rock, grasps one's nature, and, whether he will or no, compels it into stern, strong accord. Then, as you come again into softer air, and enter the comforting presence of trees, and feel the grass under your feet, one fetter after another seems to unbind from your soul, leaving it free, joyous, grateful! (emphasis added, 256)

Most critics of King have observed that the "high" moments of his life occur atop summits. King's epigraph (printed on the title page), *Altiora petimus,* or "we strive for higher things," would seem to support this, but in the presence of the lower "life region" King seems closest to some kind of spiritual self-fulfillment. Ruskin taught him that mountain peaks are supposed to be the sites of glory, but he feels more lighthearted (as opposed to feeling light-headed at high altitude) and free when back in the shade of comforting trees. Mountain peaks exalt the self, but it is lower in the "sheltered landscape" that he feels "at home" (97). At the top of Mount Shasta,

At fourteen thousand feet, little is left [of] me but bodily appetite and impression of sense. The habit of scientific observation, which in time becomes one of the involuntary processes, goes on as do heart-beat and breathing; a certain general awe overshadows the mind; but on descending again to the lowlands, one after another the whole riches of the human organization come back with delicious freshness. (269)

The heroic climb paradoxically leads to a quieting down of the ego until little is left but the physical senses and the habit of scientific observation. Then, the "human organization comes back" with renewed freshness, a "point of departure" King doesn't seem to understand, because it's not what he expected. The top of Tyndall is "inanimate" (97) while lower regions provide the "spirit of life. The groves were absolutely alive like ourselves" (255). Of course, the lower regions are likely the places where King sat down to record his experiences. This is where language makes sense again, where he is able to concentrate space in the pages of his journal. It is where *here* takes on meaning in relation to *there.*

The sense of vast space serves to heighten his sense of place, if place is defined as an area humans give value to and organize. In much the same way, King's travels from one place to another sharpen his faculty of repose. "Duty" always keeps him moving on and climbing more mountains, making him aware of the "pathos of nomadism" (253). This "pathos" afflicted much of the nation and bothered King. The Newtys of Pike (King's local color sketch of a family from Pike County, Missouri) have fallen into a "weak-minded restlessness," losing the "ideal of home, the faculty of repose, [that] results in that race of perpetual emigrants who roam as dreary waifs over the West" (123).

Although the explorer in King was always anxious to travel on, the surveyor had a mind to pause. "Against the explorer's high road," writes Paul Carter, the surveyor liked to juxtapose high peaks with fertile and protected basins, "conceptual places where the imagination might be enticed to settle" (112). To read King's descriptions of mountains is to find images of architecture and enclosure, as well as open spaces. While the view from high up gives the "vast yawning of hollow space," an "endless remoteness" of "echoes and emptiness," King also finds grottos, minarets, obelisks, and amphitheaters. Paul Shepard in *Man in the Landscape* offers a provocative suggestion for this habit of description. He theorizes that "rocks of certain angular shapes may always mean 'manmade structure' to European-Americans because of an indelible association of form with human works," and likens it to the biological syndrome of "imprinting" (245). While others of his generation—Henry James, Mark Twain, Henry Adams—were going to Europe to tour their ruins (Adams especially was studying architecture), King was finding these at home and injecting the landscape with symbolic ruin.[7] Another source of these "ruins" was the picturesque. Gilpin wrote in his *Three Essays* that the "picturesque eye is perhaps most inquisitive after the elegant relics of ancient architecture; the ruined tower, the Gothic arch, the remains of castles, and abbeys. They are the richest legacies of art" (46). The American West did not easily provide such objects of appreciation, but King found them. The inclusion of the architectural metaphors was a way to accord the land significance in relation to a European history. The land had picturesque value because of its remnants of this history. It was also a way of making the unfamiliar familiar, providing a shorthand and "interesting" description of geological formations difficult to describe.

As a geologist, King was also interested in the rocks themselves. These architectural shapes provide form against hollow space, as home and the "human organization" take on new significance for him against the inhospitable summit. On Mount Whitney in 1873, a year after the diamond triumph and weary from the pace of modern life, King once again evokes the image of the perpetual hearth against indefinite space: "Perhaps there is no element in the varied life of an explorer so full of contemplative pleasure as the frequent and rapid passages he makes between city life and home; by that I mean his true home, where the flames of his bivouac fire light up the trunks of sheltering pine and make an island of light in the silent darkness of the primeval forest" (293). Such a little "island of light" and so much space. The appearance of architectural metaphors and of the word "home," against the "primeval forest," remind the reader of the uncivilized state of that portion of the country.

Despite a desire for home building in the West, King never settled there, perhaps because, though it was a place he helped to "discover," his faith in that enterprise would be badly shaken. Although King was a hero in 1872 after exposing the diamond scam, a year later the most embarrassing moment of his career would occur. Another Geologist, W. A. Goodyear, announced in the August 4, 1873, *Proceedings of the California Academy of Sciences* that King had missed "the real peak" in his 1871 account but rather climbed one next to Whitney. That would make the venture King's second failed attempt at the highest mountain in California, for he was forced to turn back in 1864, the year he named Mounts Whitney and Tyndall. In his correction to the earlier addition of *Mountaineering* (and his response to Goodyear), King says in 1874 that he realized during his 1871 climb of the false Mount Whitney that the measurements taken with his instruments were off, but he attributed it "to some great oscillation of pressure due to storm" (291). The storm prevented him from seeing the "real" Mount Whitney with his eyes, so he relied on his map. When a sense of doubt overcame him, he "carefully studied the map" and established "beyond doubt the identity of the peak designated on the Map of the Geological Survey of California as Mount Whitney with the one I had climbed" (291). When King finally got to the real summit after Goodyear's paper in 1873, there in "uncolored plainness, stood the peak, where, in 1871, I had been led by the map, and my error perpetuated by the clouds" (298). Once again the spot on the map was an illusory mirage.

Although he charged the error to the map, King declined to disparage the work of C. F. Hoffman, chief topographer of the Survey. Hoffman's map was issued with the 1874 edition of *Mountaineering* put out by Osgood (Figure 3.1) along with King's revision of the earlier chapter on Mount Whitney and his answer to Goodyear. In Hoffman's map physical relief is expressed through elaborate brushwork, hachures (short lines used to indicate the degree and direction of a slope, as shown in Figure 3.1) and shading. In their attempts to represent landforms, these maps were works of art in themselves. The system of contour lines for showing topography was only beginning; King's Fortieth Parallel Survey, which produced the atlases for *Systematic Geology* (1878), would be among the first. It included a broad "Sketch Map" that was then broken out into a "series of geological and topographical sheets, on a scale of four miles to one inch ... in grade curves of 300 feet vertical interval" (4). Although the brushwork system is richer and has a more life-like feel for landscape, the system of contour lines can better express distances, coordinates and geologic data.

Guided by the more "picturesque" map but unable to see because of the storm (and hence verify what the map showed), King climbed the wrong mountain. King realized that he should have trusted his better instincts: "among the many serious losses man has suffered in passing from a life of nature to one artificial, is to be numbered the fatal blunting of all his senses" (296). Although his instruments and map should aid him, these crucial senses can and should be given greater weight.

By then King had been in the West for a decade. The peaks of the Sierra range had been named and were no longer "new." King was no longer in a chase to reach first summits; there were no more to reach. As so often does in *Mountaineering*, "intellectual and spiritual elevation" comes as he camps below the tree line. There, "deep and stirring feelings come naturally, the present falls back into its true relation, one's own wearying identity shrinks from the broad, open foreground of the vision, and a calmness born of reverent reflections encompasses the soul" (302). There, between the barren summits where maps betray and the modern cities with their "smothering struggle of civilization," King senses his "true home" as he prizes the "pure, simple, strengthening joy of nature" (293–94). King was finally "home on the range"—at least his own carefully defined "range." He seems to thrive in the hybrid of wilderness and home that Thoreau also enjoyed.

As John O'Grady writes in *Pilgrims to the Wild*, the pattern of "journey to strange place, the unselfing of self, and the return home in an enlightened state of being" is that of the pilgrimage (97). The story O'Grady tells is about psychological repression: King was a reluctant "pilgrim" because his unconscious kept the hostile, open space of the wild at bay (91). But how many of us are comfortable succumbing to wilderness, which is, by definition, a place where humans are not? King's text reflects how the awe-inspiring summits create an effect on him that cannot be measured or quantified, and teach him the value

Fig. 3.1. A section of the map that accompanied the 1874 edition of *Mountaineering in the Sierra Nevada*, drawn by C. F. Hoffman. Physical relief is brought out through brushwork and hachures. In 1871, King climbed what is now Mount Langley instead of Whitney, an error he attributes to Hoffman's map.

of place over space—of a sheltered landscape vs. an unbound one—even if his way of understanding place, as mapped and measured, is shaken. Like animals marking territory, humans carve up space to make a place, usually according to the experience of the shaper. We section off, inscribe, and name it. King's experiences with maps are emblematic of how that process eludes him yet lingers: He wants to feel *placed*. If King's unconscious reveals anything to us through his texts, it is that his return to images of campfire and enclosure reveal a desire to inhabit rather than view from above or quantify, as the map perspective locates and validates.

As King reflects on Mount Whitney after his 1873 ascent of the "real" peak, he writes that it is "hard not to invest these great dominating peaks with consciousness," that is, project onto them a guardian spirit or some part of the interior landscape (304). King acknowledges the tendency to myth-make, for he watches it in his Indian counterpart who intrudes upon his "hard, materialistic reality of Mount Whitney":

> At last he drew an arrow, sighted along its straight shaft, bringing the obsidian head to bear on Mount Whitney, and in strange fragments of language told me that the peak was an old, old man, who watched this valley and cared for the Indians, but who shook the country with earthquakes to punish the whites for injustice toward his tribe. (306)

King feels an "archaic impulse" take hold of him as the Indian, "who must have subtly felt [King's] condition," sat down next to him and cast a "hawk eye" toward Mount Whitney.[8]

Perhaps King liked the paradox of the moment at the base of Mount Whitney, the two interpretations clashing. Henry Adams said that above all King "loved a paradox—a thing, he said, that alone excused thought. No one, in our time, ever talked paradox so brilliant" (Hague 167). Though he doubts the Indian's interpretation of the mountain's face, King claims he can "read" the Indian's face, which has "written" upon it "a hundred dark and gloomy superstitions." Although King rejects the Indian's story of the mountain being an old man, he has himself represented the "spirit of place" throughout *Mountaineering*. As he watches the Indian walk away, King considers the Indian's "myth" for a moment, then proceeds to describe the mountain "as it really is . . . 14,887 feet high," scientifically quantified (306). The measurements of Mount Whitney determine how it will appear on the maps, but King's experiences with maps demonstrate how quantitative values don't tell the full story, nor do they bind him to place any better than the Indian's "superstitions." Places aren't found on maps, but exist in a complicated layer of affiliation and imagination—what he earlier in *Mountaineering* called the "power of local attachment" (253). This is not something easy for the surveyor/scientist to admit, but in more than one instance King expresses the attraction nature has for him over and above scientific methodology:

> No tongue can tell the relief to simply withdraw scientific observation, and let Nature impress you in the dear old way with all her mastery and glory, with those vague indescribable emotions which tremble between wonder and sympathy. (142)

Mountaineering in the Sierra Nevada stages a debate between scientific measurement and measureless emotion, between a map-bound ordering system and an imaginative one. In acknowledging the realm of experience "no tongue can tell," King brings a high level of desire and unknowability to scientific discourse. Places are named and contained by surveyors and mapmakers, but the mystery of a place, the interior landscape, must be projected by the writer. A strong sense of anticlimax pervades the chapter he inserted for the 1874 edition that describes his attempt at "the real peak." From the monuments of stones at the top of the Whitney, King discerns that he is at least the third party to reach its summit, "save Indian hunters" (302). He adds of the Euro-American ascents, "our three visits were all within a month" (302). But the magic and mystery he experienced on Tyndall is gone. Though he has named the peak, someone else has left a monument—that is, a history—on it. Whitney is not *his*, at least he can't lay imaginative possession to it, and he no longer feels the urge to tell about it: "I do not permit myself to describe details, for they have left no enduring impression, nor am I insensible of how vain any attempt must be to reproduce the harmony of such subtile aspects of nature" (304).

This is a shocking moment, a complete turnaround from the opening I quoted about the lingering effects of the sunsets. King's subject in the above passage is the difficulty in "reproducing" the "subtile aspects" of nature, but significantly he says "aspects" and not "effects," for now it has not made an impression on him. If we are talking of reproducing aspects of nature, a map might be more useful than description, since to "reproduce" is to re-create a copy or image, especially of surface features, but King says how difficult it is to "map" the "harmony" of nature. He is talking about his sense of it, since he "do[es] not permit [him]self" to put the feeling of the place in the objective description of it. As King's previous passages show, a description involving the feeling of the place and one that attempts to "map" it objectively are closely intertwined. But now, the experience is no longer exhilarating, because it is stale or because he is depressed over losing the glory of the first ascent. He no longer word-paints but proceeds to give a scientific explanation for the "atmospheric effect" at the top of summits, as if he is *not* representing its impression on him but rather its physical laws. His earlier account of Tyndall called the place into being and dramatized why it mattered, but Tyndall was unmapped and hence undescribed. Whitney has been mapped and explored—it has been made—but he is reluctant to make it his own.

His humiliation seems to cause him to turn away from his aesthetic receptiveness and word painting. As Simon Ryan writes in *The Cartographic Eye*, "the importance of sight as an element in the construction of discovery cannot be overlooked" (24). Almost all discoveries are constructed as visual events, the pleasure resulting from the fact that no Euro-American eyes have ever intruded upon the scene. If that vision of the "new" is not available, then neither are the claims of "discovery" (24). Perhaps more than the scientific embarrassment, Goodyear's discovery made it impossible for King to develop his impressionistic vista.

King stands toward the end of a long line of exploration and mapping, a tradition that began for Europeans in the 15th century and one that he carried west. Maps facilitated the colonization and appropriation of space from native peoples, but they didn't help King feel *appropriate* to that space, and King closes the revised version of the "Mount Whitney" chapter of *Mountaineering* on this melancholic note. The experience with the Indian has left him "trembl[ing] on the edge of myth-making" as it "unfold[s] the origin and manner of savage belief" (304). The Whitney experience and his embarrassment over it have clearly shaken him; he essentially renounces his own book. He says now that Ruskin "helps us to know himself, not the Alps" and accuses him of "myth making." He says he feels the "liberating power of modern culture which unfetters us from self-made myths" (306). King now claims that the "varying hues which mood and emotion forever pass before [Ruskin's] mental vision mask with their illusive mystery the simple realities of nature, until mountains and their bold natural facts are lost behind the cloudy poetry of the writer" (305). King now chooses to see Whitney as "it really is" rather than according to the self-made myths or "hues" that he has given to his other mountain experiences, or the animate spirit that the Indian gives it. Though he says in his 1874 preface that "the serious service of science must hereafter claim me," it is impossible to believe him. As he looks back over his mountaineering experiences in that preface, written after his later ascent of the "real" Mount Whitney, he also remembers the place that hangs in the gallery wall of his memory. This is the vista that props him up and guides him home. Maps are merely records of somebody else's tracks.

CHAPTER FOUR

Surveying the Sublime
John Wesley Powell's Representations of Place

Q. Then we have no official map of the United States defining its
   frontiers in respect to foreign nations, except, perhaps, on the coast?
A. No sir; no general map of the United States which gives its proper
   relation to other countries.
Q. We have no complete official map showing either the outline of our
   territory on land or sea, or showing the boundaries of the political
   divisions within the domain.
A. That is true.
—*John Wesley Powell before the Joint Committee of Congress, 1885*

John Wesley Powell was the quintessential mapmaker. In 1881, when he took over the USGS from Clarence King, Powell initiated and oversaw a plan to map the whole country according to a uniform system of mapping conventions, since none yet existed in America or Europe. The system he pushed through has remained the standard even today. Specifically, Powell's plan was to divide the map of the country into quadrangles, with smaller scales used for desert regions and larger ones, one mile to one inch, for populous regions. The maps were to represent the shape of the land by contours, the classification of it (swamp, desert, etc.) by colors, and important cultural features by lines and symbols (Wilford 214). The 54,000-map project was completed a century later in 1991 (Miller 94).[1]

He suggested America revise the rectangular system by which its landscape had been mapped since the Land Ordinance of 1785 divided land into 640-acre grids and the Homestead Act of 1862 authorized "quarter sections" of that grid, 160 uniform acres per applicant, thought to be the ideal size for a family farm. Although the quarter section could easily support a family in Wisconsin or

Iowa, in the arid West it was an abstract mathematical expression. After spending nearly a decade studying the West's topography and rainfall, Powell wrote a scientific monograph, the *Report on the Lands of the Arid Region of the United States* (1878). In that document he suggested that Americans revise the map, that we revolutionize the system of land policies, tenure and farming methods in the West—based on principles of scientific management and control—so that they comply with the topography and the conditions of the region's scarce resource, water. Powell observed that 160 acres were too many for farming and too few for grazing, and proposed gathering peoples in commonwealths organized around watersheds.[2] However, even before he wrote the *Report,* Powell published *The Exploration of the Colorado River of the West and Its Tributaries* (1875), an account of his 1869 though 1872 explorations of the last blank spot on unofficial maps of the continental United States, the Colorado River country.[3] In that narrative Powell "mapped" the nation in ways Congress didn't intend or even comprehend when he stood before them in 1885 to explain why there was no official map of "our territory" (qtd. in Stegner, *BHM,* 274–75).

Powell's story presents two problems worth attending to: First, and what I'll give most treatment to, how did the writing of the exploration through the canyon lead to his revision of the region's "maps"? Secondly, why didn't his recommendations for changes to the system of land tenure and use, based as they were on a scientific analysis of the evidence, take hold? Powell's suggestions as outlined in his *Report* were virtually ignored by Congress and the public, a fact that has been the object of extended comment among historians. According to Bernard DeVoto, in his introduction to Wallace Stegner's *Beyond the Hundredth Meridian: John Wesley Powell and the Second Opening of the West,* the *Report* was one of "the most remarkable documents ever written by an American. In the whole range of American experience from Jamestown on there is no book more prophetic ... If we could have acted on it in full, incalculable losses would have been prevented" (xxii). In *his* introduction to a 1983 reissue of the *Report,* T. H. Watkins lauds it as "quite possibly the most revolutionary document ever to tumble off the presses of the Government Printing Office.... If even half its proposals on land use had been translated into reality, it would have transformed the history of the West—and thence the United States" (xi). Historians of the West have concluded that Powell's revolutionary ideas were poorly received because they conflicted with a deep-seated and fervently held optimism about the West, and because their recommendations for commonwealths gathered around watersheds flew in the face of ethics of capitalism and resource exploitation.

The general consensus of these views has bestowed upon Powell the status of a nineteenth-century reformer who combated greed, individualism, and recklessness. From this point of view, Powell was a hero who advocated a position of "scientific realism" with regard to Western landscape and its uses. On the other hand, an assessment of Powell's career must also come to terms with his own complicity in developing the images and myths that lingered about the West. Though he helped to disprove the "myth of the garden," his writing in *The Exploration* helped to substantiate the image of the West as a place sublime and heroic, images that may have inadvertently helped bolster pioneering pride and optimism about the national landscape. Though he disproved many of the existing myths and fables about the rivers and lands of the West, Powell substituted new ones for them. When he wrote about the Colorado River country, Powell described a heroic voyage through an awesome and sublime landscape. But in doing so he also helped transform the area from a blank spot on the map to a place with story, sight, and sound, making possible his later writings on how these lands should be used. He contradicted notions of the West's fecundity and its ability to support American-style settlement in his later *Report,* but the landscape was already culturally "mapped," its destiny manifest as a "promised" land, something "commensurate to humans' capacity to wonder" as Nick Carraway says at the end of *The Great Gatsby* (182). What the Powell story demonstrates is that mythology was finally more influential than maps.

In this chapter, I aim to show that in Powell's struggle to write about the place even before it was fully mapped scientifically, and in coming to see it in figurative as well as scientific terms as his writing progressed, Powell became aware of the metaphoric nature of maps and description, of an ongoing process of identification over a fixed identity of place. Because the Grand Canyon was so difficult to assimilate into a single system (aesthetic, symbolic, visual, scientific), its identity so active and changing, he tried to *propose* rather than *impose* a system on it. Nevertheless, while Powell proposed a more "realistic mapping" of West, he also offered romantic codes—the heroic and the sublime—and failed to account for how this interior landscape had constructed the Western place and even went counter to his proposals. In the first section of this chapter, I describe Powell's preparations for exposing a scientific but also a representational truth as he described his heroic voyage. Then, I discuss how the canyon country begins to undercut notions of the grand, heroic scene. Since Powell's vantage point was constantly changing during his voyage down the river, his sublime was a decentered one, accounting for the inability to represent the canyon through a single form or "truth." Turning to its illustrations and maps, I then discuss the visual aspects of his *Exploration*. Although some of the illustrations present the grand, majestic view, others combine the imaginative stretch of the paintings with the context and accuracy of a map. Finally, I turn to the rhetoric of the scientific *Report,* which evolves from his doubts that nature can be known or represented, but also his hopes that it can—in keeping with sublime and heroic tropes he developed in *The Exploration*—and where he suggests better "maps," both cultural and cartographic.

PREPARATION FOR THE SCIENTIST: ADVENTURES INTO THE LITERARY IN *THE EXPLORATION OF THE COLORADO RIVER OF THE WEST AND ITS TRIBUTARIES*

John Wesley Powell was born in Mount Morris, New York, in 1834, but soon moved to Jackson, Ohio, with his family. His father, a Methodist minister, argued against slavery, and this public stand forced the younger Powell out of the public schools because other children threw rocks at him and called him "abolitionist." John Wesley Powell studied with his father's friend, George Crookham, a self-taught man of science who housed a private museum of Indian relics and natural history specimens. Crookham took Powell on "field trips" to places in southern Ohio, sometimes with state geologist and friend William Mather. The relationship with Crookham ended when antiabolitionists burned down Crookham's museum and makeshift schoolhouse, but the protégé's interest in natural history, geology, and ethnology had been ignited. Powell would spend the later part of his professional life as director of both the USGS (1881–94) and the Bureau of Ethnology (1894 to his death in 1902).

Fearing the same reprisals that befell Crookham, the Powell family moved to Wisconsin and then to Illinois to farm. In the 1850s, after quarreling with his father over joining the ministry, John Wesley Powell took a series of teaching jobs in Illinois. He was determined to be scientist. When the Civil War began in 1860, Powell enlisted and soon came under the command of one General John Charles Frémont, explorer and mapmaker of the West. In April of 1862, at the Battle of Shiloh, Powell took a bullet in his right arm. The battlefield surgeon promptly amputated the arm at the elbow.

After the Civil War, John Wesley Powell was one of many Americans who looked with intense expectation and interest toward the opening of the West. Along with the rest of the nation, he dreamed of what might lie there. In the summer of 1867 Powell took a group of undergraduate students west for the purpose of studying the Badlands area of South Dakota. However, discouraged by reports of growing Indian resistance to white travelers, Powell and his party turned south and headed toward Colorado. During that summer in the high country, Powell heard from trappers about the unexplored Plateau country of the Colorado River, where erosion worked on the "grandest" scale anywhere, and where the river was fabled to disappear into subterranean depths and conduits: "stories of parties entering the gorge in boats and being carried down with fearful velocity into the whirlpools" (*Exploration* 35).

According to historian Stephen Pyne, the Grand Canyon was one of the earliest of North America's natural wonders to be visited (Spanish conquistadors came to the South Rim in 1540), though it was one of the last to be assimilated (4). The context for understanding such a peculiar landscape had yet to exist. In the sixteenth century, the earth was thought to have begun a few thousand years ago, and cartographic methods were mostly suited for coastlines. Not for two hundred years would the "calculation of longitude become more or less routine," would geology enter the lexicon, and would writers and painters start using the word "sublime" for "distinctive landscapes" (9).

During the winter of 1867–68, Powell studied existing maps in order to prepare for an expedition to and down the river. According to one official map, the area had been crossed several times, with dotted lines showing routes of the previous explorations of Frémont (his third, in 1845) and Gunnison (1854), but had never been surveyed, walked, and brought within the definite and controlled lines of a knowledgeable map. According to historian of cartography Carl Wheat, the "Map for the Utah Territory showing the Routes Connecting it with California and the East . . . 1858" contained "all the latest information of the Bureau of Topographical Engineers" (104–5). It shows a "wagon road" extending from Salt Lake City to San Bernardino (likely the one King used on his way to what is now Palm Springs). In California it shows a range of mountains, but also the words "Unexplored Region" with a parenthetical note that speculates: "said to be filled with short Ranges running gradually in a direction nearly North and South." Then, for the area of the Colorado River and the Grand Canyon, there is an inviting blank space with the following words: "Region Unexplored Scientifically" (105).

While he aimed to correct some existing myths about the Colorado River country, Powell was also helping to perpetuate and construct myths about the canyon country and the American West. Powell's exploration of the Colorado River country was the final act in a long drama of clarification about *exactly* what was in the interior of the country. The fact that he was exploring the last blank spot on the map facilitated the hero motif that would long be associated with the western frontier. According to Beau Riffenburgh in *The Myth of the Explorer,* the blank-spot-on-the-map motif was a popular convention not only of nineteenth-century adventure stories but with official societies: "Subjugating nature and filling in the blank spaces had become the aim of numerous organizations, including the Royal Geographic Society (RGS) and the American Geographical Society" (34). The blankness on maps justifies, even encourages intervention by Euro-American explorers.

Powell also invoked existing myths in the first chapter of *The Exploration* to clear a space for his own narrative. He describes early Spanish adventurers and other "penetrations" into the land that fomented rumor: "all were overwhelmed in the abyss of waters, and stories of underground passages for the great river never to be seen again" (35). The myths are important contrasts for his particular representation of knowledge. They represent ignorance, an "abyss" in the known, and enable him erase the *tabula* from which the cartographic writer's project begins. Powell is the hero-scientist who unravels these myths and reveals the truth, though also a representational one.

Powell set out to explore the "blank" region scientifically. In 1869, using boats loaded with scientific instruments and with provisions for ten months, he set out with nine other men on his epic voyage down the Green and Colorado Rivers. Unlike Clarence King, Powell could make no claim for doing the formal "work of the country," as the party was not a government exploration at all. It was under the auspices of the Illinois Natural History Society.[4] In his preface Powell insists that the voyage was made "purely for scientific purposes, geographic and geologic," and that he had no "intention of writing an account of it" until persuaded to do so by the editors of *Scribner's* and congressmen.

While King was preparing his preface for the 1874 edition of *Mountaineering in the Sierra Nevada*, John Wesley Powell was called before an appropriations committee of the House of Representatives to explain the progress of his geologic and geographic work and why no published account of his 1869 exploration of the Colorado River existed. Powell wrote in the preface to *The Exploration* that he "had no interest in that work as adventure, but was interested only in the scientific results" (xv). This disclaimer, along with his apologies for the "weakness of [his] descriptive powers," add to the "immediacy and authenticity" of the "journal format," giving the impression that the text is a mere transcription of field notes, "rough and unadorned" (Tallmadge 1182).

Notwithstanding the disavowals of the preface, adventure happens to the group in spite of its putative scientific goals. Knowledge is the worthier end than the thrills that draw most to exploration, but as John Tallmadge observes, "science and adventure prove to be indissolubly linked" (1182). The Civil War veteran no doubt suspected that doing good science was like fighting a good battle: Both required constant courage, stamina, and coolness under fire. By becoming a better scientist, Powell was able to predict adventure down river and so heighten suspense (Tallmadge 1182). He learned by closely observing rock conditions how to predict the worst rapids, which often occur where soft limestone gives way to black granite or marble, causing an uplift in the strata—"Now and then we pass for a short distance through patches of granite, like hills thrust up into limestone." (268)—or where tributaries enter. From general patterns Powell draws a hypothesis, but the scientific method also aids in the drama. When black granite is sighted, imagination takes over the crew and the reader, since both have to anticipate what will happen next. Reluctant as Powell says he was to publish his account of the exploration as adventure, the first part of *The Exploration* contains some "suppressions, alterations and additions of fact" that usually aren't associated with a scientific monograph (Stegner 147).

As Wallace Stegner noted, Powell had several motivations for writing *The Exploration*: "he had his eye partly on the scientific results and the scientific reader, partly on the persuasive power the narrative might have on appropriations committees, and partly on the public impression he would make" (148). Stegner documents that Powell had been getting clips of what the newspapers were printing about *The Exploration* (Powell himself and several others in the expedition were sending and receiving reports through "wilderness mail" from towns and outposts). Emerging from the canyon when the journey was over, Powell was conscious of his status as popular figure. In the minds of the public, it seemed, he was striding the world like a colossus. He had sent seven letters to the Chicago *Tribune*, and his river exploits had captured the fancy of an audience eager for news of Western adventuring. After returning home to Illinois, "Powell promptly hit the lecture circuit" (Aton 17). Conscious of his role as hero, reinforced during his public speaking tour that he gave after the trip, Powell would incorporate elements of what his audience expected of him when it came time to write *The Exploration*. Stegner speculates especially about one section of *The Exploration* where, toward the end of the journey, the one-armed Powell reports on being "rimmed," trapped on the canyon walls, where one can move neither up nor down. According to Powell's own journals, the event happened much earlier and probably without as much drama.[5] As Powell reports it in *The Exploration*, a member of his party rescues him from falling off a cliff. He calls for help, and crewmember Bradley climbs to a rock overhead:

> Then [Bradley] looks around for some stick or limb of a tree, but finds none. Then he suggests that he would better help me with the barometer case, but I fear I cannot hold on to it. The moment is critical. Standing on my toes, my muscles begin to tremble. It is sixty or eighty feet to the foot of the precipice. If I lose my hold I shall fall to the bottom and then perhaps roll over the bench and tumble still farther down the cliff. At this instant it occurs to Bradley to take off his drawers, which he does, and swings them down to me. I hug close to the rock, let go with my hand, seize dangling legs, and with his assistance am enabled to gain the top (169, see Figure 4.1).

After the heart-stopping moment, Powell, ever the conscientious scientist, reports that they "walk out on the peninsular rock, make the necessary observations for determining its altitude above camp, and return, finding an easy way down" (169). When Powell describes hanging from a cliff or being thrown down a churning rapid, his one arm signals the heightened risk, the "heroic" element of the narrative that seems to require reinforcement for the reader, whether or not the event actually happened.

Powell took other historical liberties with the facts. Numerous incidents from the later 1871–72 expedition were placed in the 1869–70 story. Chapter 8 of the first *Exploration* ends the story of the first expedition at the mouth of the

THE RESCUE.

Fig. 4.1. Artist's rendition of the rescue of the one-armed Powell. *The Exploration of the Colorado River and Its Canyons* (1895), 169.

Virgin River without mention of a second expedition. The last journal entry is September 1. Chapter 9 picks up at the Virgin River (though over a year has lapsed), with the first journal entry being September 5, apparently continuing a consecutive narrative.[6] Some Colorado River historians like Robert Brewster Stanton and Julius Stone have criticized Powell for altering facts. After all, they claim, later expeditions incorporated in the final *Exploration* were conducted under government and public expense, and should be scientifically factual (107). Powell's argument, were he to make one, could only rest on his literary motives: that he was trying to capture the sense of the place as a "truer" representation than the actual facts. He included information from a later trip in order to make the narrative coherent and dramatic.

A scientific truth and a representational one also mix during the story's dramatic climax. Near the end of *The Exploration,* three men threaten Powell with mutiny and he considers leaving the river. Narrator Powell does some "reckoning," not only to count miles yet to cover, but also to consider what brought him there: "for years I have been contemplating this trip. To leave the exploration unfinished, to say that there is a part of the canyon which I cannot explore, having almost accomplished it, is more than I am willing to acknowledge" (279–80). Good science depends on conclusions, but so do good stories. Although the three who leave do not trust Powell's "reckoning" or the hero's "weapons" with which he calculated it, Powell had determined by sextant that they weren't far from their point of destination, so he carried on. Captain Howland, his brother, and William Dunn decided to climb out of the canyon and risk walking toward the nearest Mormon settlement. In fact, the three men who distrusted the scientific instruments died from Shivwit arrows soon after they left the canyon.

Powell's journal on this part of the trip is sparse. On August 28, 1869, he wrote: "Boys left us. Ran rapid. Bradley boat. Make camp on left bank," but *The Exploration* describes the climactic trip over Separation Rapid for four pages. When Powell wrote in his journal, he clearly intended to come back to that event, and he describes in the "revised journal" the details of how the boat is tossed by every wave: "A wave rolls over us and our boat is unmanageable. Another great wave strikes us, and the boat rolls over, tumbles and tosses, I know not how" (284). After the brave and heroic adventure through this "wine-dark" sea, Powell describes the elation he feels the next day, drawing on his experiences in the Civil War for an extended simile.

> When he who has been chained by wounds to a hospital cot until his canvas tent seems like a dungeon cell, until the groans of those who lie about tortured with probe and knife are piled up, a weight of horror on his ears that he cannot throw off, cannot forget, and until the stench of festering

wounds and anesthetic drugs has filled the air with its loathsome burthen,—when at last goes out into the open field, what a world he sees! How beautiful the sky, how bright the sunshine, what 'floods of delirious music' pour from the throats of birds, how sweet the fragrance of earth and tree and blossom! The first hour of convalescent freedom seems rich recompense for all pain and gloom and terror. (284–85)

All the senses are evoked in the passage, and the feeling of horror and imprisonment piles up in the dependent clauses until he "goes out in the open field" and sees a "world." His is the glory of the hero. Powell's pain during the war can't be diminished, but here he compares the "war-torn" river runner to a convalescent soldier rising from his hospital bed. After the trials of battle, "all pain and gloom and terror," the hero emerges, wounded but sensuously alive.

Powell would carry on with the celebration, but he remembers the three men: "We sit long after midnight talking of the Grand Canyon, talking of home, but talking chiefly of the three men who left us." The crew were getting restless from Powell's repeated stops to map or geologize, especially as rations were getting low. But, unlike their leader, they didn't understand how closely their fate was tied to heroic science. When Powell describes their location as "three quarters of a mile in the depths of the earth" (291), their fate is represented through a combination of surveyor's measurements and epic rhetoric. When the group stands by the scientist, it is led out of the underworld and the strange unknown, but when it loses faith and leaves, it meets a different fate (Aton 35).

Chapter 9 of *The Exploration* functions as a kind of "epilogue" to the story (Aton 37). Learning of the men's death, Powell seeks to discover what happened to them. Arranging an introduction to the Paiute Shivwits through the "Mormon Natty Bumpo," Jacob Hamblin,[7] Powell asks to hear some of their "mythology" (303). The story Powell relates in *The Exploration* is one of how So'-Kus Wai-un-ats, or One-Two Boys, avenges his father's death. As literary biographer James Aton has observed, in Powell's own story, through a kind of reverse irony, the roles are switched; he is the "father" as he seeks to find out how his "sons" died (37), but the pattern is not complete. Powell has learned from Indians how to better read the river and terrain, and he listens quietly as the Shivwits tell how they mistook Powell's men for the murderers of an Indian woman. Rather than seek revenge, he passes the pipe and makes peace with their killers. Powell doesn't connect his story to the Indian's mythology, but presents it as another truth-finding mission, as he does the exploration as a whole. However, that truth is located somewhere between Powell's "reckoning" and the mythology he hears and tells, his counting and his account.

NAMING THE PLACE: EXPERIENCING THE DECENTERED SUBLIME

A literary motive clearly had a more important role in *The Exploration* than Powell acknowledged. Although based on journal and field notes, the published version of *The Exploration* was edited to tell the adventure story, and early on has the tone of the nineteenth-century literary traveler with a capacity and taste for affectation:

> And what a world of grandeur is spread before us! Below is the cañon, through which the Colorado runs. We can trace its course for miles, and at points catch glimpses of the river. . . . Away to the west are lines of cliffs and ledges of rock—*not such ledges as the reader may have seen* where the quarryman splits his blocks, but ledges from which the gods might quarry mountains that, rolled out on the plain below, would stand a lofty range; *and not such cliffs as the reader may have seen* where the swallow builds its nest, but cliffs where the *soaring eagle* is lost to view ere he reaches the summit . . . Away to the east a group of eruptive mountains are seen—the Sierra La Sal. . . . Their slopes are covered with pines, and deep gulches are flanked with *great crags,* and snow fields are seen near the summits. So the *mountains are in uniform,* green gray and silver. (emphasis added, 212–13).

Powell's writing is suffused with literary self-consciousness. Journal accounts would be rendered without such an awareness of audience: "not such ledges as the reader may have seen" but ledges where gods quarry; and "not such cliffs as the reader may have seen" but where eagles soar. Although travel writing is concerned with creating a preview for future tourists, there's an odd social contract at work in the passage. In the exploration narrative, there must be a crucial separation between explorer and reader—readers are unable to view the scene as the explorer has, so they put their faith in the writer to craft not only description but also an interesting perspective on the scene. Powell takes readers on a bird's eye sweep, beginning with what is below, the canyon, then on a flight west and east, but this panoramic vision is less concerned with topographical accuracy than what eagles and gods may "quarry" there. Powell characterizes its glory as something the reader has never seen, but he also describes it in terms they would be familiar with and expect. Powell also infuses the scene with phrases borrowed from popular romantic poets he has read during calm stretches: Scott, Longfellow, and Tennyson. The last, in particular, provides an image: "[The eagle] clasps the crag with crooked hands."[8]

However, what emerges from Powell's pen is not simply a landscape that is infused with preconceptions. More important, it is a landscape that must surrender a meaning. What is notable is his impulse not to merely to "clothe" the mountains in mystery and military uniform, or give readers an impressionistic mirage, but to give them a context they can understand. Though forced, "mountains are in uniform" is the figure of speech Powell uses to translate the view into a cultural "map" his readers can comprehend.

We soon notice, however, that Powell was not able to "paint" for his readers as effectively as King.

> After dinner we pass through a region of wildest desolation. The canyon is *very* tortuous, the river *very* rapid, and *many* lateral canyons enter on either side. These usually have their branches, so that the region is cut into a wilderness of gray and brown cliffs. In several places these lateral canyons are separated from one another only by narrow walls, often hundreds of feet high,—so narrow in places that where softer rocks are found below they have crumbled away and left holes in the wall, forming passages from one canyon into another. These we often call natural bridges; but they were never intended to span streams. They would be better, perhaps, called side doors between canyon chambers. (191)

Powell finds relief in the architectural image of a door, but the style here is pedestrian, characterized by weak or vague adjectives, and the tone is dull. Whereas King consistently makes use of "metaphor, allusion and sophisticated syntactical variation" to convey a scene, taking it beyond the level that the objective map presents it, "Powell's rough takes show him wrestling with nature," "chained to the facts" (Tallmadge 1182–83). Except for his swerves into "adventure," Powell describes the location in a quasi-technical vocabulary: lateral canyons, gray and brown cliffs. In this same canyon, which they name the Canyon of Desolation, Powell's scene is hard to imagine or see without a map:

> In the Canyon of Desolation the highest rocks immediately over the river are about 2,400 feet.... This is at Log Cabin Cliff. The highest part of the terrace is near the brink of Brown Cliffs. Climbing the immediate walls of the canyon and passing back to the canyon terrace and climbing that, we find the altitude above the river to be 3,300 feet. The lower end of Gray Canyon is about 2,000 feet; the lower end of Labyrinth Canyon, 1,300 feet.
>
> Stillwater Canyon is 42 ¾ miles long; the highest walls, 1,300 feet. (209)

In passages such as this, we are given only the scientific facts, the exterior landscape, with nothing to relate them to (not even a door or a quarry), but the imagination does not take them in. At times Powell seems to be grasping for metaphors, at other times, refusing to give any, opting for little more than the repetitive cadences of heights and distances to convey his scene. As if to make amends for the times when he does use literary license, Powell inserts his sober observations in the sections on the physical features of the Colorado valley, filled with surveyor's measurements. The eye (I) must be absent for claims of scientific detachment and objectivity, but such a pose is broken down by his continual narration of the climbs necessary to obtain such views and measurements. His shifting among styles also makes it difficult to forget the author assembling the view.

Like the coordinates he produces for maps, his description is a way of ordering the landscape into a coherent system. But whereas King's narrative shows a strong element of projecting the inner landscape onto the outer, Powell's shows him grappling with nature and with a way of writing about it that is more intrinsic to what is "out there." A crucial aspect of their respective approaches to nature can be seen in the names they give places. King's names mostly honored patrons or other people he wished to honor (Mount Whitney, for example, or the Sierra peak he named after California politician John Conness). Though some of Powell's did too, he did not, as Stegner observes, "plaster politicians across the map" (195). Many more of his names evolved from some particular aspect of the landscape, as if it was speaking back to him (one place is even named Echo Park). Some of these names are scientific

(Marble Canyon and Gypsum Canyon, named for kinds of rock found there) whereas others refer to qualities or appearances of the landscape (Log Cabin Cliff, Canyon of Desolation). In one insightful instance, Powell shows his pleasure in this process of naming: "So we have a curious ensemble of wonderful features—curved walls, royal arches, glens, alcove gulches, mounds, monuments. From which of these features shall we select a name? We decide to call it Glen Canyon" (233). From the infinite number of possibilities, from the "royal" ensemble, Powell opts for one unadorned: glen, "a narrow valley," to join with canyon, "a chasm with steep cliff walls cut into the earth by water." This naming might be said to resemble the Indian practice of naming, arising from features of the landscape rather than Euro-American monumentalizing of the (irrelevant) "great ones."[9]

However, other names are derived from more anthropocentric sources, such as poems the crew could remember. The party named the Canyon of Lodore after the Xanadu-like poem by Robert Southey:

> And so never ending, but always descending,
> Sounds and motions forever and ever are blending,
> All at once and all o'er, with a mighty uproar,
> And this way the Water comes down at Lodore. (176)

Eastern audiences may have remembered the poem from their youth, and in this instance Powell reached out to poetry as a break from his more prosaic names. Perhaps realizing a missed opportunity, Powell rechristened to "Bright Angel Creek" a beautiful clear creek he had earlier called Silver on a later lecture tour about his voyage, "to make a singularly happy contrast with the Dirty Devil above" (Stegner 98). When Powell reports the incident in *The Exploration,* he glosses over the original names: "We have named one stream, away above, in honor of the great chief of the 'Bad Angels,' and as this is in beautiful contrast to that, we conclude to name it 'Bright Angel'" (259). Names are essential to the process that brings space into place, and when he prepared to write *The Exploration,* Powell was becoming conscious of how his names and his narrative would create the story of the place.

Though Powell and King were both involved in the transformation from topography to place, Powell's process ultimately differed from King's (Tallmadge 1183). Except when King describes its catastrophic power, he characteristically represented nature as an impressionist but passive portrait, and even describes himself a "sensitized photographic plate, to be influenced" (142). He portrays the catastrophic energy, nature's agency, as happening a long time ago, as in a five-act drama that included the "dragons of ice." For King in the present, nature was either an inviting place for repose or a scene to be painted. For the mapmaker and scientific cataloguer, even for the painter, mountain ranges, rivers, fossils, even Indians, might all be data to absorb. That view is static, usually gained from a bird's eye view, but Powell's view was always changing, from heights where he could look down on the space to deep in the canyon, where his view was limited, and he could not see the "uniform."

Since Powell was always moving, so too was the landscape, seen to him as a motion picture rather than a static canvas of vast proportions—a single frame. Sound was part of this "kinesthetic effect: the constant roar of the river ... the rush of the wind" (Tallmadge 1183). Also, there was no one center to it, as there is a summit to a mountain, from which one gazes on the still surroundings. Thoreau could measure the width, length, and depth of Walden Pond, map and locate its epicenter by moving around its stable presence, but the canyon country with its flowing rivers was a labyrinth that compelled a constant movement from one new point to another (related to Thoreau's "walking").

In his revised *Exploration* of 1895, Powell reflected on this constant change and its ultimate reward: a "sublime" prevision of "Paradise." "You cannot see the Grand Canyon in one view," he writes, "as if it were a changeless spectacle from which a curtain might be lifted" (397). To see it, you have to "toil from month to month through its labyrinths" (397). Powell learned that the sublime was more something the explorer earned through hard, investigative work than imported as a literary aesthetic; more a quality of the land's interior than the explorer's.

Early in the expedition, Powell expressed his confidence in his ability to "read" the canyon from one view: "All about me are interesting geologic records. The book is open and I can read as I run."[10] To presume the land is a text is to claim an ability to read it, in ways useful for the exploration or to claim power over it. But when the signs are difficult to read, the notion of the land as a decipherable "book" fades. Before completing his reading, Powell sees that all about him are "grand views," but then adds: "but somehow I think of the nine days rations and the bad river, and the lesson of the rocks and the glory of the scene are but half conceived" (263). Even when the canyon permitted a view or a truth, there was danger to worry about. The "grand view" is moderated by the dangers of the voyage and difficulty of seeing what lay ahead. Powell pushes on to get a better view, to check on the prospects to come, "but, arriving at the point, I can see below only a labyrinth of black gorges" (264).

The sublime was invoked to explain these failures of interpretation, but the sublime was not simply a construct that Powell imported. His sublime was a decentered one, gained from the shifting perspective in rivercourses rather than the view Frémont or King gains from high on summits. He could gain neither the "grand view" nor sympathetic "contact" with the canyon country. Instead of the Romantic Sublime, which according to Thomas Weiskel is an "egotistical sublime," foregrounding the human self and perceiving in one's own image and for one's benefit (48), Powell offered something closer to an ecological or decentered sublime, based on the self's relationship to what was beyond and outside it.[11]

His conception that nature was sublime, operated independently from him and wasn't to be seen from one "view" enabled Powell to draw a radical conclusion: that nature organized itself. The corollary is that humans' duty is to "read" that order. In his scientific *Report* (1878), which draws on the material he developed for *The Exploration* (1875), Powell writes that "divisional surveys should conform to the topography" (22). The terrain of the arid region should determine how settlement plots should be graphed, meaning that the long-used methods of government survey do not take into account the changed relation of water and land in the West. Powell's recognition that nature organizes its own space is clear in a later essay he did for *Century* magazine in 1890, "Institutions for the Arid Lands":

> In a group of mountains a small river has its source. A dozen or a score of creeks unite to form a trunk. The creeks higher up divide into brooks. All these streams combined formed the drainage system of a hydrographic basin, *a unit of country well defined in nature,* for it is bounded above and on each side by heights of land that rise as crests to *part the waters.* (emphasis added, 113)

Nature, not surveyors, creates boundaries, but note that Powell is bringing the sublime and the scientific together. Nature has its own "units," already well defined, though it also has a sublime force that "parts" it. Powell brings together the two codes, scientific ("hydrographic basins") and literary (the figure of a tree), to explain how nature operates. Also, a "unit" of country is different than a country that is "uniform." Perhaps most important, the interior landscape influences the practical, scientific one: Powell's sense of independent (sublime) units in nature predetermined his recommendations for alternatives to rectilinear conceptions of space and his rationale for organizing land-use in conjunction with these units and not in spite of them. In short, the sublime influences the empirical.

"Water parting" has historically been a way to talk about watersheds ("hydrographic basins"). The word "watershed" comes from the German *wasserscheide* (*wasser* = water, *scheide* = parting). The allusion is also biblical, as God is the agent at work, parting the waters for his chosen people. Reflecting about the erosion of the region in "The Grand Canyon," an essay he wrote for the revised *Exploration* (1895), Powell again asks us to consider the godlike work of nature: "the wandering clouds, the tempest-bearing clouds, the rainbow-decked clouds, with mighty power and with wonderful skill, carve out valleys and canyons and fashion hills and cliffs and mountains. The clouds are the artists sublime" (393). The sublime enabled him to help explain nature's processes. It wasn't simply to be felt, as it was for Jefferson looking down on the natural bridge ("the rapture of the spectator is indescribable,") or Cole gazing over Niagara ("we become what we behold"), but understood as an aspect of nature's fundamental phenomena.[12] It continued to refer to those thrilling emotions that Burke described, but now the sublime experience also came from grasping the full story of geologic history developing over millions of years: the full picture of how land forms pushed up and came back down, of forces of eruption and erosion working on a grand scale.

Considering all the components of the work required to know the canyon, Powell later concluded that the Grand Canyon was "the most sublime spectacle on earth" (390). A decade before, Clarence Dutton (who worked under Powell on the survey) wrote in his *Tertiary History of the Grand Canyon District* (1882) that the Grand Canyon "is the sublimest thing on earth. It is not alone by virtue of its magnitude, but by the virtue of its whole—its *ensemble*" (143). Powell, too, was interested in aesthetic questions, in how the canyon could be seen, but he was less likely to get the "whole." His sublime both competed with his wish for scientific understanding and completed it. As fact finder and data collector, Powell was not out to locate the sublime in nature, though as a writer he found it a convenient tool. The sublime descends from the sense that the supernatural lies just beneath the surface of the earth, in a place that can't be mapped topographically, but could be interpreted. In the canyon country of the West, Powell was detecting not only the motion of the river, but also the visible traces of nature's agency: geologic motion that was engraved in the rocks but whose forces were just below the threshold of consciousness or apprehension. He could see the different layers that form the canyon from above, "black gneiss below, the variegated quartzite, and the green or alcove sandstone form[ing] the foundation for the mighty red wall," but from below, and perhaps from the cumulative effect of these layers, they fade into sublime and "empyrean" blue:

> Seen from below, these changing elements seem to graduate into the heavens, and no plane of demarcation between *wall* and blue firmament can be seen. The heavens constitute a portion of the *façade* and mount into a vast *dome* from wall to wall, spanning the Grand Canyon with empyrean blue. So the earth and the heavens are blended in one vast *structure*. (emphasis added, 393)

From below, he seems to lose perspective. He sees no line of demarcation between the wall, which can be surveyed, and the heavens, which are sublime. The canyon country made the devotee of science feel that the incredible labyrinth of canyons and rivers was limitless, not to be bounded. More important, the canyon doesn't just rise into the sky, but all the way to the heavens, the empyrean. The architectural terms signify that the canyon is *built* this way, not by accident.

Although he momentarily gets the grand view here, the earth and heavens in one "building," Powell would also sense some of the lack resulting from an abstracting or "uniform" way of perceiving. As did King at the base of Mount Whitney, and Thoreau in the forests of Maine, Powell sensed that Indians knew an aspect of the land of which he had no conception:

> It is curious now to observe the knowledge of our Indians. There is not a trail but what they know; every gulch and every rock seems familiar. I have prided myself on being able to retain in my mind the topography of a country; but these Indians put me to shame. My knowledge is only general, embracing more important features of a region that remains as a map engraved on my mind; but theirs is particular. They know every rock and every ledge, every gulch and canyon, and just where to wind among

these to find a pass, and their knowledge is unerring. They cannot describe a country to you, but they can tell you all the particulars of a route.
(299–300)

The statement follows the breakup of the crew. Powell has returned, a year
later, to search for his crew with Indian guides he has employed to find the
"truth" about what happened to them. Perhaps Powell is reflecting doubts
about his "reckoning." He recognizes that he operates from the stance of the
map-reader, the bird's-eye view. Indians "cannot describe a country" because
they do not describe it mathematically as the surveyor does, spatially as the
cartographer would, nor do they draw on the scientific terms of geology or the
aesthetic of the sublime. But the map-view cannot represent the crucial details, the trail along the little-known "gulch," or the rocks that may take one
home. It orients in terms of vast distances, not in the sense of walking over the
terrain. The Indian's knowledge of place results in one that is "unerring," a
more "particular" spatialization of landscape. When he can't get the bird's eye
view, a surveillance or command of the territory, the landscape seems general,
whereas to the Indian, he thinks, the country is individuated.

   Though Powell also expresses confidence in being able to read the canyon,
in many more places in *The Exploration* Powell acknowledges his own inability
to "describe a country." Powell first experiences the sublime indescribability of
the territory he can map and measure but not possess on June 17 in the Canyon of Lodore, which has "scenic interest" that is "even beyond the power of
pen to tell" (163). About the navigation of dangerous rapids, Powell says, "It is
not [possible] to describe the labor of such navigation" (255). As the journey
progresses down the Colorado, and Powell and his men become more fatigued
and hungry, his sense of sublime wonder and dread seems to increase. He says
in an entry dated August 14: "At the very introduction it inspires awe. The canyon is narrower than we have ever before seen it; the water is swifter." (248).
More than a mile deep in the canyon—deeper than most mountains are high,
when measured from their base—the vantage point of a bird's eye view, where
Powell can survey and map (hence, *know* according to a map reader) the territory is greatly diminished, and the canyon closes in. Powell acknowledges that
he is in the realm of the "Great Unknown":

We have an unknown distance yet to run; an unknown river yet to explore. What falls there are, we know not: what rocks beset the channel, we

know not; what walls rise over the river, we know not. Ah, well! we may conjecture many things. (247)

Powell is clearly building suspense, but is also acknowledging the strange "otherness" and unknowability that the unmapped, unexperienced canyon has for him and his men. They couldn't have a way of knowing what was ahead, but Powell emphasizes the cumulative effect of this experience through the repetition of the main clause: "we know not." Some aspect of the known (falls, rocks, wall) is presented and then negated three times. As the walls close in so does the syntax, tightening and constricting, cutting off speculation in a three-syllable main clause. They can "conjecture" many things, but these are left unnamed after the empty expostulation: "Ah, Well!" When deep in the canyon, without the "grand view," Powell enters his sublime, which is associated not with what is clear and distinct, but what is vague and obscure.[13] Ironically, Powell's scientific exploration aimed to make this unknown visible, representable, and perhaps tame, but this sense of the sublime place is ambiguous, vague, and indescribable, and leads to conjecture rather than certainty.

In the earlier *Exploration* Powell says that that the gulches, canyons, and alcoves of the Grand Canyon are part of the "library of the gods." He says that "he who would read the language of the universe may dig out the letters here and there, and with them spell the words, and read, in a slow and imperfect way, but still so as to understand a little, the story of creation" (194). Powell, like other geologists and literary cartographers, senses an alphabet beneath the surface, waiting to be "dug out" and assembled into a subsequent narrative, and the narratives themselves part of a larger "library" or orderly procession. But he leaves behind the notion of land as text in his later essay on "The Grand Canyon" in the revised *Exploration,* suggesting that just as "your books may have many colored bindings and differ greatly in their contents; so these quartzites vary greatly from place to place along the wall, and in many places they entirely disappear" (379). The bookshelf metaphor was under some strain, as if Powell sensed that there were worlds overprinting other worlds, layers impinging on other geological layers too varied for analogy, or cartography, so he drew on the sublime to help tell his "story of creation."

After his thinking on the "knowledge" of Indians, Powell once again attempts to climb a summit "to obtain a view of the country." However, reaching it, he sees "once more the labyrinth of deep gorges that flank the Grand Canyon; in the multitude, I cannot determine whether it is itself in view or not" (300). After having spent months in the canyon, Powell is now not only unsure if he sees the Grand Canyon, but whether or not it can be seen.

VISUAL ASPECTS OF THE EXPLORATION: TOWARD A BETTER "MAP"

While Powell represented the canyon through a combination of scientific confidence and sublime wonder, many of the more notable visual aspects of *The Exploration* pick up on the latter sense. The first edition of *The Exploration of the Colorado River of the West and Its Tributaries* was lavishly illustrated. It contained no map, but it had pictures. Wood engravings based on Thomas Moran's sketches accompanied the articles that first appeared in *Scribner's* and were subsequently used in *The Exploration*. Moran's monumental *The Grand Chasm of the Colorado* (1873–74, Figure 4.2) was based on sketches from a trip in Powell's company to the north rim of the canyon. Though they weren't sympathetic to Powell's proposals for a revision of land use, Congress later purchased the painting for $10,000 and hung it in the Capitol, giving many Americans an image of what their greatest natural wonder looked like (Wilkins 135). It now resides in the Department of the Interior Museum in Washington, D.C.

Moran's illustrations were not realistic in the scientific sense; they proceeded from facts but attempted to transcend them. Moran once claimed that the goal of the artist was to "produce for the spectator the impression produced by nature on himself" (qtd. in Stegner 24–25). He also said that "a place, as a place, has no value in itself for the artist only so far as it furnishes the material from which to construct a picture. Topography in art is valueless. The motive or incentive for my *Grand Canyon of the Yellowstone* was the gorgeous display of color that impressed itself upon me" (qtd. in Taft 250). In other words, Moran did not wish to "realize" literal facts, but to paint the impression—not the place's topography, but the place's character. Significantly, most of the illustrations that Moran produced for *Scribner's* were painted from photographs and imaginatively refigured. In one instance Moran created a photograph of a promontory and made it look like a monument, dramatizing it by narrowing the frame, heightening the view, and adding figures and boats in what was an otherwise empty foreground, thus—in literary terms—making

Fig. 4.2. Moran's *The Grand Chasm of the Colorado* (1873). This engraving accompanied the early *Scribner's* articles and went into *The Exploration*. Congress later purchased the huge painting for $10,000. *The Exploration of the Colorado River of the West and Its Tributaries* (1875), 194.

the prosaic poetic. Considering that Powell drew from literal facts but transformed them, the "impressions" Moran took from photographs may seem appropriate. He paralleled in painting what Powell did in writing *The Exploration,* transforming his field notes into a swift-moving dramatic "picture," but
Moran's paintings were more sublime than Powell's descriptions. After reading
Powell's book as serialized in *Scribner's,* Moran even told Powell in a letter that
he should make *The Exploration* more reflective of the sublime scenery. He
found Powell's descriptions "strong and vigorous," but added:

> You do not once (If I recollect right) give your sensations even in the
> most dangerous of passages, nor even hint at the terrible and sublime
> feelings that are stirred within one, as he feels himself in the jaws of the
> monstrous chasms. It seems to me that the expression of these impres-
> sions and thoughts tend to *realize* the descriptions to the reader & are
> almost as necessary as the descriptions themselves. (emphasis added,
> qtd. in Wilkins 89)

Moran gave Powell good advice for the popular magazine where the narrative
first appeared; however, Moran's advice to give "sensations" and "impressions"
weren't necessarily among Powell's own objectives to "realize" the canyon.

To some extent, Powell responded when he revised the *Exploration* for the
1895 edition. Although Powell changed few things about the narrative of the
expedition, he revised his scientific "The Physical Features of the Valley of
the Colorado" (Part II of the of the 1875 *Exploration*) for a lay audience, adding
more from his ethnographic studies, and moved that section to the front. Then,
he added his essay on "The Grand Canyon," a concise statement and culmination of Powell's attitudes toward the region's geology and aesthetics, with the
descriptions of the area's sublimity that I have already cited (above, page 115).

Also, when he revised the 1875 *Exploration* for the 1895 *Canyons of the Colorado* (subheading: "with many illustrations"), Powell also inserted 170 more
illustrations than the eighty in the original, some of which bear no resemblance to the contiguous text. These illustrations were some of the country's
first "exposure" to the landscape and Indian artifacts of the West, and they ca-
ter to the audience's voyeuristic tendencies, as they presented not only the
views peering down into the canyon, but "gazed" at Indian rituals and artifacts,
not to mention women without clothing. Nevertheless, those illustrations

were culled from the thirteen years of the Powell surveys, and he was obviously proud of the "work" they reflected, all at his charge. The pictures of so many Indians, while not repudiating the sublime, suggest that, as Donald Worster has noted in his biography of Powell, "people belong in our pictures and places" (334).

But what was the picture of the place that was emerging? The illustrations for both the original and the revised *The Exploration* were far from a surveyor's expressions of mathematical verisimilitude, but even more oddly, maps of Powell's journey were conspicuously left out. Only one appears in the original, a foldout tucked in a back pocket titled "Green River from the Union Pacific Railroad to the Mouth of the White River. 1873."[14] But this map only covers the very northern tip of the expedition through the Uinta Mountains. One of the reasons it took so long to publish *The Exploration* (six years from the time of the first trip) is that many of the scientific findings, along with the map, were lost when the chief topographer of the first trip, Captain Howland, climbed out of the canyon and was killed. This made the second voyage necessary, and Powell made sure this time that there were duplicate versions of maps and notes. The second trip in 1872 involved nearly all the hardships of the first, but, lacking the suspense and fear, the tragedy of separation and death, it didn't make for a story. As Stegner observes, "the second passage down the river was not an exploration, but a survey; what rendered it scientifically important rendered it dramatically second-hand" (137). The routine of mapping the river—setting up baselines, taking barometric readings—rather than exploring left Powell's imagination restless. He left the party once and went to Salt Lake City to visit his pregnant wife and made several excursions to Indian villages to begin his ethnographic work, leaving his brother-in-law, Almon Thompson, in charge of the survey. Mostly under Thompson's direction, this trip produced the map that went into *The Exploration* (1875). When maps are made, as King found out, the mystery contracts: What is mapped ceases to be sublime.

Another map was included in Powell's "Overland Trip to the Grand Canyon," published in *Scribner's* in 1875 as a follow-up to the initial articles and recounting the journey with Hamblin to find out about the lost crew. Published in a popular magazine, this map, to be sure, is less useful as a scientific report than as an illustration for the narrative of the journey. It is labeled "Map of the Grand Canyon of the Colorado," with subheading, "Showing the Route

Traveled by Major Powell" (Figure 4.3). The map has no "legend" (a delicious pun in this case), but a dotted line shows the overland routes as "Powell's Line of Travel" and "Route Traveled."[15] Labels are scarce owing to the small scale of the map, but "Powell's Point" can be detected. Powell's name is there, though others' in the party are not (especially Thompson's). Powell hardly mentions his crew members by name in *The Exploration* (indeed, he leaves the second crew from the 1871–72 party out completely, to create the illusion that it was all one trip) and omits them from his original preface. With its clear lines of hierarchy and command, this practice may have come from Powell's military training. Whatever the reason, because his name only is prominently displayed, it perpetuated the myth that heroic individuals and not collaborative groups were winning the West, a myth that Powell himself would later attempt to debunk.

Even though maps are scarce in *The Exploration,* Powell put other illustrations and woodcuts in, including those by Moran. The illustrations often presented the view from above, the one the map produces. But if maps create the illusion that space is contained, most of the illustrations, especially those by Moran, present the impression of vast distances and heights, a labyrinth of unfamiliar landscape.

In some instances, we are presented with both the sense of the topography given by an artist and the factual information of a cartographer. H. H. Nichols wanted to be sure he wasn't presenting only a literal map ("topography in art is valueless").[16] From the high position, much of the canyon country, with its ledges and lines, could resemble the contours of map, but the comparison stops there. As seen in Figure 4.4, he made a compromise. Instead of labeling place-names as a cartographer would, Nichols presents "One bird, Echo Cliffs, Two birds, Kaibab Plateau . . . Five birds, Shivwits Plateau" (1st edition 186). Since pictographic symbols (birds) denote location, the illustrator is able to convey cartographic information without sacrificing a rendering of the place as it appears to the camera or naked eye. In a sense, the illustration provides a realistic "map," with a frame so that it may be read like a map, but controlling the landscape's threatening vastness (the sublime scene that Moran painted) by labeling its different sections. A map would not convey the "newness" and unfamiliarity of the scene, and a painting alone of the strange and unfamiliar landscape, without any markers, would not provide enough information. The compromise allows for both accuracy and aesthetic pleasure.

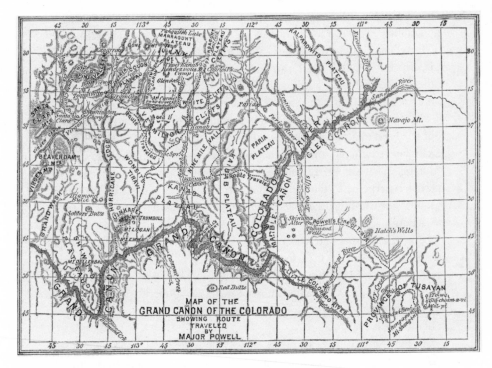

Fig. 4.3. This "Map of the Grand Canyon of the Colorado" presents visually what a summary of *The Exploration* does through writing. Powell left it out of *The Exploration,* perhaps because he felt it to be inadequate, but also because the map, in condensing the space, makes it less "grand." *Scribner's* (1875), 661.

The last illustrations to accompany Powell's closing statements on the Grand Canyon are from the sketches of William Henry Holmes, first included in Clarence Dutton's *Tertiary History of the Grand Canyon District* (1882) as double-page panoramas. The sketches are far less idealized than Moran's paintings and border on diagrams, but to view them is also to step to the edge of the canyon. Holmes raised topographical drawing to the level of art. Whereas Moran most always brought in a storm for the atmospheric background (as he did in both *The Grand Chasm of the Colorado* and *The Grand Canyon*), Holmes seemed to want to cut through the haze, to present the canyon as clearly as possible, to mark its horizontal layers and vertical panels with crispness and precision. Moran's majestic 1873–74 *The Grand Canyon* (Figure 4.5) prefaces the concluding essay by the same name, one Powell wrote especially for the new edition, but six by Holmes conclude it. If Moran's *The Grand Canyon* set up the sublime, Holmes's sketches were there for scientific purposes, to illustrate the recession of cliffs, lava flows, the forms of buttes and peaks. Indeed, Holmes seems to refuse to "improve" on the scene: His drawings were to be used for utilitarian purposes, and Holmes's three views from, ironically, Point Sublime, looking east, west, and south, come with letters to label named places and numbers to indicate geologic features (Figure 4.6). From this vantage point, Clarence Dutton concluded that the Grand Canyon "could not be comprehended in a day or a week, nor even a month." It was a "special culture, requiring time, patience, and long familiarity for its consummation" (143).

Though designed for scientific purposes, the Holmes illustrations have their own artistic devices to help us understand that "special culture." Though he did not falsify proportions, he would heighten contrasts for depth. Still, as Stegner observed, Holmes was less likely to distort details than to "move himself around indefinitely until the landscape composed itself" (illustration 6 in BHM). Holmes's drawings bring together the precision of science and the poetry of art. In moving around until the canyon "composed itself," Holmes contributed something not only to the clarification of the Colorado River country, but something closer to Powell's own objectives than Moran's "sensations": a representational "map" that found the "value" in topography but wouldn't overly distort.

CONSRVATION AND CONTROL FROM HEROIC AND SUBLIME: *REPORT ON THE LANDS OF THE ARID REGION*

Powell closed his revised *Exploration* with these more literal "maps" and with his ten-page essay titled the "The Grand Canyon." In the essay, Powell discussed the inadequacy of both verbal and visual "maps": "The wonders of the Grand Canyon cannot be adequately represented in symbols of speech, nor by speech itself," he said. Neither speech nor visual forms could fix the identity of the canyon country: "The resources of the graphic art are taxed beyond their powers in attempting to portray its features. Language and illustration combined must fail" (394). The elements that composed the Canyon country were too multifarious and diverse.

Fig. 4.4. In this "Bird's eye view of the Grand Canyon looking east from the Grand Wash" the illustrator gives both cartographic and artistic information. We are presented with both the sense of topography that an artist gives, including depth and perspective, and the factual information that a cartographer provides. Five birds signifies Shivwits Plateau. *The Exploration of the Colorado River of the West and Its Tributaries* (1875), 186.

Fig. 4.5. "Topography in art is valueless": Moran's *The Grand Canyon* (1873–74) is Figure 1, the frontispiece, of the first *Exploration* and kicks off Powell's concluding essay by the same name in his revised 1895 *Exploration*. The sun is coming out under the storm above, as the rocks look like a great city from afar. *The Exploration of the Colorado River of the West and Its Canyons* (1895), 378.

> The Cyclopean forms which result from the sculpture of tempests
> through the ages too long for man to compute are wrought into endless
> details, to describe which would be a task equal in magnitude to that of
> describing the stars of the heavens or the multitudinous beauties of the
> forest with its traceries of foliage presented by oaks and pine and poplar,
> by beech and linden and hawthorn, by tulip and lily and rose, by fern
> and moss and lichen. (394)

The Grand Canyon resisted any attempt at systemization or description, though Powell approaches one in his series of flora, punctuated in groups of three. Discarding both visual and descriptive epistemologies, Powell turns to music: "It is the land of music . . . The Grand Canyon is a land of song . . . the music of waters. The adamant foundations of earth have been wrought into a sublime harp, upon which the clouds of the heavens play with mighty tempests or with gentle showers" (394). It was a landscape of infinite variety and complexity, not to be known through a single language, verbal or visual or musical. In the passage, there are both a "mapping" and unmapping, a discrediting of verbal powers but a description, a rejecting of words and "maps" but an appeal to music. If "maps" and language couldn't adequately represent the sense of place, perhaps music was a better medium for capturing the sense of time, so detectable in the canyon's layers and audible in the river that cut it.

The canyon country was an enigma, a puzzle to be solved. It was difficult to "map" and had no one identity or way of knowing it, but it did have a system, even if a musical one. For Powell, music may be an appropriate figure for understanding nature's processes, for it can be said to be more natural than either the literary or visual arts. Powell stated these ideas in his revised *Exploration* of 1895, after the scientific "maps" in his *Report* had been rejected by Congress, as if he was now more acutely aware of how the region could not be understood. Still, he was developing such ideas earlier when he wrote about his expedition and the canyon country itself.

Since he understood the difficulty in describing and "mapping" the canyon, when he turned to *The Report*, Powell attempted to propose rather than impose a system for nature's use. He recognized that the rectilinear maps wouldn't do in the arid west, because there was no way rectangles could be formed or otherwise developed. The topography forbade it. Neither the Romantic sublime nor the Enlightenment grid nor Pioneer expectations would do in the arid country, so he suggested a new approach.

Fig. 4.6. One of the sketches, this one looking west from Point Sublime, in William Henry Holmes's three-part panorama that concludes Powell's 1895 *Canyons of the Colorado*. It positions the observer as the map does, the earth below, open to investigation. But it provides the perspective a map wouldn't. The drawings provide the depth and composition of a painting with the precision and accuracy of a map. *The Exploration of the Colorado River of the West and Its Canyons* (1895), 398–403.

Since his days of farming in Ohio and Wisconsin, Powell felt that his exploration should map the country so that its settlers could know what to expect in terms of water, forest, and grazing resources. But Powell immediately sensed a difference between his own Midwestern agrarian experience and the Western pioneer's—the condition of aridity. Though he learned about the region's aridity during his explorations, his attempt to debunk myths about a "Garden of the World" appeared not in *The Exploration* but in his *Report of the Lands of the Arid Region* in 1878.

As Michael A. Bryson has pointed out in *Visions of the Land,* Powell's rhetoric in the *Report* is characterized by two key features: "the emphasis on quantitative data and the corresponding de-emphasis upon the narrator's ... subjectivity" (88). No heroic protagonist strides through these pages. By making scientific analysis his rhetorical framework rather than the sublime or the adventure narrative, Powell was able to construct nature as an active, ordered system that can be understood, and this understanding provides the means of controlling nature for human use. The *Report* contains echoes of *The Exploration,* for it also contains doubts that nature can be known (in keeping with the assertions of sublimity in the earlier text), but also a strong feeling that it can be known and, if it can, should be controlled by humans (as the scientific and heroic in the earlier text testify). The *Exploration* focuses on where Powell has been, mapping terrain and bringing it into the realm of the known. In Powell's *Report,* on the other hand, data is more important for the trends it may predict over time (determining land policy and resource utilization) than for its variations it may map and chart over space (Bryson 94). Powell's *Report* offers not only estimates of the impact that humans have had (in passages on the Mormons and Indians), but ones they may have on the arid region, and his recommendations for how they should use it. His arguments about land use are designed to counter the myths of the "garden of the world" and the notion that "rain follows the plough," a myth promulgated by a surveyor, Ferdinand V. Hayden.[17] This "interior landscape" that Americans had of the West, the "garden of the world" notion that was fostered by boosters such as Senator William Gilpin, was in direct conflict with Powell's observations of the arid nature of the West.

The maps Powell included in the *Report* were to aid in the persuasion. Instead of giving only topographic information, Powell's maps were also designed to counter the myth. The "Map of Utah Territory representing the extent of the irrigable, timber and pasture lands" shows a dearth of all three elements. The last map, "Rain Chart of the United States showing by isohyetal lines the distribution of the mean annual precipitation in rain and melted snow," shows through blue shading how rainfall diminishes west of the 95th meridian and inland from the Pacific Coast. Powell's *Report* provided maps that not only presented topographic space but also critical environmental data about what took *place* there.

Nevertheless, the interior landscape may have rung "true," because Powell's radical proposal of the 1878 *Report* for a reorganization of the rectangular survey laws was ignored. A decade later a drought gripped the lands that Powell had classified; the aridity he warned about revealed itself with a vengeance. As he had foretold, it hit the subhumid regions, where farmers relied on rains, worse than it hit the arid ones where most farmers had made some provisions, however inadequate, for irrigation (Stegner, "Introduction" xix). From these lands came renewed demands for surveys and irrigation works. Powell was appointed director of an Irrigation Survey with federal appropriation. According to Stegner, Powell saw it as a "chance to realize a good part of his general plan for the West," but others in Congress, notably William Stewart (1827–1909) of Nevada, wanted a quick designation of reservoir sites so profit would be "prompt and easy" (xx). Powell put in a plan to complete the topographical mapping and on top of those maps, to conduct hydrographic surveys—measuring stream flow and plotting catchment basins and canal lines—all to systematically classify the lands as either irrigable or nonirrigable. He estimated the job at seven years and seven million dollars, but members of Congress grew impatient and cut his funding.[18]

In an 1890 series of articles that he wrote for *Century Magazine*, Powell restated and rewrote the essential ideas of the *Report*. He hadn't changed his mind about anything in the *Report*, but, as if now aware that scientific "maps" would not convince either the public or Congress, he changed his methods of persuasion. In the "Non-irrigable Lands of the Arid Region" (about those lands that couldn't be farmed), Powell was less likely to let numbers convince, and inserted one table with this caveat: "Numbers perhaps are more arid than lands, and hence they are appropriate here" (917). In another of these articles, Powell wrote more convincingly about the yields proper management and irrigation would produce, recasting the myth but appealing to it:

> Ultimately, the whole region will be covered with a mosaic of ponds fringed with a rich vegetation; and crystal waters, and green fields, and blooming gardens will be dotted over all the burning naked lands, and sand dunes, alkali stretches, and naked hills will be decked with beautiful tracts of verdure. ("The Irrigable Lands of the Arid Region" 770)

The West was not a garden now but could be, through proper management. Written for a popular magazine rather than as scientific report to be read by Congress, the tone and language changes greatly. There is a "mosaic" of ponds, like a work of art, and "tracts of verdure." Crystal waters, green fields, and blooming gardens will "dot" and "deck" this majesty. Powell also wrote in the same article that, after all, "arid lands are not lands of famine, and the sunny sky is not a firmament of devastation. *Conquered rivers* are better servants than wild clouds (emphasis added, 767). Where the clouds were also "artists sublime," sculpting watersheds, here they are wild, subjecting humans to their inconsistent precipitation. To solve the problem, "conquer" the rivers. Such acts require a form of heroism, whereby humans devise methods to reclaim and redeem the landscape. Powell no doubt gained such confidence of human prowess from his travails on the river, where he developed methods to negotiate and "conquer" difficult stretches of it. And, to "redeem" these lands, they must be accurately and meticulously surveyed. Powell proposed four sweeping surveys to determine how the lands could be mapped and classified: a topographic, hydrographic, engineering, and geologic survey (770–71). A topographic survey alone would not be adequate: The streams must also be gauged, the reservoirs must be planned, and the geology must by classified to learn were wells might exist. To accomplish the difficult task of surveying the "arid region" from the different positions would indeed be a Herculean and heroic task, but Powell knew that the many different kinds of surveyor-knowledge would be necessary if science was to win over myth.

Yet he continued to appeal to myth. After discussing the need for the surveys, he takes us on a "brief survey" (his words) of Western watersheds and lands, from the Rio Grande to the Snake, the peaks of the Sierra Nevada to plateaus of the Southern Utah, *cartographing* their variations in climate and terrain, suggesting their favorable development characteristics. "The Arid Land is a vast region," he ultimately concludes: "Its mountains gleam in crystal rime, its forests are stately, its cañons are made glad with the music of falling waters, its skies are clear, its air salubrious, and it is already the home of millions of the most energetic men the world has ever known" (776).

In the beginning to that essay's counterpoint, "The Non-Irrigable Lands of the Arid Region," Powell gives his own syllogistic creation myth:

Sun is the father of Cloud.
Cloud is the mother of Rain.
Wind is the ruler of Rain.
Fire is the enemy of Forest.
Water is the enemy of Fire.
Wind feeds Forest, and Rain gives it drink.
Wind joins with Fire to destroy Forest.
Constant Rain battles with fickle Wind and mad Fire to protect Forest.
So Climate decks the land with Forest. (915)

Powell wants his readers to recognize the warp of climate with the woof of vegetation, but he sets his "facts" of ecological wisdom within a narrative, in this case a kind of eco-parable. In a similar fashion, Aldo Leopold would implore us to "think like a mountain" a half-century later.

Later in the same essay, he mentions the narrative of his earlier explorations: "More than twenty years ago I entered the region for the purpose of studying its resources" (921). Without seeming to realize it, Powell then discusses the prospectors in the region in a comparison that seems to rebound on him:

Everywhere men were digging into the heart of the mountains for gold and silver, and armies of men were engaged in prospecting, lured, now here, now there, by rumors of great discoveries. These armies were composed of stalwart men, adventurous, brave, and skillful. Away in the wilderness, without capital, but endowed with brawn and brain, they established industries, organized institutions, and founded a civilization. (921–22)

A key aspect of that civilization is that it adapted to the "physical conditions of the land" (922). But the characterization above seems to apply most significantly to Powell himself. He also "dug" into the "heart" of the canyon, "without capital," and lured by rumor, all to organize institutions.

In most of his later writings, Powell critiqued the notion of heroic individuals "conquering" landscape and argued that the local community as a social structure is better adapted to living wisely and productively within the Western environment. Powell says groups of people forming commonwealths can protect against the few, and that these groups could work together in the "natural" divisions of land, the hydrographic basins (47). Powell proposed a "re-mapping" of the cultural landscape, a quasi-socialistic approach to sharing property. He called for a "system less arbitrary than that of the rectangular surveys now in vogue," one that will overlook "the interests of single individuals," the 160-acre homesteaders, for the "interests of the greatest number" (37). Powell was essentially proposing a countermyth: a collaborative model perhaps based on his observations of the Mormons—who, he says in "Institutions," borrowed the Mexican system of pueblos or "irrigating municipalities" (112)—rather than the myth of heroic individualism. He proceeded beyond the role of mapper and explorer, giving shape to the land and bringing it into the realm of the known, to that of prophet or social visionary, proposing how humans should adapt their culture and institutions to fit the patterns of nature, rather than vice versa.

But Powell's recommendations for a system of cooperative watersheds didn't take hold in the minds of the public precisely because they flew in the face of images he had already helped to promote, if inadvertently. He was, in effect, telling Americans how they could use their Western lands when he had already written that they were sublime, paradisal gardens-in-the-making, reinforcing the idea that in the West, "the mountains were bigger, the canyons deeper, the waterfalls higher—where one seemed closer to God's creation . . . an emblem of America's pride in itself" (Goetzmann, *Imagination* 190). Powell knew Americans could not farm the country's arable lands without irrigation, but its scenic value was already imprinted in the minds of the public, to manage or "see" as they wanted. Still, Powell was astute enough critique the system: He understood how fragile the western lands were. To change the system, he would have to change the cultural landscape.

Paul Shepard has written in *Man in Landscape* (1967) that the focus on the sublime in wilderness in the late nineteenth century "has created in the American character one of its few true idiosyncrasies: the emotional connection of nationalism with stupendous scenery, leading to the phenomenon of the preservation of wilderness areas" (189). As Shepard notes (and Cronon has echoed in "The Trouble with Wilderness"), celebrating the sublime led to the preservation of some of America's wilderness, notably in Yellowstone (1872)—"a

museum to American sublimity" writes art historian Robert Hughes (200)—
and Yosemite (1890), America's first two national parks.

Though Powell also celebrated the Colorado River country as sublime, it
was to meet a fate different from either Yosemite or Yellowstone. In 1964 Glen
Canyon Dam was completed to create, rather ironically, Lake Powell. The
Colorado River has otherwise been diverted, ditched, and reservoired, so that
it no longer reaches the ocean in seasons of average precipitation. Its irrigation
system has created what Donald Worster calls the "hydraulic west," its best-
known symbol the 762-foot Hoover Dam (though in a different canyon than
the Grand Canyon), which was the inspiration and pet project of one Arthur P.
Davis, Director of the Bureau of Reclamation from 1914–23, nephew of John
Wesley Powell (Worster, *Under Western Skies* 69).

Most historians argue that Powell's work on irrigation was on behalf of local and not federal control (Worster, *Unsettled Country* 22–23). Marc Reisner
argues that the "half century of dam-building and irrigation development . . .
went far beyond anything Powell would have liked . . . It is hard to imagine that
the first explorer of the Colorado River would have welcomed a future in
which there might be no rivers left at all" (53). Nevertheless, Powell added to
the image of his sublime a "taming" ideal, one of heroism and confidence. Such
a notion was continued into the image of the brave men who built Hoover
Dam during the early depression-ridden 1930s. In *The Story of Hoover Dam*
(1961) the United States Bureau of Reclamation reports that "in 21 months
5,000 men with modern equipment had built a structure greater in volume than
the largest pyramid in Egypt—a pyramid which, according to Herodotus, required 100,000 men working 20 years to build" (28). The speed with which the
dam was completed bears testimony to "grand old construction men" (30).

Explanations for why Powell's recommendations in the *Report* were not followed abound, but Powell must also bear some responsibility for an image of
the West as explorable and "mappable"—hence controllable. Though he
wanted to limit the number of settlers that could live in the arid region, he also
created the desire to see what he saw, experience what he himself experienced.
To this day, legions of faithful make boat trips down navigable stretches of the
Colorado in neoprene rafts or wooden dories, "reliving Powell's adventure in
the 'Great Unknown,' and knowing where they have been and are going by one
of the quadrangle maps of Powell's Geological Survey" (Wilford 215).

Nearly one hundred years after the first expedition down the river, Edward

Abbey invoked Powell's book—"my favorite western book," (*Journey* 189)—
for his own trip "down the river," the title of his chapter in *Desert Solitaire*.
Abbey writes that the (human) "beavers had to go and build another
goddammed dam on the Colorado." "Not satisfied," he writes, "with the enormous silt trap and evaporation tank called Lake Mead (back of Hoover Dam)
they have created another even bigger, even more destructive, in Glen Canyon"
(151). The impounded waters are called Lake Powell, "supposedly to honor but
actually to dishonor the memory, spirit and vision of Major John Wesley
Powell" (152). Abbey enters Glen Canyon "without having learned much about
it beforehand because [he] wishes to see it as Powell and his party had seen it,
not knowing what to expect" (156). Significantly (and conveniently), he and
his companion lose the Texaco road map ("there are no gas stations in Glen
Canyon anyhow" 158) that would have given them the names of tributaries as
they float "onward in effortless peace deeper into Eden" (160). Without a "map,"
Abbey rids himself of the "mental smog that keeps getting between a man and
his world, obscuring vision"(184). Eventually, they merge with the river,
"intersubjectivity," "molecules getting mixed" (185).

Abbey quotes Powell's sublimest passages ("by a year's toil a concept of sublimity can be obtained never again to be equaled on the hither side of Paradise")
while experiencing his "merging" with the river, all to make an argument about
the need for wilderness. Abbey wanted to prevent Glen Canyon Dam in the
name of wilderness preservation, and says we should "undress" the desert and
the canyon country from all the cultural baggage that is associated with it. He
says the desert "says nothing," is "completely passive, acted upon but never act-
ing," it has no heart (240). "What does the desert mean?" he asks, wary of the
ways humans have appropriated nature for human causes. "It means nothing. It
is as it is and has no need for meaning. The desert lies beneath and soars beyond
any possible human qualification. Therefore, sublime" (194). Abbey's tough
stance ignores the layers of myth, image, and belief that have made the region the
place it is, in his mind as well as others. Abbey wants the space to be blank, and, in
a symbolic gesture, tears up survey stakes for a new road into Arches National
Park. Though he wants it to be "unmapped," the canyon has already been endowed with human, cultural meanings—the sublime is one. For Powell, the
forms, colors, and sound of the canyon unite to produce something that could
only be understood as sublime; he wants to *place* the canyon country in existing
human "maps," even when modifying them. Abbey worries that, for the canyon

Fig. 4.7. Another surveyor, George Wheeler, competed with Powell's survey to produce this map. Wheeler directed a survey up the river, and like Powell's map in Figure 4.3, this map is most useful for telling a story. The "legend" gives the "dates and camps of the river party in 1871." In a sense, these European maps that tell a story more closely resemble the Indian practice of mapping, of "mapping" space through a narrative account of what has happened there. *Mapping the Transmississippi West* (1963, v5, pt2), 338.

country to become a place—endowed with human meaning—it must be misused. If Abbey unmaps the American West, we will leave to Wallace Stegner to rewrite "maps," to create a meaning that isn't harmful, and to continue Powell's hopes that we use nature wisely.

Perhaps because he was so many things—surveyor, explorer, scientist, anthropologist, philosopher, land planner, bureaucrat—Powell's writing is underappreciated, but the *Exploration of the Colorado River of the West and Its Tributaries* remains one of the great adventure stories in American literature. Powell contributed much to our scientific knowledge, but in that book he also contributed to the notion that the Grand Canyon, and by extension a whole region, was more than a spot found on a map: It was an idea, a symbol, an image; a matter of mind and of emotion, a landscape of his interior but also that of the country's. Its significance was cultivated by him but also interpreted—and misinterpreted—by the larger culture he wrote for. Before he could recommend how it should be either preserved or conserved, he had to give it a meaning. As conservationist Aldo Leopold has written, "We can be ethical only in relation to something we can see, feel, understand, love, or otherwise have faith in" (251). The history of the Colorado River country and the Grand Canyon is less contingent on the physical processes that can be mapped, than in the evolution of images and ideas through which we have seen and believed in it. That is also territory that Powell helped to "map," and Stegner, in turn, interpreted.

Both Clarence King and John Wesley Powell would serve terms as Director of the USGS, but both wrote about the sense of place that no government survey could quantify. Although both men would recognize the limitations of science, neither would fully abandon his scientific views. Writing and exploring only a few years after Darwin's *Origin of Species* (1859), King and Powell wanted to ground their responses, especially any imaginative or poetic ones, in the objective facts of a map. They stand at the other end of the spectrum of nature study and writing from Thoreau and Emerson, who were eager to see nature primarily symbolically. Nevertheless, despite their "objective" positions, both Powell and King reached for a literary or poetic "truth," created the panorama of a place rather than a factual replica and abstract representation. Never did they abandon a scientific view of the world, but each expressed ambivalence about a purely scientific understanding of nature and often wrote about it in ways that incorporated their impressions, images, and ideas of the place. Perhaps their heroism lies in a struggle to resist the "merging" that, for Joyce Carol Oates in her essay "Against Nature," exposes nature writing as easy and unearned "PIETY, MYSTICAL ONENESS" (236). In their quest to see and present things as they "really are," both Powell and King accomplish the considerable task of accommodating objective science with a subjective and even sublime experience of nature.

CHAPTER FIVE

Geography of Repose
Wallace Stegner's Middle Ground

When Bruce Mason drove west in June . . . the names flowed in his head like a song, like the words of an old man telling a story, and his mind looked ahead over the long road . . . west beyond the Dakotas toward home. —from *The Big Rock Candy Mountain*

We have examined at least two kinds of surveying in this book. One is the map survey, which seeks to impose an order on landscape, sees it from afar, and is objective and quantifiable. The other is the denizen's survey, which also seeks an order, but one closer to the way an insider knows the landscape ("denizen" from Old French *deinz* = within, from Latin *dêintus* = within), perhaps even belongs to it, and is subjective and qualifiable. Whereas the map survey is concerned mostly with space, with quantifying and containing it, the denizen's survey wants to know the space as place, to comprehend its meaning and particulars.

Thoreau had trouble understanding the Maine Woods because he wanted it to remain an unmapped wilderness to make way for "contact"; his map of Walden Pond didn't necessarily help him to know the pond better, because he was more interested in the order he created from his calculations rather than the place itself. Even his walks that follow the contours of the land allowed him to transform landscape to imaginative and unfamiliar spaces: Because he knew it mostly from within, the place itself failed to be defined. King was out to know places scientifically, to observe the mountain as it "really is," but was often at odds with this mission, finding a denizen's repose in the "sheltered landscape" beneath summits. Still, he was hardly conscious of this desire, and customarily saw landscape from the distance of his impressionistic mirage. Of the three literary cartographers, Powell tried harder to understand the landscape he traveled through on its own terms and sensed the ways that both maps and familiar aesthetic categories failed in the arid West; nevertheless, his recommendations for changing the map surveys didn't change minds because the cultural canyon—the view from afar—had already been "mapped." Powell may have been too chained to the facts to recognize the interior landscape, the country of the mind that mingles with the exterior one to construct a "place."

In this chapter, I examine the "cartographic" work of Wallace Stegner. Although Stegner wasn't a surveyor in the map sense, he was no less a cartographer in the stories and essays he wrote about his place and region. He wrote, of course, about John Wesley Powell, learning from the surveyor's life story what Powell learned too late: Narratives about place "map" landscape better than maps can. Stegner did not characterize land according to the sublime, but understood how it—like myths of the Garden of the World or the Big Rock Candy Mountain—was a template to cut the future and shape the land, often in spite of what was really there. His overriding concern was with *placing* the West, with reclaiming it from a view that misreads it as space to a view seen according to the denizen: with sound local knowledge and a more particularized version of place, accomplished through his essays, history, and fiction. Following the others in this book, Stegner gives us a richer and more precise "survey" of the American West.

Wallace Stegner is arguably the most important of the West's novelists and one of its most preeminent historians. As the author of ten novels and the recipient of a Pulitzer Prize, a National Book Award, a Senior Fellowship from the National Endowment for the Humanities (NEH) and numerous other prestigious awards, his accomplishments as a fiction writer have been recognized. More recently, Stegner has received his due as a historian. Several articles collected by Charles Rankin for *Wallace Stegner: Man and Writer* acknowledge Stegner's contributions to the field of American history, and there is now an endowed chair in his name in the Department of History at Montana State University. In addition to his literary and historical pursuits, Stegner has been widely acclaimed for his work as a conservationist. His rational and eloquent statements on land use once prompted former student Edward Abbey to pronounce him "the only living American worthy of the Nobel" Peace Prize (qtd. in Hepworth "QR" 17). His famous wilderness letter[1] ends with a plea for wilderness preservation as a "geography of hope," one of his most memorable phrases and the title of another recent tribute, edited by his son Page. While the "hope" has been identified with the conservationist's desire to save the environment, a key aspect of that phrase, geography, deserves more attention as it pertains to Stegner's work. Geography (literally meaning writing about the earth) commonly refers to the study of the physical features of an area, but it is also concerned with how humans transform these physical environments to places, that is, endow them with some name or meaning. The relationships of people to their places, including how they perceive them and how these places in turn shape character, life, and expression (otherwise known as humanistic or behavioral geography) has been one of Stegner's principal concerns and is often the site where his imaginative writing, historical scholarship, and environmental concerns converge.

Geographical boundaries and mapmakers are the subjects of a good deal of Stegner's writing, both fiction and nonfiction. He has written about what it means to be "beyond the hundredth meridian" and to live on the 49th parallel. He was fascinated by such surveyors and geologists as John Wesley Powell, about whom he wrote a book-length biography; Clarence Edward Dutton (1841–1912), on whom he wrote his dissertation; and Clarence King, whom he mentions in several essays and who appears as a character in Stegner's historical novel about an engineer-surveyor-geologist, *Angle of Repose*. *American Places*, the book he cowrote with his son, Page, looks at relationships between people and the land, "how the American people and the American land have interacted, how they have shaped one another" (vii). One of the books Stegner often quotes in his essays is George R. Stewart's *Names on the Land*, a study of "how we went about putting our marks on the unnamed continent, and in doing so both added ourselves to the continent and added the continent to ourselves (LS 127).[2]

His stories and novels often move over landscapes in cartographic sweep. In his novella "Genesis" (in *Wolf Willow*), his "tenderfoot" narrator muses over "places where anything could happen, and from the *sound* of them, had happened—Jumbo's Butte, Fifty-Mile, Pinto Horse Butte, Horse Camp Coulee, the War Holes" (emphasis added, WW 141). When Bruce Mason drives "west beyond the Dakotas toward home" in *The Big Rock Candy Mountain*, after his first year away, "the names flowed in his head like a song, like the words of an old man telling a story" ("Northfield, Fairbault, Owatonna, Albert Lea . . . Blue

Earth, Jackson, Luverne ... Sioux City, Yankton, Bridgewater, Mitchell, Chamberlain, Rapid City ... Sugar City, Blackfoot, Pocatello" 457–64). Like the songlines of the Australian aborigines, the names of places inscribe a song, or tell a story, in Stegner's writing: They aren't just spots on the map but places of rich linguistic and historical association, markers in a journey toward "home."

Amidst the catalog of names, there is a yearning to know well the sites they signify. Narrator Lyman Ward has returned to a significant place at the outset of *Angle of Repose*. A deep relationship and knowledge of one's place is what Elsa Mason craves in Stegner's autobiographical epic, *The Big Rock Candy Mountain*, and that desire is replicated in her son Bruce: "To know always ... that there was one place to which you belonged and to which you would return ... to love and know a single place, from the newest baby-squall on the street to the blunt cuneiform of the burial ground" (460). This is the place to which Bruce would return, if he knew where it was, but he and thousands like him had missed it: "The whole nation had been footloose too long, Heaven had been just over the next range for too many generations" (460). The "home" place is where literary agent Joe Allston would go, in *All the Little Live Things*, during the weeks following the death of his son. "If I had a home town, I would have gone straight back to it" (137). But he also spent his childhood on the move, in "shallow, laborious, temporary ruts, and over their rims ... was always . . . some dawn or rainbow, the kind of rainbow that brought [his mother] to the States" (137). Both characters, like the young Stegner himself, are caught between staying and going, between living in a place and knowing it *deeply*, and moving to a new one in *hopes* of a better life. Staying has positive connotations, because as we live in the place we derive satisfaction from our connection to it. Going can be harmful—to us and to the place—since our hopes for new places break that connection and bond, and without that connection we are less likely to care for any place. The former involves an association with the past, the knowledge of the denizen, whereas the latter looks to the future, the anticipation of the explorer or settler, the "pleasure of hope" (from Thomas Campbell via railroad surveyor John Lambert). However, some might argue the reverse: that our long association with places has actually caused harm ("familiarity breeds contempt," "Ktaadn" 75).

Stegner's concept of place represents a paradox, or at least a puzzle, for how in Stegner's writing can places be both deeply lived in, known through long association, and containers of future hope, known for what they might be?

How can they be both surveyed from within, like Thoreau's "intelligence" of place, and surveyed from without, like Powell's physical features? These are questions that I want to deal with, for they occupied Stegner as a literary cartographer, one who writes about places and what and how they mean.

What follows is an examination of Stegner's aesthetics and philosophy of place. I will first turn to the memoir section of *Wolf Willow* (1962), in which Stegner expresses his view that his experiences as a child on the Saskatchewan prairie imprinted in him a sense of place. The contours of this subjectivity influenced how he viewed geography and how he thought it should be written. I will then look at the historical and fictional sections of the book to see how they relate to the kinds and forms of knowledge that constitute a relationship to place. I argue that the fictional portion of *Wolf Willow,* or at least the imaginative faculty necessary to create it, is important for any attempt to appreciate and understand Stegner's aesthetics of place as bound to narratives, both fictional and historical. As a work of metafiction, Stegner's historical novel *Angle of Repose* confirms my view that he is interested in the way we write (or imagine) stories that fix place and time, often "warped" by the perspective of the viewer, the interior landscape from which explorers "see" their places. Despite the efforts of Powell to map more realistically, the West as a place has always existed in a "middle ground" between the realistic/scientific contact of explorers such as King and Powell and the imaginative/mythological contact of explorers such as Thoreau ("The West of which I speak...."). As a literary cartographer, Stegner is concerned with writing the interior landscape, the "deep maps," stories, and myths humans develop about places, but he sees some versions as qualitatively better than others, adjusted for how they conform to the exterior landscape.

EXPERIENTIAL GEOGRAPHY: LEARNING
THE PLACE IN *WOLF WILLOW*

Wallace Stegner was born in 1909 in Lake Mills, Iowa. For the first five years of his life, the family moved frequently, to North Dakota and then to Redmond, Washington; George Stegner, Wallace's father, had an eye toward moving to Alaska and searching for gold. Instead, he settled for seeking gold in the wheat harvest of Saskatchewan, and Stegner's mother and her two sons joined him there in the summer of 1913. When that "gold" ran out, the family moved to

Great Falls, Montana, in 1920, and then, fifteen months later, to Salt Lake City, where they moved from house to house (over a dozen in ten years), as George Stegner tried one get-rich scheme after another, from gambling to bootlegging. In 1930, after receiving a B.A. from the University of Utah, Stegner completed his M.A. at the University of Iowa, and then his Ph.D. at the University of California at Berkeley in 1935. Stegner then taught writing at the University of Wisconsin, Harvard, and at the Bread Loaf Writer's conference with Robert Frost and Bernard DeVoto. In 1945, he returned to the West to begin the eminently successful writing program at Stanford (1945–71). Some ten years later, in midlife, Stegner returned to one of the places, Eastend, Saskatchewan, where the family "stayed long enough to put down roots and develop associations and memories" to see what he had missed, and remembered (LS 4).

Among his other works, he had already written a novel on place, *The Big Rock Candy Mountain* (1943), and two nonfiction books: one on the Mormons, *Mormon Country* (1942), and one on John Wesley Powell (1954), both of which could be read as examinations of place. In *Wolf Willow* (1962) Stegner returns to his hometown to recall deep associations and attachments with it and to write a work that is part memoir, part history, and part fiction, a work that succeeds as a layered look at the knowledge composing our sense of place. The work is a "denizen's survey" of Stegner's place as he knew it as a boy, with the added "map" and historical knowledge that he acquired much later. That knowledge is not as romantic as some of the stories he used to hear. He writes of the map/survey party that struggled to put up the international boundary near which he lived as a child:

> The mythic light in which we have bathed our frontier times . . . does not shine on the surveyor as it does on the trapper, trader, scout, cowboy, or Indian fighter. Surveyors do not even acquire the more pedestrian glamour of the farming pioneer, though they make him possible, and though their work is basic not merely to his conquering of the frontier, but to some of the mistakes he has made in trying to break it (86).

Surveyors interest Stegner because they are the ones responsible for imposing order, limitations, or even fictions upon landscape (85). They have failed to receive the attention of other frontier figures, but surveyors like Thoreau, King, and Powell not only fixed boundaries, but also set places in motion. They provide an initial conceptual framework for place.

Stegner is interested not only in the consequences of surveyors' borders, in the roles they play in history, but also in how geography affects character and belief. On a personal level, geographical borders, specifically the 49th parallel, "exerted uncomprehended pressures of affiliation and belief, custom and costume" (ww 84). As the southern boundary of his family's land, while he lived on it, "I accepted it as I accepted Orion in the winter sky. I did not know that this line of iron posts was . . . one of the strings by which dead men and the unguessed past directed our lives" (ww 85). The 49th parallel divided him in two, he says, between the United States and Canada, Montana and Saskatchewan. He would also be caught between the internal, subjective associations he had with his place, and the more objective map facts he would discover about it much later. For one, he discovers that the "Whitemud" (now the Frenchman) River he knew as a child "has changed its name since my time to conform with American maps" (6).

To begin *Wolf Willow* Stegner inserted such a map on the end papers of the book showing the geography of Eastern Montana and of Saskatchewan. The first lines of the text acknowledge the importance of maps as the starting point for information about a place. "An ordinary road map of the United States, one that for courtesy's sake includes the first hundred miles on the Canadian side of the line, will show two roads, graded but not paved, reaching up into western Saskatchewan to link U.S. 2 with Canada 1, the Trans-Canada Highway" (3). The map provides routes for commerce and shows political divisions, but doesn't successfully evoke the real place. The "block" of country on the map to which Stegner refers is what his book is about. To look at it from the perspective of a map, it is blank space or "block," but it is also one of the places— specifically the Cypress Hills—where the western Plains, as an ecology, as an Indian culture, and as a process of white settlement, came to a climax and end.

The place is indelible to Stegner's memory, but as to its history or geography he had no knowledge of the region while growing up there: "the information I was gaining from literature and from books on geography and history had not the slightest relevance to the geography, history, or life of the place where I lived" (27). School knowledge of place meant knowledge of the far and foreign. The assumption for him and for those he grew up with was that the region in which they lived was a "new" one and that new countries have no history. His relationship to both geography and history was personal and limited. However, even though he did not know these "map facts," geographical and historical markers that seemed to only exist on paper, he carried with him a personal relationship to place that comes back to him when he returns, in the scents of the "Whitemud" river—especially the pungent smell of wolf willow. That smell comes back until a "contact has been made, a mystery restored. For a moment, reality is made exactly equivalent with memory" (19).

Stegner did not have to explore and map like the others, but he had to use a map to start an exploration of the place of his youth. And he, too, begins with the image of a blank spot. But unlike Thoreau, who made contact with an un-mapped wilderness, Stegner makes *his* "contact" with a place he thought he already knew. He relates this contact to a phase ethnologists have identified in the development of both birds and humans: "expose a child to a particular environment at his susceptible time and he will perceive in the shapes of that environment until he dies" (21). Likewise, the lasting impressions of our origi-nal place can come to color our physical environment, influence our attitudes, and penetrate our behavior. Stegner is analytical about these relationships to place in ways the others in this book are not:

> A good part of my private and social character, the kinds of scenery and weather and people and humor I respond to, the prejudices I wear like dishonorable scars, the affections that sometimes waken me from middle-aged sleep with a rush of undiminished love, the virtues I respect and the weakness I condemn, the code I try to live by, the special ways I fail at it and the kinds of shame I feel when I do, the models and heroes I follow, the colors and shapes that evoke my deepest pleasure, the way I adjudicate between personal desire and personal responsibility, have been in good part scored into me by that little womb-village and the lovely, lonely ex-posed prairie of the homestead (23).

His early experiences there *shaped* him, literally gave him an internal geogra-phy from which to see the world. What Stegner describes is close to what hu-manistic geographer Yi-Fu Tuan calls topophilia, "the affective bond between people and place" (*Topophilia* 4). For Tuan, all subsequent understanding of nature derives from this early emotional union with one's environment, here both a natural and cultural place, an idea represented by coupling a biological process with a cultural one to form "womb-village."[3]

The interaction with and influence of the physical environment also occu-pies Stegner's early autobiographical novel, *The Big Rock Candy Mountain*

(1943), which is full of finely drawn details of landscape and place. His stand-in, Bruce Mason, gives his impressions of the Canadian homestead, the one Stegner would return to in *Wolf Willow*. Bruce describes the "mousy smell of the house, the musty smell of packed quilts," the Russian thistle he hoes out of the garden, the "grass-grown wagon track," "the way the grass grew curling over the lip of a burnout, and how the prairie owls nested under those grassy lips." Bruce feels that the "the yapping of coyotes on a moonlit night was lonely and beautiful to him, and the yard and chicken house and fireguard and coulee were as much a part of him as his own skin" (182–83).

The place haunts Stegner's dreams, and he came to ask in *Wolf Willow:*

> [Why should] this dead loop of river, known only for a few years, ... be so charged with potency in my unconscious—why around it there should be other images, almost all from the river valley rather than from the prairie, that constantly recur in dreams or in the images I bring from up off the typewriter onto the page. They lie in me like underground water; every well I put down taps them ... why does that early imprinting, rather than all later experience, so often dictate [my dreams'] form? (22)

On that prairie, he concludes, the river provided shelter and safety from the wind and open space. E. O. Wilson writes in his *Biophilia* that the human sense of place is embedded and instinctual. For Stegner, that embeddedness matters mostly for how he writes about places, for "the images [he brings] from up off the typewriter onto the page."

The particulars of Stegner's place shaped his perception and the way he responded to and created environments, in fiction and in his own life. However, a crucial aspect of his knowledge of his place was missing: He had no conception of the area's history. Without such knowledge, Stegner saw his former self as a "sensuous little savage." Like R. W. B. Lewis's American Adam, Stegner was "an individual emancipated from history, happily bereft from ancestry" (5). But the Adamic man myth is one Stegner would dispel: he doesn't believe we can wipe the slate clean of the past and return to a condition that existed before humans began to leave their "marks on the world" (Cronon, "Wilderness" 484). Despite his assumption as a child that his was a "new country," a blank spot on the map, it did have history, one that Stegner uncovered years later, and wrote about in the second section of *Wolf Willow*. Stegner's "contact" is part sensuous—as it is when we are young and when we recover the sensations of youth, as he does when he comes back to Eastend—but also part intellectual, the contact made through understanding and interpreting the region's history.

The first white visitors in that part of the West just missed the region in the surveys and explorations of 1805 (by Lewis and Clark), and the fur trade stayed further west. Nevertheless, Lewis and Clark were close to one of the geographical secrets they were looking for, one of those heights of land that can change both politics and history. A little pond in the Cypress Hills was balanced on the Continental Divide, hills that also separated "the Gulf of Mexico from the Hudson Bay" (ww 43). The Cypress Hills form the northern edge of the Missouri watershed, and if political boundaries on maps were established by "topography and logic rather than by expedient and compromise," the North Bench of those hills would carry the international boundary, "and the lower fifty miles of Saskatchewan would be politically what they are geographically—an uninterrupted part of the American High Plains" (45). As they are, the hills form a completely different ecosystem than the Great Plains, though a human line, a boundary, seems to say otherwise.

Stegner learned that the survey to set up that line was sped up by the Canadian government because of violence in the territory. They established the international boundary and the Royal Mounted Police, which patrolled the northern side. The line would be called the "Medicine Line" by the Crow, Gros Ventre, Sioux, Blackfoot, and Assiniboin, because they could not be pursued by the "long swords" over that line. Once Stegner uncovers it, the history starts to fill in the details of the "block" of space and deepens his sense of it, adding meaning to the significant boundary he lived near. Once discovered, the history has relevance because it reconnects Stegner to his place and region. The history and geography of the Cypress Hills offers Stegner connectivity: "a past to which I could be tribally and emotionally committed" (111). All of the history was there, the stories of hope, loss, and defeat, but not known to him as a child. "I think you don't choose between the past and the present," Stegner has written, "you try to find the connections" (mw 200). Connecting the past with the present could create a continuity of experience, and connectivity, as Rob Williams has shown, was one of Stegner's primary goals in writing history. He aimed not only to survey the surfaces of his Western place, but its long history and traditions: to add nuance to the names on the map.

In a 1967 essay, "History, Myth and the Western Writer," Stegner observes that: "In the old days, in blizzardy weather, we used to tie a string of lariats from house to barn so as to make it from shelter to responsibility and back again. With personal, family, and cultural chores to do," he concluded, "I think we had better rig up such a line between past and present" (MW 201). History provides continuity between past and present and contributes to the relationship between people and places. In *Wolf Willow*, Stegner also characterizes "history" as a "pontoon bridge," where "every man walks and works at its building end, and has come as far as he has over the pontoons laid by others he may never have heard of" (29). Continual work at the building end creates a "usable" or "possessed past." But that past doesn't really become "usable" until Stegner derives some meaning from it. The contact and connection occurred with the experience of the "tantalizing and ambiguous and wholly native smell" of the wolf willow growing along the creek bed, "where reality is made exactly equivalent with memory" (19). To be useful, the history must be attached to the many points of his personal and experiential connection to the place.

Stegner realizes in *Wolf Willow* that although he didn't know the outward historical narrative, the objective history of his place, he knew his own inward narrative, which is no less "real" because of the information he discovered. Knowledge of place can be historical, but is also grounded in those aspects of the environment that we appreciate through the senses, such as the sound and feel of the wind. "You don't get out of the wind," says Stegner, "but learn to lean and squint against it. You don't escape sky and sun, but wear them in your eyeballs and on your back" (WW 8). For geographer Tuan this *sense* of place "is made up of the experiences, mostly fleeting and undramatic, repeated day after day and over the span of years. It is a unique blend of sights, sounds, and smells, a unique harmony of natural and artificial rhythms such as times of sunrise and sunset, of work and play. The feel of a place is registered in one's muscles and bones" (*Space and Place* 183). This is a contact that Thoreau knew, but Stegner adds to the sensory experience a thick layer of memory, history, association, and affection.

Stegner's mental or "cognitive map" retains such information. Cognitive maps depend on experience and on narrative: Something happened to me in some place and there is an association that I have with it that forms the story and image I retain about that place. These narratives deliver a more particular orientation to our surroundings than topographical maps, providing the central means through which we organize our surroundings. Stegner and the people he grew up with had no "history" that they knew about, but they had cognitive maps of their region. The shrub he calls wolf willow is a case in point. The name Stegner calls a gray-leafed bush that grows along the waterways in the region is not the scientific one, but one local people gave to that specific physical thing, because of its rank, "wolfish" smell and greyish foliage. The naming constitutes the beginnings of a folklore and fiction of place. According to Kent Ryden, these kinds of vernacular names for local flora and fauna, "as opposed to formal biological taxonomies and more widely known common names, provide an especially good indication of environmental literacy" and a good "indication of regional consciousness and a sense of living in a distinctive place" (78).

In his essay on "The Sense of Place," Stegner writes about such a process of becoming placed. "No place is a place until things that have happened in it are remembered in history, ballads, yarns, legends, or monuments" (LS 202). A place involves not only the fact that it is a name on a map, or the accumulation of events that happened on that spot of the map, but the meanings, perception, and emotion of individuals responding to their surroundings and events. If a place is to be told, it might best be told through fiction. "Fictions serve as well as facts" Stegner observes in the same essay (202). History does not in itself provide the link that Stegner wants with the geographical facts of his region. Historical or topographical knowledge alone does not make geography meaningful until there can be a personal or imaginative connection with place. Stegner means to dig out the narratives and images which give the world meaning and definition, preventing it from becoming flat, smooth "blocks" of space.

WARPING HISTORY: TELLING
THE TOPOGRAPHY

In novels such as *Joe Hill* and *Angle of Repose*, in which he draws extensively upon historical documents, Stegner makes no attempt to cover up the fact that though he has "[selected] facts from … real lives," he has not "hesitated to *warp* both personalities and events to meet fictional needs" (emphasis added, AR ix). In *Wolf Willow*, in which he also uses historical documents, Stegner acknowledges that he "occasionally *warped* fact a little in order to reach for the fictional or poetic truth" that he ranks "a little above history" (emphasis added,

307). And about *Beyond the Hundredth Meridian* Stegner has said, "I may have been *warping* . . . nearly a third of the book" (emphasis added, MW 207).[4] Since his sense of place was personal and experiential, Stegner's mingling of fact with fiction came from an awareness that all narratives, including historical (or geographical) ones, are individual constructions (F. Robinson, "Essay" 204), turned, or warped, to show the human meaning inside the obscure details presented for inspection. In the same way explorers see from an interior landscape, Stegner presents places through a narrator's cognitive and fictional "map."

To interpret the history of the Cypress Hills, Stegner developed a fictional lens through which to see his place. "If we want to know what it was like on the Whitemud River Range during that winter [of 1906–7] when the hopes of a cattle empire died, we had better see it through the eyes of some tenderfoot, perhaps someone fresh from the old country, a boy without the wonder rubbed off him and with something to prove about himself" (138). He then proceeds to tell two fictional accounts of what life was like in that region during that winter. The two stories that form part three of Wolf Willow, "Genesis" and "Carrion Spring," are designed to transport a reader beyond the factual, historical account of part two to a more vivid, phenomenological rendering of a catastrophe on the frozen, desolate grasslands. Historical facts alone would fail to capture the complex interplay of courage, individualism and cooperation that characterized life on the frontier towns of the Great Plains in the early 1900s. Set in the frozen frontier earth, these stories combine the researched and remembered facts of the first two sections. As fictions, these stories are juxtaposed with a larger, omnipresent narrative, the cowboy myth, fostered in dime novels and Hollywood movies. Stegner says he has spent a good deal of time "putting on [his] armor and breaking a lance against the windmill of the cowboy myth that dominated not only much western writing but almost all outside judgment of western writing," but the cowboy was always a faster gun than he. "Genesis," Stegner notes, is one of two stories with cowboys in them "and probably as good a story as I ever wrote" (LS 136–37). Against the backdrop of the living Western prairie and the cowboy myth, Stegner's story intends to be more "real" than either the facts of Western history or the fantasies associated with it. Between the two extremes lies Stegner's "middle ground" (MW 205), where a better understanding of place will emerge.

To achieve something both more objective than myth and more subjective than history, Stegner finesses point of view. "Genesis" is focalized through a "tenderfoot." Because he is new to America, he might allow Stegner to present the story as disinterested observer. But because he is newly arrived to the West, he comes with a heightened set of expectations about his place, as did the mapmakers I have written of in earlier chapters. When he sits down to write about his new experiences to his family back home, he is conscious of what they expect of him: "to fill pages with cowboys and Indians and wild-game and the adventures and observations of a well-educated young gentleman in the North American wilderness" (170). Only after a personal trial of extreme cold and near starvation during a blizzard is he able to see and tell the "truth."

This fictional portion of *Wolf Willow* has equal status with the autobiographical and historical sections of the book. About his fictional narrator in "Genesis," Stegner has said, "let it be admitted that I have also put into him something of myself" (138). The tenderfoot English boy learns through the test of experience what it means to be a "man" in terms that fit the circumstances of a "real" cowboy rounding up cattle in the worst winter imaginable. In that respect, he is closely related to the larger movement of the book: the search by Stegner himself to find out who he is and what the circumstances are of the environment that made him.

His search for the meaning of his place is best conveyed in the stories told by the people who live there and experience it. For Stegner, any landscape is composed not only of what lies before our eyes but also what lies within our heads. The function of a literary cartography for Stegner is not only the delineation of the external landscape, but also an exploration of the interior landscape that was given shape within a particular environment. For Thoreau, the exterior landscape could almost be evacuated to make way for a new, unfamiliar place ("The world with which we are commonly acquainted leaves no trace, and it will have no anniversary," "Walking" 217). But for Stegner, the external landscape regulates the stories of place.

An example from "Genesis" will illustrate this point. From the beginning of the story the narrator senses that he will have to cross some border or threshold, "as one would enter a house" (143). Meanwhile, the earth is borderless and signless, "the earth showed him nothing" (151). Like Stephen Crane's "The Blue Hotel"—also taking place on the cold, frozen plain and also dealing with heightened expectations from dime novels—there is a sense of cosmic indifference in the story ("whirling, fire-smote, ice-locked, disease-stricken, space-lost bulb," "The Blue Hotel"). The earth in Stegner's story is "big and pale," and the only thing that stands out is the crew's fragile camp, which "stamped itself in Rusty's mind and memory" (161). However, as Rusty thinks more about his "test," "to be invincibly strong, indefinitely enduring, uncompromisingly self-reliant, to depend on no one," Stegner lets us know that such a notion, "stamped" on Rusty's mind, is flimsy on the frozen plain. Here the shelter is fragile and penetrable: "nothing between them and the stars, nothing between them and the North Pole, nothing between them and the wolves, except a twelve by sixteen house of cloth so that that every wind moved it and light showed through it" (165). Stegner makes it clear that there is little barrier between human hopes and expectations and the exterior landscape: They exist in a dialectical relationship.

When the blizzard comes, the first thing to go is the tent, and along with it Rusty's expectations of heroism and grandeur. In the whiteout, as the cattle crew makes their way back to the ranch, they lose all sense of place and of time: "in an hour, or four hours, or ten minutes" (204). Rusty's enemy in the camp, Spurlock, the senior cowboy with whom he wants to pick a fight and test his mettle, is the first to be weakened by the cold and fall to the hard ground. Rusty waits with him while someone else goes for help and the mechanical processes of thought and breathing come to a halt: "[he] simply waited, without mind or thought, no longer afraid, not hopeful, not even aware or sentient, but simply waiting while the gasp of breath and hammer of heart labored toward some slowing point" (212). His life is "driven inward from its frontiers"—literally from its physical extremities, but also from the frontiers and edges of the cold landscape that regulate human hope, feeling, and thought. After they rest, Rusty and Spurlock make it to the cabin to join the rest of their crew, but more than the cattle has been lost. Human hopes, human expectations, human stories (the test Rusty wants to write home about) have been altered by their environment. The landscape speaks back; according to legend and told through the cook, Jesse, this is a place cold enough that if you yell into the cold air, your words will freeze and be heard again—come back to you—during the spring thaw.

The story illustrates what the Stegner family learned while trying to make a living on the frozen prairie. Stegner writes in the last chapter, "The Making of Paths," that his family was victimized by the "folklore of hope," notions of what the land could provide that were essentially false. When the Stegner family left their homestead, we knew, we all knew, that we wouldn't be back any more than the families of our acquaintance who had already left; and I imagine we obscurely felt that more than our personal hope had died in the shack that stayed in sight all the time we were bumping down along the field to the border. With nothing in sight to stop anything, along a border so unwatched that it might have been unmapped, something really had stopped there; a crawl of human hope had stopped. (283)

Stegner implies that, without a better internal "map" of the country, hopes about places are doomed to get lost.

If we turn briefly to Stegner's Pulitzer Prize–winning novel, *Angle of Repose,* we see again someone negotiating between exterior and interior landscape. The novel is about someone who comes to know more facts about his grandparents' history, but superimposes his own cognitive map on the information he receives. In this historical novel (based on the journals of Mary Hallock Foote, a nineteenth-century writer and illustrator[5]), Lyman Ward pieces together the facts of his grandparents' lives ostensibly to write a history of them, but also for his own sake: "I realize it is not backward that I want to go but downward. I want to touch once more the ground I have been maimed away from" (17). Lyman is literally removed from the ground as he is confined to a wheelchair, but is also seeking a connection to his time and place in the history of his grandparents. He is hoping to find his "angle of repose," a geological term for the slope of an incline where sediment comes to rest. Lyman is a surveyor only in the denizen's sense; he is less concerned about mapping the future than he is filling in the blanks on the map, to see how the past informs the present.

The story Lyman seeks to know and tell is about a marriage of a fiction writer/illustrator and a surveyor/geologist. It records the couple's trek from mining town to mining town during Oliver Ward's stint as an overseer: New Almaden, California; Leadville, Colorado; Santa Cruz, California; Boise, Idaho; Michoacán, Mexico, (along the way they meet up with then director of the USGS Clarence King). As Lyman's research into his grandparents' lives and their quest to live with each other and in one place progresses, he reveals his personal dilemma—his wife has left him and his son wants to commit him to a nursing home. He gradually learns of his grandmother's infidelity and his grandfather's cruel silence in return. The stubbornness and hard-headedness he uncovers in his grandfather proves to be what he is also guilty of. Though "Genesis" is focalized through the "tenderfoot's" third-person perspective, *Angle of Repose* is seen through a first-person narrator, to better present "warpings." Lyman's personal investments in the story underscore a theme of the novel: We invest, like the "tenderfoot" narrator or the "real" explorers King and Powell, "in the stories we tell" (Graulich 92). Lyman's grandmother (Susan Burling Ward) is a genteel Easterner who comes to the West with a heightened set of expectations. By contrasting Susan's perceptions with those of the people who live there, Stegner shows how Eastern visions shaped what the West symbolized for Americans, a process we saw often with King and with Thoreau. With Susan's perceptions and her grandson's commentary, Stegner constructs a novel about how personal experience and personal geography inform our thinking and determine our stories (Graulich 88).

Early in the novel, when Lyman Ward reassembles his grandparents' early courtship, he imagines them on an excursion to a pond, "eight miles back in the woods, a wild romantic place where a waterfall poured into a marble pool and then fell through diminishing pools into the lake" (61). Lyman says that there they sat, "confronting nature," doing what poets and philosophers did outdoors in the "early years of the picturesque" (61). They see landscape in the ways their culture has conditioned them to—"incorrigibly Hudson River School." They want to see landscape in terms of an aesthetic, the picturesque or the sublime. Their Victorian culture also gives them "no acceptable way of expressing their feelings directly," so "they probably vented them on nature" (61). Lyman says he can see "a lot of [Romantic] tableaux" while his grandparents are sitting by the pond, misreading nature and misreading each other. When Lyman Ward's grandmother moves west with her engineer husband, she sees the West through the filter of her eastern "tableaux."

The parallax of perspective as it pertains to knowing both place and history becomes a major theme of the novel.[6] As Lyman reads the text of Susan's life, his own present text is transposed onto her historical one; the topographies overlap, making it hard to determine where the *facts* of Susan's life become speculative *fictions* based on his own. Stegner employs his narrator in this way to emphasize that history is dependent on what Lyman calls the "ocular illusion of perspective." Through the conscious manipulation of point of view, the third-person narrative constructed by the first-person narrator-agent, Stegner presents history as he presents geography: as meaning different things to different people.[7] Relationships to place and time are ongoing negotiations between shifting, changeable perspectives. The "angle of repose" is Stegner's metaphor for the way we balance these social and physical ecosystems. "The West," he once said, "is less a place than a process" (LS 55), a continuing adaptation.

GEOGRAPHIES IN MOTION:
WESTERNIZING THE PERCEPTIONS

As *Angle of Repose* involves competing geographies and histories, and moves from one site to another, Lyman's stories are always in motion across the landscape's surface. The places tell a story that Lyman has to interpret, and variations on the history of the American West often result from different interpretations of geography. When Stegner comes back to Eastend, Saskatchewan, in *Wolf Willow,* he is pleasantly surprised that it has a history. But the story is depressing. He discovers a "capsular history of the [American] frontier experience" in general: from myth of paradise to the true story of gullibility, individualism, violence toward Indians and finally, fatally, drought (Robinson, *Stegner* 65). Stegner's West is not colored by the optimism that characterizes much Western history. Nor is it entirely pessimistic: Just as his stories, essays, and novels expose failures, greed, self-serving illusions, and violence, they also acknowledge human triumph, hope, cooperation, and redemption.[8] The history of the West is "torn between powerfully competing versions" of the same story (F. Robinson, "New" 88).

Different versions of the West's geography are already present in Stegner's *Beyond the Hundredth Meridian* (1954). Stegner begins the book with a dichotomy of vision located in opposing individuals: John Wesley Powell and the first territorial governor of Colorado, William Gilpin. Stegner presents Gilpin as a tireless promoter of the West as Canaan, pastoral Arcadia, an enormous garden, "tooting the horn of Manifest Destiny" (MW 15). Where soil was inadequate for crops or livestock, the land would provide a limitless store of minerals and precious metals. Gilpin and those with his mindset envisioned hundreds of millions of Americans finding happiness and prosperity in the land of infinite promise. In his look back at this vision in his preface to *Where the Bluebird Sings to the Lemonade Springs* (the title taken from the Harry McClintock song, "The Big Rock Candy Mountains"), Stegner writes: "From before it was ever known, the West had been a land of Cockaigne ... a Big Rock Candy Mountain where the handouts grow on bushes and the little streams of alcohol come trickling down the rocks" (LS xix).

At the other end of this political propaganda line stood Powell, who was one of the first to recognize how the limitations of the West's aridity would affect the dreams of settlement and prosperity. Nineteenth-century laws of the region were premised on the myth of inexhaustible resources. Powell responded with the *Report on the Lands of the Arid Region of the United States,* which he presented to Carl Schurz, the Secretary of the Interior, in 1878. As discussed in the last chapter, his report recommended a revolution in the system of land policies and farming methods in the West that would have them comply with the conditions of the region's scarce resource, water. According to Stegner, the document was a "denial of almost every cherished fantasy and myth associated with the Westward migration" (212). The Secretary of the Interior would be sympathetic to Powell, but the document was too revolutionary for Gilpinites in Congress.

In the settlement of the West, the story would be the same, as Stegner understands it; the fictions would, time after time, suppress the facts. He recognized the Gilpin dream of easy wealth and easy escape in his father and people he called "boomers." Stegner's father wanted to make a killing and end up on Easy Street; he was driven first by hope, then by failure, from one money-making scheme to another, and finally to ruin. This is the same expectation that led to the settlement of the American West on the basis not of sound local knowledge, but of presumption and "arrogant pipedreams" (LS xviii). Out of his father's life, Stegner writes, he made a novel, *The Big Rock Candy Mountain,* "my most heartfelt commentary on western optimism and enterprise and the common man's dream of something for nothing" (LS xxi). What lured his father and many people to the West "has been, and still is, mirage." "Finally, like Clarence King," Stegner writes, his father "died broke and friendless in a flea-bag hotel, having in his lifetime done more human and environmental damage than he could have repaired in a second lifetime" (LS xxi).

Stegner told Richard Etulain in his "Conversations" that a book on Clarence King was a project he would like to get around to:

[King] seems to be a variant of the Big Rock Candy Mountain theme— the big, quick, easy splurge of fortune-making and ultimately the way in which that fortune-making subverts and ruins a considerable talent. A potentially great man goes down on the basis of the profiteering of his place and time. It seems to me a nice moral fable, the reverse of the Powell story." (195)

The restlessness and energy demonstrated by Stegner's father and the real-life Clarence King were pervasive in the West. But there was also a counter-narrative, one of settlement that we also saw in King. Stegner saw that second story in Powell and was born into it as well; he knew it in his mother who, "would have loved to get herself expressed in all the pleasant, secure details of a deeply lived-in [place]." Not all came to the West to plunder and run. Some came with the hope of staying; these Stegner called the "stickers" or "nesters." Of himself, he said, "I was at heart a nester, like my Mother" (LS 12).

For Stegner and for millions of others, their image of the West has always been warped by prejudgments. "The West has had a way of warping well-carpentered habits, and raising the grain on exposed dreams," Stegner writes, in "Living Dry" (LS 57). Millions of Easterners read about the West and fantasized about it before ever having been there. Those versions of the West may in fact be more "real" than the actual West because of their hold on the imagination. "It's hard to take in," Stegner said in *American Places,* "the land and its rivers and forests may have been tamed, but our minds have not" (247). Americans still dream of a spaciousness when they think of the West, but Western realities often don't conform to those expectations. Stegner thinks the dream of what lay in the West as having its origins in the earlier dream of what lay in the New World, a process and desire that kept repeating itself: "And dream kept opening into further dream, chaos often led on to more confusing chaos" (AP 7). Early explorers cared more for the land as resource bank than as a place to live in. Barry Lopez makes a similar point on the early Spanish explorers in *The Rediscovery of North America:* "the Spanish experience was to amass wealth and go home."[9] The New World optimism continued through Manifest Destiny and the settlement of the West, a process Stegner has called a "series of raids made by people of power" (Video interview).[10] "The fact is," he writes in "Living Dry," the West "has been as notable for mirages as for the realization of dreams" (LS 57).

The dream of a Northwest Passage was but an early example of what "flickered along just ahead of knowledge" in early exploration, "just beyond the next day's sail, beyond where vision blurred with fog and distance" (AP 8). In both *Wolf Willow* and "Thoughts in a Dry Land," Stegner quotes from William F. Butler, a surveyor of the Canadian West. Writing about early maps, Butler notes in *The Great Lone Land* (1872) the "tricks" they played with geography: "the center of America was represented as a vast inland sea whose shores stretched far into the Polar North; a sea through which lay the much-coveted passage to the long-sought treasures of the old realms of Cathay." Butler continues to say that they weren't far off, "for an ocean there is, and an ocean through which men seek the treasures of Cathay, even in our own times. But the ocean is one of grass, and the shores are the crests of mountain ranges, the dark pine forests of sub-Arctic regions" (qtd. in LS 48 and WW 37–38). Butler articulates something crucial for Stegner: Geography was often drawn according to hopes and expectations. The maps of early explorers were drawn and interpreted according to not only what was out there, but also what they *hoped* to find there. The motives and goals of exploration and even future settlement were based on some imponderable combination of real and imaginary geography.

In "Thoughts in a Dry Land," Stegner writes about the need to understand landscape better as it is. He pieces together the history of exploration in the West, from Lewis and Clark to Powell. "The surveying and mapping of great areas of the West was not completed for decades after real exploration had ended; and the trial and error (emphasis on the error) by which we began to be an oasis civilization was forced on us by country and climate, but against the most mule-headed resistance and unwillingness to understand, accept, and change" (49). Perceptions that were trained in another climate and another landscape had to be modified. As writers, artists, and citizens, "our first and hardest adaptation," he writes, "was to learn to all over again how to see." For that to happen, we had to "learn new techniques, a new palette, to communicate them" (52). Lastly, writers needed an audience who would respond to "what we wrote or painted" (52).

One of the writers who recognized the need to re-see was a surveyor, Clarence Dutton (on whom Stegner wrote his dissertation), whose forms and colors, Stegner notes, "are as far from Hudson River School standards as any in the West" (LS 53). From Point Sublime, the one William Henry Holmes sketched, Dutton writes about a landscape that may clash with an Eastern audience's perceptual habits: "The lover of nature, whose perceptions have been trained in the Alps ... or New England ... would enter this strange region with a shock, and dwell there for a time with a sense of oppression, and perhaps with horror. Whatsoever things he had learned to regard as beautiful and noble he would seldom or never see, and whatsoever he might see would appear to him as anything but beautiful and noble" (qtd. in Stegner, LS 53). What the observer has learned is beautiful will not be found there; the colors are "tawdry and bare" according to his learning. This is the canyon country that shocked John Burroughs, who was reared in the Catskills and wrote out of a pastoral tradition, in *Far and Near* (1904).

> Indeed, never before have I seen the earth so vivisected, anatomized, gashed,—the cuts all fresh, the hills looking as new and red as butcher's meat, the strata almost bleeding.... In places, the country looks as if all the railroad forces of the world might have turned loose to devil and rend and pile in some mad, insane carnival and debauch. (7–8)

But, with time, according to Dutton, could come a "gradual change": The outlines that seemed harsh and trivial come to have grace and meaning, a response that must "be understood before [it] can be estimated, and must be cultivated before [it] can be understood" (qtd. in Stegner 54). For Stegner, what Dutton describes is a "westernization of the perceptions," a process of becoming placed. For that process to occur, "you have to get over the color green; you have to quit associating beauty with gardens and lawns; you have to get used to an inhuman scale; you have to understand geological time" (LS 55). The problem is, people don't stay in one place long enough to cultivate that understanding, to cultivate deeper "maps": "especially in the West, what we have instead of place is space" (LS 72).

The surveyors that Stegner writes about relied heavily on empirical knowledge, on using precise instrumentation to verify the measurements of a particular place. Powell could see that institutions and laws would have to change if people wanted to settle the West, as Stegner writes, proposing his "surveys and political divisions not by arbitrary boundaries but by drainage divides" (LS 50). Stegner writes how the rectangular surveys would "cut across the little farms that the *métis* had established on the Assiniboine, the Red, and the other rivers." The cooperative system that Powell proposed was much like the system of land division the *métis* used:

Long strip farms, each with a frontage on the river which gave not only a canoe landing but an access to water for the irrigation of gardens. The strips ran far back and were combined in common pastures like the *ejidos* of Spanish New Mexico, and on these pastures the *métis'* stock could run freely while people were off on the annual hunts ... their system of land division was appropriate to their life. As a matter of fact, it was far better adapted to the arid and semi-arid plains than the rectangular surveys were, but nobody in Canada or the United States understood that. (*ww* 59)

Powell understood it, but his recommendations flew in the face of blind desire, desire Stegner saw in his father, who led the family on a chase for rainbows across the West, and ended up drunk, then dead, in a cheap, transient hotel.

Though Stegner condemns the fantasies of "visionaries" like his father because of their destructiveness to the land and people, he understands how imagination and myth plays a role in our knowledge of a place. Since he had no formal history of the place he grew up in and learned about it through the stories he either read or heard, Stegner understands the power stories have in shaping perception. He admits what was only implicit in the other surveyors we have seen: The interior landscape resolves external geography. Stegner knows of the power of an imaginary or interior landscape because much of his information came from stories. He talks about his "Fenimore-Cooper-trained sensibilities" (*ww* 114) and how "it was the cowboy tradition, the horseback culture, that impressed itself as image, as romance, and as ethical system upon boys like me" (*ww* 134). That image and the romance of the cowboy culture came from dime novels readily available to Stegner as a youth, and they impressed upon him a landscape that mixed with facts to produce his "middle ground."

Getting to know a place may depend on every kind of knowledge, including some reports that are unreliable or biased.

Across a century and three quarters since Lewis and Clark pushed into the Missouri, we have had multitudinous reports on the West—Pike and Long; Catlin and Maximilian of Wied Neuwied; Ashley and Jedidiah Smith and Frémont; Bonneville and the Astorians and Nathaniel Wyeth; Spalding and Whitman; the random Oregon and California gold rush diarists; the historians of the compact Mormon migration; the Pacific

Railroad Surveys of the 1850s, which for many areas were the basis of precise knowledge; the Powell, Hayden, King, and Wheeler surveys and the U.S. Geological Surveys that united and continued them. (LS 48)

However, not only these "factual" reports but also the fictional and artistic ones have constructed a "place."

The dime novels and the Currier and Ives prints; the reports of missionaries and soldiers; the reporters and illustrators for *Leslie's* and *Harper's Weekly*; the painters, from Catlin and Miller and Bodmer to Bierstadt and Moran; the photographers, from Jackson and Hilliers and Haynes and Savage onward; the Fenimore Coopers, Mark Twains, Bret Hartes, Dan de Quilles, Horace Greeleys; the Owen Wisters and Frederick Remingtons; the Andy Adamses and Zane Greys and Eugene Manlove Rhodeses. (LS 49)

Some accounts were more true than others, some observant and some not able to "see," as Dutton wanted us to, some impartial and some interested, some factual,—such as the railroad surveys that John Lambert participated in, though his report also contained some of the fanciful ("the enchantment that distance lends"), like the sublime landscapes of a Bierstadt. As Stegner sees it, "it has all gone into the hopper and influenced our understanding and response" (49). The problem becomes one of sifting through the knowledge, asking what kinds of knowledge and writing about place we should honor. Place-writing that concentrates only on minute, observant description cannot always account for the "myths" beneath its acts of representation, but place-writing that relies too heavily on myth warps what it sees out of recognition.

GEOGRAPHIES OF HOPE: FIELDS OF CARE

Since stories impress themselves on us as well as facts do, and since the stories we tell emerge as powerful expressions of desire (often warping the facts behind them), it would follow that humans need to be careful of the stories they create. Humans will inevitably make paths and marks, Stegner has said, in the last chapter of *Wolf Willow*, "The Making of Paths." Stegner writes about the paths to the privy, the wagon tracks to his house, as they are indicative of "the folklore of hope": "the pioneer root-cause of the American cult of Progress, the satisfaction that *Homo fabricus* feels in altering to his own purposes the virgin earth." Like a pictograph on a wall, the tracks demonstrated his family's existence, said, in effect, "See? We are here" (272). Though the wearing of paths in "the earth's rind is an intimate act, an act like love" (273), he also senses, as do the surveyors, a deep "inescapable ambivalence" about leaving such marks, boundaries, borders (282). The question becomes, what kind of marks should we leave?

At a speech Stegner gave in 1988, he examined the dream of profit and bonanza that had powered much of the move across the nation. He ended the speech by quoting Mark Twain's Satan, in *The Mysterious Stranger,* that we "dream other dreams, and better" (qtd. in Limerick 116). Constructing a new ethic for a relationship to place requires telling stronger stories, having morally better fantasies. It involves some middle ground between the empirical, verifiable knowledge of place and how it is imagined, experienced, and perceived.[11] *Wolf Willow* attempts to account for both the real and imagined aspects of place through its combination of history and fiction. Like a folklorist or oral historian, Stegner interviewed people of his region to write his stories. In inventing his "tenderfoot" for "Genesis" he put in something of Corky Jones, whose narrative serves as the epigraph to "Genesis": "The winter started early with a light snow on the 5th of November, followed by a terrific three-day blizzard that started on the 11th. From then till Christmas was a succession of bad storms. The range cattle were dying in December" (139).

Stegner insists that the sense of place is in large part a creation of folklore and can be expressed most eloquently through its narrative. Indeed, a sense of place can emerge from writing, since it derives geographical meaning from a fusion of imaginative and physical geography. The stories give visibility to "deeply lived in" landscapes that we carry in our minds. Writing about one's place includes this kind of insider's knowledge. Historian Elliott West writes about Stegner's fiction:

> The accretion of experience, the accumulation of perceptions and response, including wind on the face and willows smelt, the weathering of the memories—all that is part of the making of a place. Knowing a place, and telling intelligent and true stories about it, must take that process into account. (70)

Stegner used his insider's knowledge to write "Genesis," a title that should indicate his concern that we be attentive to these particulars of lived experience when creating new cultural myths. "Genesis" shatters the romantic myth of frontier individualism, and "Carrion Spring" is about a couple that decides to "stick"—to make a living in that place even though they lost their cattle to the winter—while others are moving on.

As writing about place, Stegner's geography understands more than the "block" on the map that Stegner presents on the endpapers of *Wolf Willow*. From this perspective places are not just geographical objects, but subjects realized through history and narrative. In my introduction I quoted from geographer Yi-Fu Tuan to define "place": "What begins as undifferentiated space becomes place as we get to know it better and endow it with value" (6). But to that we should add, the *right* kind of value, since early explorers had differing ways of defining value. Their versions of landscape diverged from those of the Indians already living there. The Indian's version was an "insider's landscape" of regions they were intimately familiar with. The competing view came from the "outsider's landscape," the view superimposed from afar rather than seen through extensive personal experience. Stegner once said, in an interview with Suzanne Ferguson, that there is a need for writing with a "land ethic" (Aldo Leopold's phrase) or Indian religious perspective:[12]

> [Euro-Americans] don't have any religion of the earth. When we came here, I suppose Europeans had it about their own earth. British plough-men had it about their fields, but when they got into Virginia, they just didn't carry it over. Because there it was, all that plenty . . . and you didn't know it . . . but the Indians presumably did. They had a kind of reverence for the earth that took a long time developing. So I suppose what I'm looking for in the long run is development of reverence (you can put that down). (19)

Writing about place should involve some knowledge of the facts of the region, some intimacy with the land as the insider knows it, an ethic built on close association with the land's details, and finally, a reverence for its capacity. Stegner "wonders" if surveyors Lewis and Clark shouldn't have filed an environmental impact study before they headed west. Before surveys are undertaken, before new places are to be constructed, we ought to evaluate their impact to the "splendid, spacious, varied, magnificent and terribly fragile earth that supports us" (LS 55). If we can't find an appropriate agency to with which to file it, "we can file it where an Indian would have filed it—with our environmental conscience, our slowly maturing sense that the earth is indeed our mother, worthy of our love and deserving of our care" (LS 56).

Stegner prides himself on being a "realist with a vision," as do the engineers of *Angle of Repose* who compare their visions with the "grandiose" ones of politicians that are "based on far less knowledge of the limiting facts" (486). In that novel he investigates the process by which we compose something like reverence, or, rather, repose. Lyman comes to history in *Angle of Repose* as Stegner does in *Wolf Willow,* years after they have already ignorantly lived through it. Their task involves a piecing together of that history so that it is also personal and relevant, which involves interpretation of historical facts—a reading of the "map" so that the *space* becomes more of a *place.* But interpreting facts or tracks, be they historical or geographical, can lead us down the wrong path if we "warp" them too far. A geography of hope should include not the old optimism, or an abstract "pleasure of hope," but a new one based on more "realistic visions." This middle ground, between the "limiting facts" and the fictions we invent, has the potential to protect places instead of destroying them. "Visionary expectation[s]" fueled western migration, but too often "exaggerated, uninformed, unrealistic and greedy expectations have been a prescription for disappointment" and for harm (LS xvi). In gaining as much knowledge as he can about place, Stegner is a new kind of writer, says Wendell Berry: "one who not only writes about his region, but also does his best to protect it . . . from its would be exploiters and destroyers" (55).[13] To be protected, it has to be known well. Surveyors such as Powell or famous Western guide Jed Smith (who dispelled the myth of the Rio Buenaventura)[14] are "not available these days as [guides]," but Stegner is, through his writing. "I accept the duty," he writes, "as least as much for what I myself may learn as for what I may be able to tell others" (LS 58).

The stories and myths developed for places have the potential to do harm particularly when it comes to the environment. Stegner's best-known comment on conservation is his 1960 "Wilderness Letter," published as the "coda" of *The Sound of Mountain Water.* It argues forcefully for the abstract notion of wilderness: "the idea alone can sustain me." When Stegner talks about protecting wilderness areas as a geography of hope, he is talking about places that, though protected, are no less human in their creation. As people warp history to meet their own ends, they warp geography and landscape. "The deep ecologists warn us not to be anthropocentric," Stegner writes, "but I know no way to look at the world, settled or wild, except through my own human eyes" (LS 201). Even wilderness areas, those supposed enclaves of pristine nature, are products of human culture and imagination. We construct them even as they help sustain our imagination: "We simply need that wild country available to us, even if we never do more than drive to its edge and look in" (MW 153). Stegner's defense of wilderness is based on a land ethic that is not "exploitation or 'usefulness' or even recreation," it is based on the notion that an area of public land that is cared for can be psychologically satisfying (MW 153).[15]

In his writing Stegner is preoccupied with the danger of perceiving a place as somewhere to pass through. Since perception plays such a strong role in defining place, he would have us perceive better, by considering what is inviolate about the relationship between a people and the place they occupy, and how the destruction of the relationship, or the failure to attend to it, wounds people. Stegner's early experiences on the prairie inform his belief that wilderness is necessary, but not as something *out there* blank but something also *in here,* known not as a "tourist but as denizen" (282).[16] His early experiences imprinted upon him an interior landscape that went into making him who he is, and that continually renews him. He connects with it when he returns to his place in *Wolf Willow* and understands how important that experience had been in shaping his identity and his perception. As the reality of the place was "made exactly equivalent with memory" when Stegner came back to it, wild places can be an idea, an imaginative fiction, that informs our relationship to the places we live in, so that they can be preserved—not only in our minds.

The information that goes into places, both the ones we "deeply live in" and the wild places we do not, should be as accurate as it should be layered and storied. "Wilderness" and "home" need not exist in binary opposition to one another, since the manner in which we care for places we deeply live in is also a metaphor for the manner in which we care for our larger home. Stegner's philosophy of conservation is part physical and emotional—formed from early experiences on the prairie—and part intellectual and rational, taken from surveyor scientists such as John Wesley Powell, who understood the "limiting facts." Stegner witnessed the ravages of landscape caused by early pioneers whose dreams of creating a Garden of the World in the arid West led to the Dust Bowl and other environmental degradations. His "hopefulness" about geography comes more than one hundred years after early optimism led people to the West. "I really only want to say," writes, "that we may love a place and still be dangerous to it" (*LS* 55).

Possibly, Stegner overemphasized motion as a defining aspect of Westerners and as a hindrance to "placedness." ("Migrants deprive themselves of the physical and spiritual bonds that develop within a place and as society" (*LS* 72.) After all, even though he moved constantly as a child, he was able to cultivate a sense of place (Vale 177). But he may not only be talking about putting down roots but knowing how to slow down and look, rather than plunging headlong into the future. Some surveyors covered vast distances of space through the techniques of triangulation, but some were inclined to slow down, inspect, and look. "In geographical terms, the frontiers have been explored and crossed. It is probably time we settled down. It is probably time we looked around instead of looking ahead" (181).

He advocated, as well, looking with a different set of eyes, eyes conscious of the past and conscientious of the future. Summarizing Aldo Leopold's impact on American culture, Stegner notes that "it was not for its novelty that people responded to Leopold's call for a land ethic. It was for his assurance . . . that science corroborates our concern, not our optimism: that preserving the natural world we love has totally practical and unsentimental justifications" (*MSF* 16). The affective and hopeful responses to landscape, what Tuan calls "fields of care," provide the emotional investments in place, while the scientific provides the critical faculty that keeps place from lapsing into total fantasy, the "big rock candy mountain," or empathic, Thoreauvian overidentification. As a "geography of hope," Stegner's wilderness is situated between a place as it is both imagined by the denizen and verifiable by the mapmaker. As geographer Thomas R. Vale writes, Stegner's sense of place seems to embrace what are usually contrasting poles, wilderness and civilization, past and present, the stories of triumph and of loss, "the high culture of poets and the wildness of mountain water" (178), into a geography of wholeness and repose. Wallace Stegner was shaped by his place as he went about shaping and writing it: His philosophy of place recognizes the spiritual and psychological dimensions of geography, where the hopes that are put on it—the stories that write it and sing its songs—are more realistic and less destructive, and provide better "maps" in a journey home.

Conclusion
"A Map of Connextion"

Your confidence in these finely etched maps is understandable, for
at first glance they seem excellent, the best a man is capable of; but
your confidence is misplaced. Throw them out. They are the wrong
sort of map. —Barry Lopez, *Desert Notes*

The broad-shouldered frame of North Carolina's Mount Mitchell rises to
6,684 firm feet pressed solidly against the sky, above all other mountain peaks
in the East. The summit is a narrow band of cool, heavily shadowed forests of
spruce and balsam fir spread along the ridgeline. This is a boreal habitat, one
closer in character to parts of Canada and Katahdin than to most of North
Carolina—crowded with cold-loving plants, birds, and trees—though a map
says otherwise.

Mount Mitchell is located in the southeastern corner of one of the U.S.
Quadrangles, a project begun by Powell, so only the tip of the peak is on my
map. Unless I had the other three (east, south, and southeast), my way up here
has been "off the map." However, my way is well marked by a trail. If there was
not one, and I had to scramble through thick mountain laurel (as early surveyors had to), I would experience firsthand how important mapping strategies
are to finding and recording the way up. I have hiked here under the influence
of these literary cartographers who could not just see their places through the
map but had to experience them, and, having experienced them, had to tell
about their experience. This mountain was named for a surveyor, Elisha
Mitchell (1793–1857). Mitchell taught at the University of North Carolina in
Chapel Hill, was a Presbyterian minister, and a scientist. In 1825 he took charge

of the North Carolina Geological Survey, the first statewide survey to be organized anywhere in the nation. During his early years in the survey, he made
several trips into the Black Mountains for the purposes of measuring elevation.

Like the summits of other mountains, this one is extreme, cut by cold, im-
placable wind and the saturating fog of clouds. But because of dangerous levels of ozone, pollution, and acid rain, Mount Mitchell's sere landscape is also
dying. The sense of mortality struck Mitchell even then. In a letter written to
his wife on July 14, 1844, Mitchell describes an ascent to what he thought was
the highest mountain in the range.

> I went up the main stream—then up a fork and over the spruce pine
> mountain ridge to another fork—then over another high mountain to a
> third for[k] ... and all the way through the laurels, and I still had the
> whole Black [M]ountain before me. I could not help thinking as I crawled
> along over the leaves under a shelving rock what a comfortable place it
> would be to die in. (qtd. in Schwarzkopf 32)

Those words, about a place in which to die, would prove prophetic. Twelve
years later he would slip and fall to his death while trying to prove that he had
indeed climbed the highest peak in the Black Mountains and consequently the
East. Though he believed otherwise, the peak Mitchell ascended in 1844 was
not the highest in the range but a nearby complex (with two peaks) known as
Mount Gibbes, though he had, on an earlier excursion in 1835, climbed the
"real" Mount Mitchell and published his results in the *Raleigh Register:*

> The Black Mountain [range] ... has some Peaks of greater elevation than
> any point that has hitherto been measured in North-America, East of the
> Rocky Mountains, and is believed to the be the highest Mountain [range]
> in the United States. (qtd. in Schwarzkopf 29)

Among those colonies and territories that had achieved statehood, Mitchell
was right. Though he had taken measurements, Mitchell still wasn't sure *which*
peak was highest, making the 1844 trip necessary. The one he ascended then
was the one that became associated with his name (next to Mount Gibbes),
but it wasn't the highest peak, even though, after measuring it, he was sure it
was. Meanwhile, a former student and United States Congressman, Thomas
Clingman (1812–97) was also interested in determining which peak in the

Black Mountains was highest. In 1855, Clingman reached what is today known as Mount Mitchell and concluded, like Goodyear about King's ascent of Mount Whitney, that Mitchell had missed the "real" peak. Clingman submitted his findings to be published by the Smithsonian. As a result of his 1855 visit, the peak formerly known among Highlanders as Black Dome now became known locally as Clingman's Peak, whereas the peak Mitchell climbed in 1844 was known among local inhabitants as Mount Mitchell.

The controversy continued, as both men defended their "claims" to having reached the highest peak. Finally, armed with his old field notes, Mitchell made another excursion in 1857 to prove that he had in fact already climbed the present-day Mount Mitchell (then Clingman's Peak), and to once again take measurements and draw maps. Apparently, while descending the mountain, after confirming that he had already been there, Mitchell slipped and fell.

During his earlier visits, Mitchell procured the services of local guides. A guide by the name of "Green Silver" helped Mitchell to the top of Celo Knob in 1835, and locals William Wilson and Adoniram Allen accompanied Mitchell to the range's highest peak (now Mount Mitchell) during that same year. During the 1844 trip, William Riddle and his son escorted Mitchell up Mount Gibbes. But for his 1857 ascent Mitchell took no such guides, though his body was found by one. After Mitchell was discovered to be lost, and the search party hunted in vain for signs of him, "local settler and mountain guide" "Big Tom" Wilson joined the effort (Schwarzkopf 62). About halfway down the mountain, Wilson discovered some tracks that led off the trail and down a creek bed where, at the base of a waterfall, Mitchell's body lay. The party speculated that someone would only take that route if "darkness had overtaken them" (Schwarzkopf 64).

Mitchell's death and the circumstances surrounding it excited much attention. According to the *Asheville Spectator,* Mitchell died a "martyr to science and scientific knowledge" (qtd. in Schwarzkopf 65). Because of such a feeling, the professor was buried atop the high peak of the range, today known as Mount Mitchell, where there stands a permanent monument to his "martyrdom." Now, his name was on the peak and on the map, and more importantly, was associated with the legend that took *place* there.

A place isn't a place, Stegner says, until it has had a poetry. There is a poem about Mitchell called *Floreen; or, The Story of Mitchell, A Legend of the 'Hand of the Sky'* (1916), by G. W. Belk: "And over the mountains, by night and by day, /

They sought for him, thinking he'd lost his way. . . . / But in his confusion he missed the trail / That led down safely to the vale (sec. xiv, xii). Not until his death in 1857 did denizens commemorate Mitchell by conferring his name upon the mountain. A generation later would come the poem by Belk. The story of Mitchell's ascents, the controversy with Clingman, his death, and the search party to find him, including the tracking by local legend "Big Tom" Wilson to find Mitchell's body, are all part of the record, and part of what made Mount Mitchell a place to local residents and a protected state park in 1915.

Mitchell's story illustrates a "landmark" for literary cartography: places can reach deep into us, though a surveyor's instruments might not provide the best means to measure them. The place sank deep into Mitchell, though his quantifications got it wrong. And without a "guide"—though not necessarily a map—Mitchell lost his life. His story contrasts two different kinds of knowledge we have seen: that of the scientist, surveyor, academic, and that of the hunter, denizen, native. "Big Tom" would have known how to find a way down through the twilight, or would have known to get down before darkness came. Places enter these kinds of mappers in excruciating detail, though are perhaps only seen momentarily, through the corner of the eye rather than through the transit. The surveyors in this book did not have to die to be associated with their places; rather, they left behind a different legacy—their written texts— that contributed to the "placing" of the lands they represented.

Mitchell's 1844 trip predated Thoreau's climb of Katahdin by just two years when Thoreau exclaims: "What a place to live, what a place to die and be buried in!" (81).[1] Thoreau cries out about his place to die with much more energy than Mitchell, because Thoreau's enthusiasm is for a natural space he can make "contact" with, one without human history. He then writes, "I am reminded by my journey how exceedingly new this country is. You have only to travel for a few days into the interior . . . to come to that very America which the Northmen, and Cabot, and Gosnold, and Smith and Raleigh visited" (81). The journey Thoreau has taken "into the interior" leads him to the site of American discoveries. However, Bruce Greenfield has shown in *Narrating Discovery* (1992) that the accounts of both Smith's Virginia and Gosnold's Cape Cod recorded clear evidence of earlier human habitants (192). The map in Smith's *Map of Virginia* (1612) even shows towns and names that preceded his arrival in 1607. On that very map, the lettering of "Jamestown" is comparatively small to "Powhatan."

Thoreau actually journeys through a mapped landscape strewn with ring-bolts and branded logs, though he also "unmaps" these signs to arrive at the point of contact he believes of earlier explorations. According to Greenfield, Thoreau's moment of discovery, when he stands in awe of a purely present landscape, detaches that landscape from the context that drove Europeans across the ocean and into unfamiliar countries (198–201). Mitchell, too, ignored those Cherokee residents who were living in the Black Mountain region. Three years after his ascent in 1835, the U.S. government forcibly removed the Cherokee and sent them walking to Oklahoma along the "the trail of tears," in part because a surveyor had mapped and measured the unknown-to-whites area, making it possible for future settlement and pushing the Indians farther west beyond the boundaries. Many whites erased the mythic interpretation of Indians to create a blank geographical space to move into, as if, without lines on paper, Indians' minds were also blank (Ryden 292). As Greenfield and others have argued, the story of continental conquest became the master narrative for nineteenth-century commentators, but, as we have seen, there are sources of contradiction and resistance within this history.

Even William Clark, who did most of the surveying for the Lewis and Clark expedition, used *all* the information he received, from Indians and trappers, to draw his "Small Map of Connextion" [*sic*] (73). Clark writes on December 17, 1804, that he obtained sketches from the "Indins [*sic*]." Then, on January 5, 1805, Clark writes: "I imploy my Self Drawing a Connection of the Countrey [*sic*] from what information I have rec[ei]ved" (74). His "Map of Connextion" involved a close cooperation of local peoples, a relationship that contradicted the scientific and legal authority of the expedition and its claims to the land.

The literary cartographers in this book recognized that Indians had a conception of the land for which they had no explanation. We saw it in Thoreau in the woods of Maine, King at the base of Mount Whitney, Powell in the Grand Canyon, and Stegner in the Cypress Hills and in his comments on Indian "reverence." There can be no doubt that maps facilitated the objectives of an expansionist government. However, these literary cartographers also expressed a strong ambivalence about their maps. They were sometimes able to look beyond them, or those of the official government survey, to include the "maps" of others, viewing the landscape through as many eyes and ways of knowing as possible.

This has not, however, been primarily a book about multicultural views of place. It has, rather, investigated how maps and writing express a powerful desire to know, represent, and live on the land. Maps and mapping "connect the countrey" and these writers, but just as they recognized that there was no unitary "place" or even "America," they also recognized that there was no one way to know or represent it. Beneath the smooth surface of the maps was a land of infinite variety and complexity.

Though he appreciated the area's beauty, Mitchell was a practical man, pursuing the goals of science, and so, unlike the other surveyors, he did not express the sublime. Still, he sensed how difficult the long Black Mountain ridge was to map:

> It is a matter of considerable difficulty . . . to ascertain which it is that overtops the rest. . . . Counting [southward] from [Celo Knob]: one low one; one low one; two in one, the northernmost pointed; a round knob, same height; a double knob; then the highest; then a long, low place, with a knob on it; then a round three knobby knob, equal to the highest, after which the ridge descends. (qtd. in Schwarzkopf 26)

Mitchell was also not a great chronicler of his experiences, and so, writing in his journals, he expresses not only his frustration about knowing which peak is the highest, but also, it appears, his frustration about how to distinguish one peak from another, with one a more "knobby knob."

Mitchell ventured into the Black Mountains to trace geographical boundaries and to determine elevations because existing maps for the area were either blank or inaccurate. Although the surveyors in this book first envisioned the land as blank on maps, and that blankness pulled them in, cartographic devices alone would not get them out. Writing for them was a way of "deep mapping," a way to encompass all the details in the life of a place that maps could not, though Mitchell didn't go further than his "counting." Ultimately, they chart for us not a route through the unknown, but through the *partly* known landscape, where its landmarks and natural features need to be more carefully understood as they constitute what gives a place its "sense."

The toponymy of early maps produced by surveyors such as Lewis and Clark and John Charles Frémont often had little success in assigning place-names that would hold up from generation to generation. Places and the names associated with them came to be not because a surveyor or cartographer suggested an appellation or wrote it on his map, but because a culture, a community of shared beliefs and ideals, stayed long enough to make the names stick. Mitchell's name didn't become attached to the highest peak until he died. A sign doesn't become a useful until some shared meaning is attached to it, and a visual depiction of a space with place-names alone doesn't become meaningful unless there is a narrative to go with those names, a literature to go with the cartography.

These writers perceive places though a fusion of geography and imagination, and their writing is cartography of this country of the mind. Although the places they see are often "warped" by their own interior landscape or the discursive formations such as the sublime that they drew on for "contact," these literary cartographers are also changed by their experiences, and they express a timeless reverence in the natural world. Surveyor Clarence Dutton had to apologize for such a "point of departure":

> I have perhaps in many places departed from the severe ascetic style which has become conventional in scientific monographs. Perhaps no apology is called for. Under ordinary circumstances the ascetic discipline is necessary. Give the imagination an inch and it is apt to take an ell, and the fundamental requirement of the scientific method—accuracy of statement—is imperiled. But in the Grand Canon district there is no such danger. The stimulants which are demoralizing elsewhere are necessary here to exalt the mind sufficiently to comprehend the sublimity of the subjects. (xvi)

As surveyors with a literary sensibility, they consistently "exalt" their readers' minds. Their scientific explanations arise out of descriptions that depart from "severe ascetic style" or an objective mapping. Instead, they are narrated in such a way that readers might "discover" the place presented before them. To comprehend the "sublimity of the subjects," exaltation was as necessary to these literary cartographers' method as the scientific one, because they worked to both expand knowledge and enlarge the spirit.

However, as the country became more known, and as the spaces were filled in, theirs was not the sublime "unislanded by the recorded deeds of man" (Cole 108). Especially for Powell, who could see traces of geological history in the strata and human history carved into the walls, the land was already, in a sense, "mapped." That is, it wasn't up to the perceiver to impose a design on nature but to draw out the shape and contour of the land that was already there. What

Powell was able to do, and Stegner following him—what we might also learn to do—was to cultivate mystery and enchantment in places they came to know better, rather than in places they "discovered." In the end, what maps may tell us about places, if we pause long enough to look at them, is how much we don't know. To really know a place may be to know that it cannot be completely understood, or captured.

Finally, I have tried to show some points of reference in stages of an American writing about place. First, there was the "unmapped" continent that needed shape and design for Jefferson. For Thoreau, no presettled shapes would do to experience "contact," so he, in a sense, unmapped his place. King tried to "map" his place again, to paint and shape the impression it made on him, though, like Thoreau, he rejected maps when they got in the way of his being the "first." Powell was less concerned with how nature could be "discovered" than detecting how it already shaped itself. Stegner, heir to all the others, thought it necessary to understand all the responses that created a place, the contact with the place when we/it are young, but also the history and story that are found there that we can appreciate as we/it grow older. If Thoreau displaces history, Stegner re-places it within a literary cartography to develop a map that reaches not only out far but down deep.

Stegner's place-sense requires an understanding of the cultural values that have shaped definitions, perceptions, and interactions with the natural world to create a place. These are the "maps" that have brought us this far, and the lines on them may reveal "the scale at which we are discerning" (Lopez 259). Although disciplines such as surveying and cartography give us the empirical tools for objectively measuring nature, we also bring our attitudes, assumptions, and anticipations to bear on our world. The key, for Stegner and others, is to investigate those aspects of human language and culture that we bring to nonhuman nature. Scott Russell Sanders writes that "we need new maps" for our places, "living maps, stories and poems, photographs and paintings, essays and songs. We need to know where we are, so that we may dwell in our place with a full heart" (8).

Because maps can be such poor, flat representations of the places we know, they are a particularly apt metaphor for writers seeking to exploit the distances, ambiguities, or contradictions between the way we apprehend the world and they way it gets represented, between cognitive maps and cartographic ones. For that reason "mapping" comes up frequently in a library search for titles, usually with those associated with postmodernism; for example, "Mapping the Postmodern" by Andreas Huyssen. As Jose Litse Noye has commented in "Mapping the Unmappable," an article on Thomas Pynchon's *Gravity's Rainbow,* the map as an unstable representation appears frequently in postmodern criticism and fiction. "The Map, its iconic status apparently assured, seems to proffer cognitive control over a geographical correlate" (512). There is also Thomas Pynchon's recent book about two surveyors, Mason and Dixon, one of which has a "Map entirely within his mind, of a World he could escape to, if he had to. If he had to, he would enter it entirely but never get lost, for he would have this Map, and in it, spread below, would lie everything" (242). And so, "mappings" of the postmodern play on the conventions of "mapping" and of representation.

I have also played with the conventions of "mapping" these writers employ, to show that places are fluid and imagined. But the point I hope I've arrived at is not that such worlds are *merely* invented, which would hardly be a radical claim on my part, or to assert, as Frederic Jameson has, that "there can be no true maps" (52).[2] In contemplating these literary cartographers, who are mostly writing in a tradition of literary realism rather than postmodernism, it is not, in the end, the futility of maps and "mapping" that we are left with, or with a delight (or postmodern "play") in the distance between our "maps" and the world.

Rather, it is the sense of impotence (or, more accurately, the potency they confront) that these texts register, the sense that they can't "get it all in" ("The wonders of the Grand Canyon cannot be adequately represented in symbols of speech, nor by speech itself") that carries important implications. That the world is out there evident to the senses but cannot be "mapped" leaves us not with a "legacy of conquest" but with a kind of environmental humility, or, perhaps, the ecological sublime of Powell. Within the difficulty of both mapping and writing the world out there lies an awareness not of mastering the environment but of entering it through a variety of forms, maps included, to realize the sense of place.

What can we expect of a literary cartography in the future? It seems likely that the lines that separate disciplines and genres will continue to blur, as Wallace Stegner blurred them, and as literary cartographers seek new ways to write and understand places. John McPhee's *The Pine Barrens* (1967) begins with the map view, invoking the image of the space on maps of the Eastern megalopolis (Boswash, to some). After also looking down on the New Jersey forest from a fire tower, he proceeds to enter the local language and landscape, "pry[ing] the landscape loose from its anonymity" (Lopez 260). McPhee combines reporting with a novelist's sense of narrative and character. In the book, he profiles both Fred Brown and Bill Wasovich, who can find their way through a "fantastic ganglia" of roads and forest without maps (19). Most people would need to study their maps, but "Fred kept calling out directions," narrating the stories of place as they drove (19). Although some places are not even identified on maps, "not even on large-scale topographic maps, [as they moved along], Fred had a name for almost every rise and dip in the land" (21).

The last chapter returns to the image of cartographic space as McPhee again describes the view from high on a hill and how planners of a new jetport conceived of the Pine Barrens. Though McPhee's own position is characteristically difficult to detect in such matters, through his attention to both the natural and cultural history of the region, he has represented it as something more than "barren." The pines are a landscape endowed with value and central to the lives of the people who live there. By the end of the book, he has transformed the view from above or afar, revealing the depth of the interior landscape in such detail that we realize how much would be lost if the Pine Barrens were paved over. He again evokes the map of the East Coast: "people may one day look back upon the final stages of the development of the great unbroken Eastern City and be able to say at what moment all remaining undeveloped land should have been considered no longer as asset to individuals but an asset of the society at large" (156). Meanwhile, he calls out the names of new subdivisions, disorienting the orderly pattern that maps create, and he leaves us with one last image of map space: "At the rate of a few hundred yards or even a mile or so each year, the perimeter of the pines contracts" (157). Those "blank" spaces on maps once so inviting to early explorers, and once again to planners and developers, are now a powerful argument for preservation.

McPhee has also profiled Alaska in *Coming into the Country* (1977) and combines geology and biography in *Rising from the Plains* (1986). In the latter work, McPhee profiles a surveyor, David Love, who works in the field with the USGS. Though he could use satellite technology and computer microprobes, Love insists on walking the topography, getting a feel for the land. Love is a clear descendent of earlier members of the Survey, King and Powell, and he has revised earlier maps to account for subsurface movement, the geological theory known as plate tectonics, to come up with perhaps not a "true" map but a "truer" one: "The 1955 Wyoming map [by Love] set a standard for state geologic maps in the detail of its coverage, in its fossil-dating, in its delivery of the essence of the region—a standard set anew in the 1985 edition" (144). To draw such a map, "of the essence of the region," Love spent countless days studying the dramatic landscape that he grew up in. He told McPhee, while looking out on the Tetons from a high piece of ground: "I guess I've been on every summit I can see from here." (149). Love has, McPhee claims, a "geologic map of Wyoming in his head" (23). Love has firsthand geology, "all in one mind," rather than "pieced together from papers and reports," maps, and atlases (144). "To compete with Dave," a fellow geologist says, you'd have to do a lot of walking" (144).

McPhee has collected all his writing about geology in his Pulitzer Prize–winning *Annals of a Former World* (1998). The 600–plus page volume is an attempt to understand how, over geologic time, physical America came to be as it is today. McPhee writes that geologists are often able to see something they call the Picture. "The oolites and dolomite—tuff and granite, the Pequop siltstones and shales—are pieces of the Picture" (62). The creatures and the chemistry that goes with them are parts of the composition. The problem with the picture is that 99 percent of it is missing, washed away, melted down, or broken up. "The geologist discovers lingering remains, and connects them with dotted lines." (62). At this point, geology becomes more imaginative than descriptive. "Geologists," he writes, "inhabit scenes that no one ever saw, scenes of global sweep, gone and gone again, including seas, mountains, rivers, forests, and archipelagoes of aching beauty rising in volcanic violence to settle down quietly and then forever disappear—*almost* disappear" (emphasis his, 64). In the subjective imagination, McPhee goes on to say, the geologist rebuilds the archipelago (64).

In doing so, McPhee describes how geologists draw inferences from available facts: "To go back this way, retrospectively, from scene to shifting scene, is to go down the rock column, groping toward the beginning of the world. There is a firm ground some of the way. Eventually, there comes a point where inference will shade into conjecture. In recesses even more remote, conjecture may usurp the original franchise of God" (217). Geologists "see, infer, extrapolate, conjure, discover, and describe" long-veiled and innumerable worlds

(641) until they get the "Picture." But the Picture, for McPhee and the geologists he profiles, is more like a moving one. In *Rising from the Plains*, the third book of the *Annals*, McPhee shifts the master metaphor from "picture" to "narrative." David Love assembles "a story in his mind," a "sequential narrative" of the history of the Yellowstone Valley, and McPhee writes that Love can "see it in motion now, in several ways responsively moving in the present" (374). Eldridge Moores, central character of book four, *Assembling California*, also sees something more like a moving picture: "like most geologists, [Moores also] carries in his head a portfolio of ancient scenes, worlds overprinting previous worlds. He sees tundra in Ohio, dense forestation on New Mexican mesas, the Persian Gulf in the Painted Desert." (541)

To read these geological volumes "assembled" together by McPhee is to come away with the feeling all writers—especially all literary cartographers— strive to attain: For a brief moment, the earth moves. In fact, the single most important accomplishment of the *Annals* may be to add the notion of "deep time" to a study of a literary cartography and deep maps. McPhee explodes the passive, static map-view, creating a volatile, organic sense of place beneath the map's smooth skin:

> If you look on a world map at Antarctica, South America, Africa, and Australia, you virtually see them exploding away from one another. You can reassemble Gondwana [a former continent] in your mind and then watch it come apart. (560)

Maps deal with surfaces, showing the "uppermost formations in present time, while indicating little of what lies farther down and less of what is gone from above" (185). But at any given coordinate on a map, the "world will have changed too often to be recorded in a singe picture," writes McPhee. It will have been at one time below fresh water; at another, brine "will have been mountainous country, a quiet plain, equatorial desert, an arctic coast, a coal swamp, and a river delta, all in one Zip Code" (185). Below this surface is an alphabet, "phrases and clauses" not yet assembled into a narrative. These stories bring the dead strata to life, evoking a changing sense of place in ways that maps or static taxonomies never can. A picture or a map would provide a fixed, authoritative representation, but geology depends on a fluid, variable language to make its subject known, as the rocks themselves are moving. As such, "there remains in geology plenty of room for the creative imagination"

(185), as there remains in cartography plenty of room for the literature. In bringing together the science of geology with the language of literature, McPhee brings together two seemingly incompatible modes of expression, rhetoric and science, to show that rhetorical and literary devices are necessary components to a linguistic understanding of complex geological concepts. McPhee and other literary cartographers write of a richly diverse land and of the ways that we might know it—especially as knowing places in order to care for them becomes more and more urgent.

The literary cartography that McPhee practices probes beneath the surface for the text underneath. Beneath my hometown are layers of experience and story that an outsider wouldn't understand the full meaning and nuance of. And on the nearby section of the Delaware are places rich with association and personal history: the spot I once saw an osprey dive, the rocks where a drowning occurred, and the island where, out of curiosity, we rubbed ourselves with nettles and soothed our burning skin with the cool river mud, not to mention the many swimming and fishing holes. Geology, to McPhee, is a metaphor for that kind of experience, extracting and writing the accretion of stories that comprise this insider's landscape. Once we know the events that took place, our sense of place is enriched, as is our respect for the infinite complexity of the dynamic processes of the earth.

After all, you may see the country from an airplane, or through the windows of a passenger train, or perhaps by boat on one of the navigable rivers. Or you may see it by car, using a map or familiar sign to guide you. You may also hike a historic trail, or even travel the country by reading, examining the literary cartographers and their representations of place. Or, you may walk the country using the senses of proprioception, where the landscape unfolds before you, rolling this way and that. You might even get "down to the eye level of rat and squirrel kind," as Mary Austin advised, where "one perceives what might easily be wide and winding roads." From this height, trails are indeed highways, "with scents as signboards." "Man-height," Austin continues (and map-height), "is the least fortunate of all heights from which to study trails" (9).

Eventually, if you concentrate and gather this information, gathered from man and mole height, a strong presence, the seed of idea, the sense of place may begin to reveal itself. The word "topic" is derived from the greek word for place, *topos*—also a way to talk about a literary convention or theme. Though "topography" commonly refers to the surveying of surface features of a particular terrain, the view a map would give, it can also mean a writing of place, a literary cartography that, if successful, will evoke not only relative positions and elevations, but the ideas, thoughts, topics, and interior of that place, so as to render them less vulnerable.

Today, there is hardly a square foot of American landscape that has not been surveyed, digitized, and made readily available on the Internet. But there are still places where one can stand and imagine how wonderfully sublime it must have seemed to early surveyors, and still does. But whereas early explorers navigated by way of rivers, mountains, or other landmarks, today global positioning systems (GPS) can accurately determine location—longitude, latitude, altitude—of people and places almost instantaneously. Technology is also introducing new ways to chart human places, with new kinds of surveyors creating precise three-dimensional maps of the earth and geneticists mapping the human genome. These latter "mappers" should remind us of earlier surveyors, charting the "unknown" when there were already sufficient descriptions and "maps" in place. They focus on one sort of knowledge at the expense of other perspectives, such as other ways of knowing the human interior.

Possibly, these technologies will help us to better improve our health and understand our environmental predicament, such as the infrared maps used by oceanographers to measure the surface temperature of the ocean. And in *Boundaries of Home: Mapping for Local Empowerment,* Doug Aberley describes ways to use mapping "as one of many tools bioregionalists can use in reinhabiting place" (3). Maps can display the destruction of land, they can show a vision of the future, and they can depict undeveloped areas to become foci of resistance. To restore or protect an ecosystem, Aberly writes, you must be "sufficiently familiar with your place to know what there is to work with" (35). And to reinhabit place, we can employ alternative forms of mapping, including our personal geographies, the ones we carry in our minds and our desires, the cartographies that bind us to our sacred places and to each other. This is the interior landscape that always orients less in terms of latitude and longitude, but more in terms of the landmarks we know intimately: the cracks in sidewalks, a split rail cedar fence, honeysuckle, a berry patch.

In many ways this project has been my own "map of connextion." It began when I "explored" and developed an allegiance to a place along the Delaware River in New Jersey, and developed when I encountered a different landscape in the West, where I went to school. I moved to Columbus, Ohio, where I worked as a writer for surveyors and scientists, and then to Cleveland, Ohio (named for surveyor Moses Cleaveland), where this project began to take shape, and where I began to examine the literary cartographies that will re-main woven together with my own conception of the places represented. Now I am on Mount Mitchell, a place I "discovered," and that is now also a part of my interior landscape, and from where I will go back to Virginia, where the national survey was conceived, and where I now reside. These places are far apart on maps, but the journey has been valuable if I can now see them more closely, close together, and up close—each deserving of a unique awe that maps fail to provide.

NOTES

PREFACE

1. Others have more thoroughly demonstrated how maps take possession of land. See for example William Boelhower, *Through a Glass Darkly: Ethnic Semiosis in American Literature*: "the map was above all a national signature of possession and a public declaration of the right to settlement" (48).

CHAPTER ONE. INTRODUCTION

1. Yet, in "Some Principles of Ecocriticism," William Howarth notes (and here he borrows from Donald Marshall's *Contemporary Critical Theory*) that such tropes may have no geographical referent. Howarth also quotes from Leah S. Marcus, who calls attention to a "set of geographic metaphors . . . that suggest [the humanities'] continuing engagement on one level with a cast of mind we have rejected on another" (qtd. in Howarth, 77).

2. The phrase is in the first line of William Cowper's poem, "Lines of Solitude," ("I am monarch of all I survey") based on Alexander Selkirk, also the prototype for the marooned traveler in Daniel Defoe's novel *Robinson Crusoe* (1719). Thoreau cites the poem in reference to the interior and mental landscape he takes with him without tools: "But I retained the landscape, and I have since annually carried off what it yielded without a wheelbarrow. With respect to landscapes,—'I am monarch of all I survey, / My right there is none to dispute.'" (*Walden* 82). Mary Louise Pratt also uses the phrase in her *Imperial Eyes* (204).

3. Roger M. Downs and David Stea argue that a "cognitive map" is a person's organized representation of a particular environment. Cognitive maps depend largely on experience and our needs in a particular environment, and tend to be highly subjec-

tive. The cognitive map differs from the cartographic one in that it is full of personal meaning—not written down. Anyone from out of town who has ever asked directions from those who have lived in that town for long time can understand these "mental maps" (6–7).

4. Jefferson includes a correction to this in his later notes. In 1815, with a theodolite, he measured the north peak of Otter at 3103 feet, and notes in a footnote that "the highest of the White mountains in N.H. by barometrical estimate made by Capt. Partridge was found to be 4885 f. from it's [sic] base" (263). Mount Washington is 6,288 feet above sea level, and the north peak of Otter is now recorded at 3,875 feet.

5. As to whether Jessie added a "literary" or poetic flair to John's writing, see Henry Nash Smith, *Virgin Land,* 27.

6. Others can summarize the difference between the terms better than I can, but generally, in aesthetics, the sublime refers to the nonhuman or infinite, the beautiful to the human or humanized, and the picturesque to something in between. For an analysis of the various landscape aesthetic controversies and definitions, see Walter Hipple, *The Beautiful, the Sublime, and the Picturesque in Eighteenth-Century British Aesthetic Theory* (83–98).

7. I do not know how well known the poem was in America, but in his biographical sketch, the Rev. W. M. Hill writes that it was among the popular lines of British poetry. He also writes that the poem was well liked by Madame de Stael, an eminent Swiss-French literary critic who was also fiercely anti-Napoleon in her politics. "Few were the political reunions, on the liberal side at least, where some quotations were not made, from language which marked a generous heart and an ardent love of liberty" (xxii).

8. For more on "the role of place in literature" (the book's title), see Leonard Lutwack. "In the final analysis all places in literature are used for symbolical purposes" (31).

9. Surveying and exploration in nineteenth-century America can be understood by some similarities and important differences to that process in Australia, so nearly concurrent. R. V. Tooley has pointed out in *The Mapping of Australia* that Australia was imagined before it was discovered (ix), as was the New World. Simon Ryan, author of *The Cartographic Eye: How Explorers Saw Australia,* has noted that the imaginative construction of a *terra australis* took shape according to an antipodality or upside-downess, a "place were everything was reversed" (105–7). Such a prejudice can be seen on medieval maps, where Europe embodied what was human and all that was not belonged to regions thought abnormal or perverse (107). European surveyors and explorers expected the unexpected in Australia: "Trees seemed to keep their leaves and shed their bark, swans were black, eagles white, bees were stingless, mammals had pockets, it was warmest in the hills and coolest in the valleys" (110). Ryan quotes from John Lort Stokes's *Discoveries in Australia; with an Account of the Coasts and Rivers Surveyed During the Voyage of H.M.S. Beagle, in years 1837–47:* "the voyager knows,

from the best authority, that upon the coasts, and within the heart of Australia, nature seems to delight in contradiction" (qtd. in Ryan 111). The land is seen through "the best authority," so their contact with it is influenced by this prevailing discourse.

10. Hayden is not one of the literary surveyors covered in this book, but he wrote *The Great West: Its Attractions and Resources. Containing a Popular Description of the Marvelous Scenery, Physical Geography, Fossils, and Glaciers of This Wonderful Region: and the Recent Explorations in the Yellowstone Park, "The Wonderland of America"* (1880).

11. Surveyor Veplank Colvin, too, was influential in creating Adirondack Park in 1892.

12. Compare with David Mazel, who says that the landscapes of King and Powell, "however much [they] may be exalted, [are] also passive and objectified," fixed in the position of spectacle (141). I argue that the two surveyors may have begun with that view, but they did not end there because of their growing recognition that the landscape wasn't static, able to be freeze-framed in a map.

CHAPTER TWO. SURVEYING THE STRANGE

1. In 1847, when Thoreau described his life for the members of his Harvard class, he listed "writer" as only one occupation among many: "I am a Schoolmaster—a Private Tutor, a Surveyor—a Gardener, a Farmer—a Painter, I mean a House Painter, a Carpenter, a Mason, a Day-Laborer, a Pencil-Maker, a Glass-paper Maker, a Writer, and sometimes a Poetaster" (*Correspondence* 196).

2. "The map is not the territory" is attributed to Alfred Korzybski (1879–1950).

3. There is as of yet no adequate account of the relationship between Thoreau's vocation, surveying, and his avocation, writing. Robert Stowell and William Howarth have collected some of Thoreau's maps in a thorough and useful collection, *A Thoreau Gazetteer* (1970), whose primary aim "is to give its readers an idea of the places Thoreau describes in his books" (xi). The book displays maps Thoreau drew with present-day maps and other pictures and illustrations of place, but is not concerned with how mapping influenced Thoreau's aesthetics of place. Thoreau's surveys have been collected in *A Catalog of Thoreau's Surveys* (1976), edited by Marcia Moss. The volume includes his early survey of the pond in 1846 and his last survey on August 20, 1860 of the "Nathaniel Hawthorne Estate," but is primarily a reference guide. One of the best and most recent books to deal with Thoreau's surveying and its relationship to his place-sense is Lawrence Buell's *The Environmental Imagination,* but Buell is primarily concerned with *Walden.* Buell makes a case for how environmental writing locates itself in "actual environments" and is referential, Thoreau's map being an example, but I try to show how the "actual world" is off the map, and ultimately how Thoreau aban-

doned the surveying and mapping aesthetic for a walking one that allowed him to perceive places as active and strange rather than fixed and familiar.

4. From their introduction to a 1970 reprint of *Survey of Maine*, curators of the Maine State Museum write that Greenleaf was a tireless promoter of Maine, spending a good deal of his time "procuring settlers" and supporting his "visionary promotional activities": "Greenleaf was, in a sense, a man captivated and obsessed by the potentialities of the Maine environment" (ii).

5. For Christopher Hitt, in "Toward an Ecological Sublime," Thoreau's "contact" on Katahdin is the moment when "the speaker transcends *logos*" (616). He adds that "a sublime encounter with nature seems to have the power to jolt us momentarily out of a perspective constructed by reason and language, a perspective that, in modern Western culture, has rendered nature mute." I would agree that Thoreau is jolted, but he has called attention to language and its inadequacy, through the vehicle of the map, not transcended it. Nature can only be rendered nonmute through an act of representation.

6. This passage is identical to one in his journal and is an extension of the passage I quoted earlier (January 1, 1858), in which he sees woods as wood-lots. Clearly, the woods of Maine were liberating him from this perspective.

7. In "Walking" Thoreau will say "in wildness is the preservation of the world," though he's talking about a particular state of mind that keeps the world alive, if only in thought, and not necessarily wilderness preservation.

8. For a thorough discussion of Thoreau's attitudes towards Indians, including his "savagist" prejudices, and for a discussion of Thoreau's "Indian books" (and a discussion of whether or not Thoreau was planning a book on Indians), see Robert F. Sayre, *Thoreau and the American Indians*.

9. Thoreau probably redrew the first map early in 1854, before he sent the *Walden* manuscript to press. The map was also literally "reduced," as it was on a smaller scale than the first, forty rods to an inch rather than ten.

10. See Christ's advice to follow him: "Whoever loves father or mother more than me is not worthy of me, and whoever loves son or daughter more than me is not worthy of me" (Mathew 10:37). Emerson also references the quote in "Self-Reliance."

11. At issue in describing the "arc" of Thoreau's career is when you date Thoreau's "Walking." Though it appeared one month after his death in June of 1862, much of the material in "Walking" was recycled from earlier lecture notes and his journals. The "Walking" manuscript in the Concord Free Public Library has notes from Thoreau's hand and some from his sister Sophia. Still, though he used earlier notes, it is accurate enough to date it as 1862 since that is when he put it together. If read as a final, concise statement on Thoreau's philosophy, he was clearly moving away from surveying, as I have argued in this chapter.

CHAPTER THREE. MAPPING THE MIRAGE

1. A key difference is that the "lakes" King sees on maps may actually have been there at one time and weren't just drawn in to help sell the land. Many of the lakes in the region are dry, a phenomenon King the geologist could surely have predicted if he had read his Frémont and studied the drainage characteristics of the Great Basin.

2. Although speculation on my part, the account of the desert crossing that King gives here, written five years later for the May, 1871 edition of *The Atlantic Monthly* (and later published as the first chapter of *Mountaineering*, "The Range"), seems to be a composite of the accounts he gave to his supporters to convince them of the need for the project. King was a much better politician than Whitney. He named a Sierra peak after California statesman John Conness and impressed congressmen and business leaders by putting the "practical" ahead of the purely scientific. William Goetzmann notes that King, remembering Whitney's mistake of publishing paleontology first, pushed the publication of a report that studied the Comstock Lode region to the front of his official reports to please politicians and businessmen (445).

3. Gould discusses Lyell in *Time's Arrow, Time's Cycle: Myth and Metaphor in the Discovery of Geologic Time*. For a discussion of the uniformitarian/catastrophism debate in King, see Keith R. Burich, "'Something Newer and Nobler is Called into Being': Clarence King, Catastophism, and California."

4. Engraved in 1865, it accompanies "The Yosemite Guide-Book," published by the State Geological Survey in 1869.

5. Moran is the most celebrated of the survey artists. He accompanied both the Hayden (1871, 1874) and Powell surveys (1873). Bierstadt traveled with King, though King found that "his mountains are too high and too slim; they'd blow over in one of our fall winds. He hasn't what old Ruskin calls for" (qtd. in Wilkins 174). Encouraged by the success of Moran's *Grand Canyon of the Yellowstone,* which was purchased by Congress in 1872, Bierstadt commemorated the King survey in his *Autumn of the Sierras* both in choice of site and by adding the survey party in the background. The painting hung in the House of Representatives, along with *Discovery of the Hudson River,* but was later returned to the artist (Rindge 62–63). King purchased three of Bierstadt's paintings for his personal art collection.

6. Janin was hired by the San Francisco Mining and Commercial Company to check out the claim and make sure it would be safe (Goetzmann 453).

7. Shepard writes that finding "architectural" ruins in the landscape also had a patriotic cause: "the haunting architecture of the Yellowstone's filigreed cliffs delighted Americans who were wistfully conscious of a national cultural shortcoming. Entertaining the pleasant illusion that the rocks were the ruins of buildings led to an equally

gratifying dream that the area had formerly been inhabited by a highly civilized and artistic people who, like the ancient Greeks and Romans, had vanished, leaving their works to the amazement of future generations" (252).

8. Racism in *Mountaineering* is flagrant, "casual but constant" (Howarth xix). King's casual use of racial slurs, "greasers" and "tar-heads" for example, suggests a "a bigotry consistent with his self-presentation as a genteel aristocrat" (Tallmadge 1179), but it was also a prejudice consistent with his way of classifying landscapes on his own terms. His prejudice against Indians is peculiar in light of his fascination with dark-skinned people. (In 1878 he entered into a secret marriage with Ada Todd, a young African American from Brooklyn; they eventually had five children. The shame of this double life and the failure of his business ventures landed him in an asylum. He died of tuberculosis in Phoenix on Christmas Eve, 1901.) Such ambivalence was due in part to King's mercurial nature and in part to his being a product of his day. For most survey-ors/explorers, Indians were at once savages and guides—a hostile threat and a valuable source of information about the land. For example, despite his claim that "the Quakers will have to work a great reformation in the Indian before he is really fit to be extermi-nated" (60), King also sought out a tribe of Paiutes to settle a legal battle between two mining companies over possession of a silver-laden hill, needing them to verify place names that were found on the maps (Wilkins 189). However, the general practice of the U.S. Geological Surveys was to "survey" Indians as if they were a part of the landscape itself rather than acknowledge that they were skillful "surveyors" and mapmakers themselves. Lieutenant George M. Wheeler was instructed by the Amy Corps of Engi-neers to obtain "everything relating to the physical features of the country, the num-bers, habits, and disposition of the Indians who may live in this section" (qtd. in Bartlett 338).

CHAPTER FOUR. SURVEYING THE SUBLIME

1. Powell also compiled a map of the "linguistic stocks of North American Indians north of Mexico" in 1891 when he was director of the Bureau of Ethnology.

2. A complete overview of the scope and content of the *Report* is beyond my pur-pose here. For a comprehensive analysis, see Wallace Stegner's *Beyond the Hundredth Meridian: John Wesley Powell and the Second Opening of the West.*

3. In 1895, after Powell retired from the USGS, he published a revised *Canyons of the Colorado,* complete with more photographs and illustrations culled from two decades of government exploration. Known now as *The Exploration of the Colorado River and Its Canyons,* this is the version widely circulated today and the one I refer to unless otherwise indicated.

4. Powell explains in a letter to the *Chicago Tribune,* dated from Green River Wyo-

ming, May 24, 1869, and published on May 29, that funding came from the Illinois Industrial University and the Illinois Natural History Society.

5. The journals of the first trip, including those of other crew members, are collected in *The Great Unknown: the Journals of the Historic First Expedition Down the Colorado River.* Bradley makes no mention of the rescue in his entry of the same day.

6. In the later *Canyons of the Colorado* (1895), Powell begins the chapter with "A year has passed" but changes little else.

7. Hamblin was born in 1819 in Salem, Ohio, and went to Utah with the original band of Mormon emigrants. He said an angel of the Lord appeared and told him that he if he never drew the blood of an Indian, no Indian would draw his. The "buckskin apostle" dedicated his life to securing peace between whites and Indians (Darrah, *Powell* 154).

8. Of course, as Stegner acknowledges, Powell had every justification for the high tone. He was on a hazardous and exciting voyage, and in territory that could "stir the superlatives out of almost anyone" (Stegner 149).

9. For more on Indian practices of naming, see William Cronon, *Changes in the Land* (65–66).

10. The nature-as-book metaphor was probably cliché by the time Powell used it, since it was no doubt exploited by Thoreau's famous "leaf" passages on the melting railroad bank in "Spring" and Whitman's "leaves" of grass. Both use the pun to suggest that leaves of nature are like leaves of a book, implying an accessible natural order. However, Powell would have been reading the "pages" of geologic evolution, whereas Thoreau and Whitman were reading something more divine. The "book of nature" was one of the "three books of God" in early Protestant meditation in the 1600s (Huntley 9). Barton St. Armand has shown that Ernst Robert Curtis dates the first secular use of the term as occurring before 1499, but Armand suggests it goes back to Pliny, as it is implicit in the very idea of natural history (30). Sir Charles Lyell used it in his *Principles of Geology* (a book Powell would have been familiar with), but not optimistically. "The book of Nature is the book of fate," he said, and tells us not of the divine but of the end of the human species (336). Interestingly, in Powell's earliest account, for W. A. Bell's *New Tracks in America,* which appeared in 1870 in England, he wrote that "the canyons of this region would be a book of revelations in the rock-leaved Bible of geology" (qtd. in Darrah, "Exploration" 21), suggesting that Powell thought the trip was apocalyptic or "messianic" (Aton 39).

11. Donald Worster, in his new biography of Powell, *A River Running West* (2001), has reached a similar conclusion, though he calls it a secular sublime: "[Powell's] emotions were completely secular and always checked by scientific reason" (309). True enough, but I wouldn't want to de-emphasize the thrill, nor the sense of the extraordinary power beyond the human, brought on by the sublime. Worster also notes that

Powell's sublime has people in it: "Powell's mission was to promote a more secularized, more inclusive, deeper understanding of human settlement and inhabitation" (335)

12. With an echo from Kant: "Sublimity, therefore, does not reside in any of the things of nature, but only in our mind" (504).

13. As Thomas Weiskel writes, to experience the sublime is to experience the unrepresentable: "The true function of the sublime is to legitimate the necessary discontinuities in the classical scheme of signification" (17).

14. For a discussion of whether or not Powell "fictionalized" the date of this map, see Wheat, 357–58.

15. Perhaps the practice of maps showing not necessarily the lay of the land but the routes explorers took was the practice of the day. In this sense, they told stories better than they presented topographical information. The "Map for the Utah Territory showing the Routes Connecting it with California and the East . . . 1858," referred to earlier, shows Frémont's third expedition and Gunninson's trail through the Sangre De Cristo Pass and on to the Sevier River where he died. George Wheeler produced a map of the same region as Powell. Upon hearing of Powell's exploration, Wheeler directed a survey *up* the river in 1871. As with Powell's map, the label demonstrates its purpose: "Map Showing Routes of the River and Land Parties Engaged in Exploring the Grand Canyon of the Colorado Under the Command of Lieut. Geo. M. Wheeler, Corps of Engineers, U.S. Army" (Figure 4.7). The "legend" on this map also tells the story. It gives "Dates and Camps of the River Party in 1871."

16. The illustrations are not attributed to anyone in Powell's "list of illustrations," but Nichols's name appears at the bottom left.

17. Hayden stated in 1867 that "the planting of ten or fifteen acres of forest trees on each quarter-section will have a most important effect on the climate, equalizing and increasing the moisture and adding greatly to the fertility of the soil." Hayden goes on to claim that the settlement of a portion of Nebraska has already changed the climate for the better (qtd. in Smith 180).

18. An 1890 Sundry Bill reduced the Irrigation Survey budget from the $720,000 that Powell had asked for to a mere $162,500, "enough to reduce the whole grand scheme to an aimless mapping of reservoir sites" (Stegner xxiii).

CHAPTER FIVE. GEOGRAPHY OF REPOSE

1. Written by Stegner in 1960 to David Pesonen of Wildland Research Center, it was first collected in his book of essays, *The Sound of Mountain Water,* in 1969.

2. Stegner calls the book a gloss on one of his favorites poems, Frost's "The Gift Outright," with its theme of "possessing what we were still unpossessed by" (LS 157).

3. Other "prairie" writers have noticed such imprinting. Kem Luther observes in *Cottonwood Roots*: "They say that the place where a child is living when she is ten is most likely to become the place she will say that she is 'from.' Some kind of domestic imprinting happens about that age which turns earlier and later homes into transient location" (10). The remembrance of place makes up a good part of Willa Cather's writing too. Antonia tells the narrator in *My Antonia*, "if I was put down there in the middle of the night, I could find my way all over that little town; and along the river to the next town, where my grandmother lived. My feet remember all the little paths through the woods, and where the big roots stick out to trip you" (237–38).

4. He has also said that too often writers "warp [reality] arbitrarily" (Hepworth diss. 319).

5. Mary Ellen Williams Walsh has severely criticized Stegner for his use of Foote's documents, as if he made them up. For Walsh, because Stegner's character is so close to the historical person, readers mistake Ward's life for Foote's.

6. Other scientific metaphors Stegner employs include the angle of repose and the Doppler Effect.

7. For more on Stegner's manipulation of point of view, see articles by Kerry Ahearn and Audrey Peterson.

8. Stegner is especially interested in debunking the myth of frontier individualism. He has Lyman Ward say, "I am impressed with how much of my grandparents' life depended on continuities, contacts, connections, friendships and blood relationships. Contrary to the myth, the West was not made entirely by pioneers who had thrown everything away but an ax and gun" (41).

9. Lopez may have borrowed the title from Stegner, who wrote an essay called "The Rediscovery of America: 1946."

10. For a discussion of how American visions of land transformation were energized by New World and millennial thinking, from the Puritans to the mid-nineteenth century, see Cecelia Tichi, *New World, New Earth*.

11. Geographer Edward Soja calls this "Thirdspace," a conception of geography that is both real and imagined rather than either/or. "Thirdspace builds on Firstspace perspective which builds on the 'real' material world and a Secondspace perspective that interprets this reality through 'imagined' representations of spatiality" (37).

12. Elizabeth Cook-Lynn, a Native American writer, has severely criticized Stegner's attitudes toward Indians in the title essay to her book, *Why I Can't Read Wallace Stegner and Other Essays* (1996). The essay exaggerates Stegner's supposed inadequacies and minimizes points of agreement he has with the "Indian point of view." As C. L. Rawlins has written, "her main point that Stegner is a literary conquistador is mistaken" (294). Throughout *Wolf Willow*, Stegner is coming to grips with the absence of a

history that Cook-Lynn accuses him of leaving out. Here is Stegner on the mistreat-
ment of Indians, an omission in Cook-Lynn's essay: "No one who has studied western
history can cling to the belief that the Nazis invented genocide. Extermination was a
doctrine accepted widely, both unofficially and officially, in the western United States
after the Civil War" (73–74). The crux of Cook-Lynn's argument comes from a single
de-contextualized passage: "like so many American writers and historians had said
before him, 'The Plains Indians were done'" (32). What Stegner says, in context, is that
as a "pure" culture uninterrupted by the advances of white settlement, Indians were
finished. "The white man literally created the culture of the Plains Indians by bringing
them the horse and gun; and just as surely, by conquest, disease, trade rum, and the
destruction of the buffalo, he doomed what he had created" (53). After Sitting Bull ca-
pitulated, the Indian resistance to white domination collapsed, and they become a
subjugated people (120). Nowhere does Stegner say that Indians stopped existing,
but—and not without opprobrium toward the laws and men who made it happen—
that they were herded in reservations, their freedom and identity obliterated beyond
repair.

Gerald Vizenor, another important Indian scholar and critic, also cites Stegner out
of context. He claims that Stegner "situates the western landscape in the literature of
dominance," a subtler form of Manifest Destiny Vizenor calls "manifest manners," because Stegner pronounces the land unnamed, without history. Vizenor's proof:
"Plunging into the future through a landscape that had no history, we did both the
country and ourselves some harm as well as some good" (qtd. in Vizenor 8). Stegner's
point is that we failed to recognize a history already there. Stegner's next sentence, not
quoted by Vizenor: "Neither the country nor the society we built out of it can be
healthy until we stop raiding and running" (*LS* 206).

13. Berry wrote to Stegner, after reading *Wolf Willow*, on October 4, 1963: "I would
like to do as well, sometime, with the facts of my own little neck of the woods"
(Stanford special collections).

14. Read about Stegner's comments on Smith in "Buenaventura and the Golden
Shore" in *Mormon Country*. See also note 7 in this book.

15. Wilderness is also, by definition, land exempt from private ownership. Stegner
talked about preserving more than just rugged mountain landscapes: "Other kinds [of
wilderness] will serve every bit as well . . . perhaps even better" ("Coda" 152).

16. As William Cronon has written in "The Trouble with Wilderness," "if [wilder-
ness] can stop being (just) out there and start being (also) in here, if it can start being
as humane as it is natural, then perhaps we can get on with the unending task of strug-
gling to live rightly in the world—not just in the garden, not just in the wilderness, but
in the home that encompasses them both" (45). In the essay, Cronon cites one of
Stegner's conservation pieces from *This is Dinosaur* as part of the problem with the

myth of wilderness, that humans can somehow "leave nature untouched by our passage" (493). But Cronon sees a deeper message in the same words: "If living in history
means that we cannot help leaving our marks on a fallen world, then the dilemma we
face is to decide what kinds of marks we wish to leave" (493).

CHAPTER SIX. CONCLUSION

1. Though Thoreau said earlier that man was not to be associated with this place:
"not for him to tread on, or be buried in" (70).

2. In *Postmodernism, or, The Cultural Logic of Late Capitalism,* Jameson develops a
postmodern "cognitive mapping."

WORKS CITED

ABBREVIATIONS FOR WALLACE STEGNER

AR   *Angle of Repose.* 1971. New York: Penguin, 1992.

BHM *Beyond the Hundredth Meridian: John Wesley Powell and the Second Opening of the West.* 1953. New York: Penguin, 1992.

BRCM *The Big Rock Candy Mountain.* 1938. Lincoln: Nebraska UP, 1985.

LS   *Where the Bluebird Sings to the Lemonade Springs.* New York: Penguin, 1992.

MSF *Marking the Sparrow's Fall.* Ed. Page Stegner. New York: Henry Holt, 1998.

MW   *The Sound of Mountain Water.* 1969. Lincoln: Nebraska UP, 1980.

WW   *Wolf Willow.* 1962. New York: Penguin, 1990.

Abbey, Edward. *Desert Solitaire.* 1968. New York: Simon and Schuster, 1990.
———. *The Journey Home.* New York: E. P. Dutton, 1977.
Aberly, Doug, ed. *Boundaries of Home: Mapping for Local Empowerment.* Gabriola Island, British Columbia: New Society Publishers, 1993.
Abram, David. *The Spell of the Sensuous.* New York: Vintage, 1996.
Abrams, Robert E. "Image, Object, and Perception in Thoreau's Landscapes: The Development of Anti-Geography." *Nineteenth Century Literature* 46.2 (1991): 245–62.
Adams, Henry. *The Education of Henry Adams.* 1918. Boston: Houghton Mifflin, 1973.
Ahearn, Kerry. "*The Big Rock Candy Mountain* and *Angle of Repose*: Trial and Culmination." *Critical Essays on Wallace Stegner.* Ed. Anthony Arthur. Boston: G. K. Hall, 1982. 109–24.

Allen, John L. "Lands of Myth, Waters of Wonder: The Place of Imagination in Geography." *Geographies of the Mind: Essays in Historical Geosophy.* Ed. David Lowenthal and Martin J. Bowden. New York: Oxford UP, 1976. 41–61.

Ambrose, Stephen E. *Undaunted Courage: Meriwether Lewis, Thomas Jefferson, and the Opening of the American West.* New York: Simon & Schuster, 1996.

Arensberg, Mary. Introduction. *The American Sublime.* Ed. Mary Arensberg. Albany: State U of New York P, 1986. 1–20.

Aton, James M. *John Wesley Powell.* Boise: Boise State U Western Writers Series, 1994.

Austin, Mary. *The Land of Little Rain.* 1903. New York: Penguin, 1997.

Bartlett, Richard A. *The Great Surveys of the West.* Norman: U of Oklahoma P, 1962.

Belk, G. W. *Floreen; or, The Story of Mitchell, A Legend of the 'Land of the Sky.'* Charlotte: Stone, 1916.

Bergon, Frank. "The Journals of Lewis and Clark: An American Epic." *Old West—New West.* Ed. Barbara Howard Meldrum. Moscow: U of Moscow P, 1993: 133–46.

———. "Wilderness Aesthetics." *American Literary History.* 9:1 (Spring 1997): 128–61.

Berry, Wendell. "Wallace Stegner and the Great Community." *What are People For?* San Francisco: North Point, 1990: 48–57.

Bickman, Martin. *Walden: Volatile Truths.* New York: Twayne, 1992.

Boelhower, William. *Through a Glass Darkly: Ethnic Semiosis in American Literature.* New York: Oxford UP, 1987.

Branch, Michael P. and Daniel J. Phillipon, eds. *The Height of Our Mountains: Nature Writing from Virginia's Blue Ridge and Shenandoah Valley.* Baltimore: Johns Hopkins UP, 1998.

Brush, Stephen J. *The History of Modern Science: A Guide to the Second Scientific Revolution, 1800–1950.* Ames, Iowa: Iowa State UP, 1988.

Bryson, Michael A. *Visions of the Land: Science, Literature, and the American Environment from the Era of Exploration to the Age of Ecology.* Charlottesville: U of Virginia P, 2002.

Buell, Lawrence. *The Environmental Imagination.* Cambridge: Harvard UP, 1995.

Burich, Keith R. "'Something Newer and Nobler is Called into Being': Clarence King, Catastophism, and California." *California Historical Society* 72.3 (1993): 234–50.

Burke, Edward. *A Philosophical Inquiry into the Origins of Our Ideas of the Sublime and the Beautiful.* 1757. Ed. J. T. Boulton. London: Routledge and Kegan Paul, 1958.

Burroughs, John. *Far and Near.* Boston: Houghton Mifflin, 1904.

Campbell, Thomas. *The Poetical Works.* New York: Crowell, 1851.

Campbell, Tony. "Portolan Charts from the Late Thirteenth Century to 1500." *The History of Cartography.* Ed. J. B. Harley and David Woodward. 2 vols. Chicago: U of Chicago P, 1987: 371–463.

Carter, Paul. *The Road to Botany Bay: An Exploration of Landscape and History.* New York: Knopf, 1988.

Chatwin, Bruce. *The Songlines.* New York: Viking, 1987.

Cole, Thomas. "Essay on American Scenery" (1835). *American Art 1700–1960: Sources and Documents.* Ed. John W. McCoubrey. Englewood Cliffs: Prentice Hall, 1965: 98–109.

Colvin, Verplanck. *Adirondack Explorations.* Ed. Paul Schaefer. Syracuse: Syracuse UP, 1997.

———. *Report on the Progress of the Adirondack State Land Survey to the Year 1886 with an Historical Sketch of the Work and Table of Elevations.* Albany: Pearsons, 1886.

Conrad, Joseph. *Heart of Darkness.* 1901. London: Penguin, 1995.

Cook-Lynn, Elizabeth. *Why I Can't Read Wallace Stegner and Other Essays.* Madison: U of Wisconsin P, 1996.

Cooper, James Fenimore. "American and European Scenery Compared." *The Home Book of the Picturesque.* 1852. Ed. Motley F. Deakin. Gainesville: Scholar's Facsimiles, 1967: 51–71.

Cosgrove, Denis. "Introduction: Mapping Meaning." *Mappings.* Ed. Denis Cosgrove. London: Reaktion, 1999.

Cronon, William. *Changes in the Land: Indians, Colonists, and the Ecology of New England.* New York: Hill and Wang, 1983.

———. "The Trouble with Wilderness, or, Getting Back to the Wrong Nature." *The Great New Wilderness Debate.* Ed. J. Baird Callicot and Michael P. Nelson. Athens: U of Georgia P, 1998: 471–99.

Curtius, Ernest Robert. *European Literature and the Latin Middle Ages.* New York: Pantheon, 1953.

D'Abate, Richard. "On the Meanings of a Name: 'Norumbega' and the Representation of North America." *American Beginnings: Exploration, Culture, and Cartography in the Land of Norumbega.* Ed. Emerson W. Baker et al. Lincoln: U of Nebraska P, 1994.

Darrah, William Culp. *Powell of the Colorado.* 1951. Princeton: Princeton UP, 1970.

———. "The Exploration of the Colorado River in 1869." *Utah Historical Quarterly* 15 (1947): 1–153.

Debenham, Frank. *Map Making.* London: Blackie and Son Ltd., 1955.

DeBlieu, Jan. "Sacred Cartographies: Mapping Your Most Intimate Terrain." *American Nature Writing 2000: A Celebration of Women Writers.* Ed. John Murray. Corvalis: Oregan State UP, 2000.

de Niza, Fray Marcos. "Report of Fray Marcos de Niza, August 26, 1539." *Narratives of the Coronado Expedition, 1540–1542.* Ed. George Hammond and Agapito Rey. Albuquerque: U of New Mexico P, 1940.

DeVoto, Bernard. "Introduction." *Beyond the Hundredth Meridian: John Wesley Powell and the Second Opening of the West.* 1953. New York: Penguin, 1992: xv–xxiii.

———. "Introduction." *The Journals of Lewis and Clark.* New York: Houghton Mifflin, 1953: xxii–lx.

Dillon, David. "Time's Prisoners: An Interview with Wallace Stegner." *Critical Essays on Wallace Stegner.* Ed. Anthony Arthur. Boston: G. K. Hall, 1982: 47–60.

Downs, Roger M. and David Stea. *Maps in Minds: Reflections on Cognitive Mapping.* New York: Harper and Row, 1977.

Dutton, Clarence E. *Tertiary History of the Grand Canyon District.* 1882. Santa Barbara: Peregrine, 1977.

Dykeman, Wilma. *Explorations.* Newport, Tennessee: Wakestone, 1984.

Elder, John. Foreward. *The Height of Our Mountains.* Ed. Michael P. Branch and Daniel J. Philippon. Baltimore: Johns Hopkins UP, 1998: xvii–xix.

Emerson, Ralph Waldo. *The Complete Essays and Other Writings of Ralph Waldo Emerson.* New York: Random House, 1940.

Exploring the West from Monticello: A Perspective in Maps from Columbus to Lewis and Clark. Ed. Guy Meriwether Benson. U of Virginia Library. July 10–September 26, 1995 <http://www.lib.virginia.edu./exhibits/lewis_clark/index.html>.

Ferguson, Suzanne. "History, Fiction, and Propaganda: An Interview with Wallace Stegner." *Literature and the Visual Arts in Contemporary Society.* Ed. Suzanne Ferguson and Barbara Groseclose. Columbus: Ohio State UP, 1985: 3–22.

Frémont, John Charles. *Narratives of Exploration and Adventure.* Ed. Allen Nevins. New York: Longmans, Green and Co., 1956.

Garber, Frederick. *Thoreau's Fable of Inscribing.* Princeton: Princeton UP, 1991.

Gilpin, William. *Three Essays on Picturesque Beauty; on Picturesque Travel; and on Sketching Landscape.* London: R. Blamire, 1794.

Goetzmann, William. *Exploration and Empire: the Explorer and the Scientist in the Winning of the American West.* New York: Knopf, 1966.

———. *The West of the Imagination.* New York: Norton, 1986.

Gould, Stephen Jay. *Time's Arrow, Time's Cycle: Myth and Metaphor in the Discovery of Geological Time.* Cambridge: Harvard UP, 1987.

Graulich, Melody. "The Guides to Conduct that a Tradition Offers: Wallace Stegner's *Angle of Repose.*" *South Dakota Review* 23 (Winter 1985): 87–106.

Greenfield, Bruce. *Narrating Discovery: the Romantic Explorer in American literature, 1790–1855.* New York: Columbia UP, 1992.

Greenleaf, Moses. *Survey of Maine.* 1829. Augusta: Maine State Museum, 1970.

Hague, James D., ed. *Clarence King Memoirs.* New York: G. P. Putnam and Sons, for the King Memorial Committee of the Century Association, 1904.

Harley, J. B. "Deconstructing the Map." *Human Geography: An Essential Anthology.* Ed. John Agnew, David N. Livingstone, and Alisdair Rogers. Cambridge, Mass.: Blackwell, 1996: 422–43.

Heat-Moon, William Least. *PrairyErth.* Boston: Houghton Mifflin, 1991.

Hepworth, R. James. "Wallace Stegner's *Angle of Repose.*" Diss. Arizona State U., 1989.

———. "Wallace Stegner, The Quiet Revolutionary." *Wallace Stegner: Man and Writer.* Ed. Charles Rankin. Albuquerque: U of New Mexico P, 1996.

Hill, W. A., Rev. "Biographical Sketch." *The Poetical Works of Thomas Campbell.* New York: Crowell, 1851.

Hipple, Walter John. *The Beautiful, the Sublime, and the Picturesque in Eighteenth-Century British Aesthetic Theory.* Carbondale: Southern Illinois UP, 1957.

Hitt, Christopher. "Toward an Ecological Sublime." *New Literary History* 30.3 (1999): 603–23.

Howarth, William. "Introduction." *Mountaineering in the Sierra Nevada.* New York: Penguin, 1989: ix–xix.

———. "Some Principles of Ecocriticism." *The Ecocriticism Reader.* Ed. Cheryll Glotfelty and Harold Fromm. Athens: U of Georgia P, 1996. 69–91.

———. "'Where I Lived': The Environs of *Walden.*" *Approaches to Thoreau's Walden and Other Works.* Ed. Richard J. Shneider. New York: MLA, 1996.

Huggan, Graham. *Territorial Dispuates: Maps and Mapping Strategies in Contemporary Canadian and Australian Fiction.* Toronto: U of Toronto P, 1994.

Hughes, Robert. *American Visions: The Epic History of Art in America.* New York: Alfred A. Knopf, 1977.

Huntley, Frank Livingstone. *Bishop Joseph Hall and Protestant Meditation in Seventeenth Century England.* Binghamton, New York: Center for Medieval & Early Renaissance, 1981.

Ihde, Don. *Technology and the Lifeworld: From Garden to Earth.* Bloomington: Indiana UP, 1990.

Jackson, Donald, ed. *Letters of the Lewis and Clark Expedition with Related Documents, 1783–1854.* Urbana: U of Illinois P, 1962.

Jacob, Christian. "Toward a Cultural History of Cartography." *Imago Mundi.* 48 (1996): 191–98.

Jameson, Frederic. *Postmodernism, or, The Cultural Logic of Late Capitalism.* London: Verso, 1991.

Jefferson, Thomas. *Notes on the State of Virginia.* 1787. Ed. William Peden. New York: Norton, 1954.

———. "Jefferson's Instructions to Lewis." *The Journals of Lewis and Clark.* Ed. Bernard DeVoto. New York: Houghton Mifflin, 1953.

Johnson, Hildegard Binder. *Order Upon the Land: The U.S. Rectangular Land Survey and the Upper Mississippi Country.* New York: Oxford UP, 1976.

Kant, Immanuel. *Critique of Judgement.* 1790. Trans. and introd. Werner S. Pluhar. Indianapolis: Hacket, 1987.

King, Clarence. *Mountaineering in the Sierra Nevada.* 1872. Ed. Francis Farquhar. Lincoln: U of Nebraska P, 1997.

———. *Mountaineering in the Sierra Nevada.* Boston: J.R. Osgood and Company, 1874.

———. "Catastrophism and Evolution." *American Naturalist* 11.8 (August 1877): 449–70.

———. *Systematic Geology.* Vol. I of *Report of the Geological Exploration of the Fortieth Parallel.* Washington, D.C.: U.S. Government Printing Office, 1878.

Lambert. John R. "Report of the Topography from the Mississippi River to the Columbia." *Reports of Explorations and Surveys to Ascertain the Most Practicable and Economic Route for a Railroad from the Mississippi River to the Pacific Ocean.* Vol 1 of 11. Washington: Nicholson, 1855. 160–77.

Lewis, Meriwether, and William Clark. *The Journals of Lewis and Clark.* Ed. Bernard DeVoto. Boston: Houghton Mifflin, 1953.

Lewis, R. W. B. *The American Adam: Innocence, Tragedy, and Tradition in the Nineteenth Century.* Chicago: U of Chicago P, 1955.

Limerick, Patricia Nelson. *The Legacy of Conquest: the Unbroken Past of the American West.* New York: Norton, 1987. 105–18.

———. "Precedents to Wisdom." *Wallace Stegner: Man and Writer.* Ed. Charles Rankin. Albuquerque: U of New Mexico P, 1996. 105–19.

Lopez, Barry. *Arctic Dreams: Imagination and Desire in a Northern Landscape.* Toronto: Bantam, 1986.

———. *Desert Notes: Reflections in the Eye of a Raven.* Kansas City: Andrews and McNeel, 1977.

———. *The Rediscovery of North America* (1990). New York: Vintage, 1992.

Lukens, Erick Jon. *Shaping California: Landscape and Literary Form in Clarence King, Frank Norris and Raymond Chandler.* Ann Arbor: UMI Dissertation, 1995.

Luther, Kem. *Cottonwood Roots.* Lincoln: U of Nebraska P, 1993.

Lutwack, Leonard. *The Role of Place in Literature.* Syracuse: Syracuse UP, 1984.

Lyell, Sir Charles. *Principles of Geology, Being an Attempt to Explain the Former Changes of the Earth's Surface by Reference to Causes Now in Operation.* London: Murray, 1830–33.

Lynch, Tom. "The 'Domestic Air' of Wilderness: Henry Thoreau and Joe Polis in the Maine Woods." *Weber Studies* 14.3 (Fall 1997): 38–48.

Magoon, E. L. "Scenery and Mind." *The Home Book of the Picturesque.* 1852. Ed. Motley F. Deakin. Gainesville, Fla.: Scholar's Facsimiles, 1967: 1–41.

Marshall, Ian. *Story Line: Exploring the Literature of the Appalachian Trail.* Charlottesville: U of Virginia P, 1998.

Mazel, David. "American Literary Environmentalism as Domestic Orientalism." *The Ecocriticism Reader.* Ed. Cherly Glotfelty and Harold Fromm. Athens: U of Georgia P, 1996: 137–46.

McPhee, John. *Annals of the Former World.* New York: Farrar, Straus and Giroux, 1998.

———. *Coming into the Country.* New York: Farrar, Straus and Giroux, 1976.

———. *The Pine Barrens.* New York: Farrar, Straus and Giroux, 1967.

———. *Rising from the Plains.* New York: Farrar, Straus and Giroux, 1986.

McQuade, Donald, et. al. *The Harper Single Volume American Literature.* 3rd ed. Longman: New York, 1999.

Melville, Herman. *Moby Dick* (1851). 2nd Norton Critical Edition. New York: W. W. Norton & Co., 2002.

Merchant, Carolyn. *Ecological Revolutions: Nature, Gender, and Science in New England.* Chapel Hill: U of North Carolina P, 1989.

Miller, Perry. *Errand into the Wilderness.* Cambridge: Harvard UP, 1956.

Miller, Peter. "John Wesley Powell: Vision of the West." *National Geographic* 185.4 (1994): 89–114.

Moldenhaur, Joseph. "The Maine Woods." *The Cambridge Companion to Henry David Thoreau.* Ed. Joel Myerson. New York: Cambridge University Press, 1995.

Monmonier, Mark. *How to Lie with Maps.* Chicago: U of Chicago P, 1996.

———. *Mapping it Out: Expository Cartography for the Humanities and Social Sciences.* Chicago: U of Chicago P, 1993.

Moss, Marcia. *A Catalog of Thoreau's Surveys in the Concord Free Public Library.* Geneseo, NY: Thoreau Society, 1976.

Muir, John. *Steep Trails.* Boston: Houghton Mifflin, 1918.

Nabokov, Peter. *Native American Testimony* (1978). New York: Penguin, 1991.

Nash, Roderick. *Wilderness and the American Mind* (1967). New Haven: Yale UP, 1982.

Novak, Barbara. *Nature and Culture: American Landscape and Painting, 1825–1875.* New York: Oxford UP, 1980.

Noye, Jose Liste. "Mapping the 'Unmappable': Inhabiting the Fantastic Interface of Gravity's Rainbow." *Studies in the Novel* 29.4 (Winter 1997): 512–38.

Oates, Joyce Carol. "Against Nature." *On Nature.* Ed. Daniel Halpern. New York: Antaeus, 1986: 236–44.

O'Grady, John P. *Pilgrims to the Wild.* Salt Lake City: U of Utah P, 1993.

O'Toole, Patricia. *The Five of Hearts : An Intimate Portrait of Henry Adams and His Friends, 1880–1918.* New York: C. Potter, 1990.

Peterson, Audrey. "Narrative Voice in Wallace Stegner's *Angle of Repose.*" *Critical Essays on Wallace Stegner.* Ed. Anthony Arthur. Boston: G. K. Hall, 1982: 176–83.

Poulsen, Richard C. *The Landscape of the Mind: Cultural Transformations of the American West.* New York: Peter Lang, 1992.

Powell, John Wesley. *The Exploration of the Colorado River and Its Canyons.* New York: Penguin, 1987 (*Canyons of the Colorado* 1895).

———. *The Exploration of the Colorado River of the West and Its Tributaries.* Washington, D.C.: G P O, 1875.

———. *Report on the Lands of the Arid Region of the United States, with a More Detailed Account of the Lands of Utah, With Maps.* 1879. Intro. and ed. T. H. Watkins. Harvard: Harvard Common, 1983.

———. "Institutions for the Arid Lands." *Century* 40 (1890): 111–16.

———. "The Irrigable Lands of the Arid Region." *Century* 39 (1890): 766–76.

———. "The Non-Irrigable Lands of the Arid Region." *Century* 39 (1890): 915–22.

———. "An Overland Trip to the Grand Canyon." *Scribner's* 10 (1875): 659–78.

Pratt, Mary Louise. *Imperial Eyes: Travel Writing and Transculturation.* New York: Routledge, 1992.

Pyne, Stephen J. *How the Canyon Became Grand: A Short History.* New York: Penguin, 1998.

Rawlins, C. L. "Essay Review." *Western American Literature* 32.3 (November 1997): 293–96.

Reisner, Marc. *Cadillac Desert: The American West and Its Disappearing Water.* New York: Viking, 1986.

Relph, Edward. "Place." *Companion Encyclopedia of Geography.* Ed. Ian Douglas, Richard Hugget, and Mike Robinson. London: Routledge, 1996: 906–24.

Riffenbaugh, Beau. *The Myth of the Explorer.* Oxford: Oxford U P, 1994.

Rindge, Debora Anne. *The Painted Desert: Images of the American West from the Geological and Geographical Surveys of the Western Territories, 1867–1879.* Ann Arbor: U M I Dissertation Services, 1993.

Robinson, Forrest G. "Essay Review." *Western American Literature* 30.2 (August 1995): 203–5.

———. "The New Historicism and the Old West." *Old West—New West: Centennial Essays.* Ed. Barbara Howard Meldrum. Boise: U of Idaho P, 1993. 74–97.

Robinson, Forrest G. and Margaret G. Robinson. *Wallace Stegner.* Boston: Twayne Publishers, 1977.

Robinson, Jeffrey Cane. *The Walk: Notes On a Romantic Image.* Norman: U Oklahoma P, 1989.

Ruskin. John. *Modern Painters.* 1843. 5 vols. New York: Dutton, 1906.

Ryan, Simon. *The Cartographic Eye.* Cambridge, Eng.: Cambridge U P, 1996.

Ryden, Kent. *Mapping the Invisible Landscape: Folklore, Writing, and the Sense of Place.* Iowa City: U of Iowa P, 1993.

"Samuel de Champlain's 1607 Map." American Treasures of the Library of Congress. 10 Sept. 2001 <http://www.loc.gov/exhibits/treasures/trr009.html>.

Sanders, Scott Russell. *Writing from the Center*. Bloomington: Indiana UP, 1995.

Sayre, Robert F. *Thoreau and the American Indians*. Princeton: Princeton UP, 1977.

Schneider, Richard J. *Henry David Thoreau*. Boston: Twayne Publishers, 1987.

Schwarzkopf, S. Kent. *A History of Mt. Mitchell and the Black Mountains*. Raleigh: North Carolina Division of Archives and History, 1985.

Shepard, Paul. *Man in the Landscape: A Historic View of the Esthetics of Nature*. New York: Ballantine, 1967.

Silko, Leslie Marmon. "Landscape, History, and the Pueblo Imagination." *On Nature*. Ed. Daniel Halpern. New York: Antaeus, 1986: 83–95.

Simpson, Jeffrey Edward. "The Walking Muse in America." Diss. Brown U., 1991.

Soja, Edward W. *Thirdspace: Journeys to Los Angeles and Other Real-and-Imagined Places*, Cambridge, Mass.: Blackwell, 1996.

Southey, Robert. *The Poetical Works of Robert Southey*. New York: D. Appleton, 1839.

St. Armand, Barton Levi. "The Book of Nature and American Nature Writing: Codex, Index, Contexts, Prospects." *Interdisciplinary Studies in Literature and the Environment* 4.1 (Spring 1997): 29–41.

Stanton, Robert Brewster. *Colorado River Controversies*. Ed. James M. Chalifant. Dodd, Mead & Company: New York, 1932.

Starr, Kevin. *Americans and the California Dream: 1850–1915*. New York: Oxford UP, 1973.

Stegner, Wallace E. *All the Little Live Things*. New York: Viking, 1967.

———. *Angle of Repose*. 1971. New York: Penguin, 1992.

———. *Beyond the Hundredth Meridian: John Wesley Powell and the Second Opening of the West*. 1953. New York: Penguin, 1992.

———. *The Big Rock Candy Mountain*. 1938. Lincoln: U Nebraska P, 1985.

———. *Conversations with Wallace Stegner*. 1983. Ed. Richard W. Etulain. Salt Lake City: Utah UP, 1990.

———. "Introduction." *A Report on the Lands of the Arid Region of the United States*. By John Wesley Powell. Ed. Wallace Stegner. Cambridge: Harvard UP, 1962.

———. *Marking the Sparrow's Fall*. Ed. Page Stegner. New York: Henry Holt, 1998.

———. *The Sound of Mountain Water*. 1969. Lincoln: U Nebraska P, 1980.

———. *Where the Bluebird Sings to the Lemonade Springs*. New York: Penguin, 1992.

———. *Wolf Willow*. 1962. New York: Penguin, 1990.

Stegner, Wallace E., and Page Stegner. *American Places*. Moscow: U of Idaho P, 1983.

Stilgoe, John R. *Common Landscape of America, 1580 to 1845*. New Haven: Yale UP, 1982.

Stowell, Robert and William Howarth. *A Thoreau Gazetteer*. Princeton: Princeton UP, 1970.

Taft, Robert. *Artists and Illustrators of the Old West: 1850–1900*. Princeton: Princeton UP, 1982.

Tall, Deborah. *From Where We Stand: Recovering a Sense of Place*. Baltimore: Johns Hopkins UP, 1996.

Tallmadge, John. "Western Geologists and Explorers: Clarence King and John Wesley Powell." *American Nature Writers*. Vol. 2. Ed. John Elder. New York: Charles Scribner's, 1996: 1173–87.

Thoreau, Henry David. *The Maine Woods*. Ed. Joseph Moldenhauer. Princeton: Princeton UP, 1972.

———. *A Catalog of Thoreau's Surveys in the Concord Free Public Library*. Ed. Marcia Moss. Geneseo, New York: The Thoreau Society, 1976.

———. *Early Essays and Miscellanies*. Ed. Joseph Moldenhauer and Edwin Moser, with Alexander C. Kern. Princeton: Princeton UP, 1975.

———. *Essays and Other Writings*. Ed. Will H. Dicks. London: Walter Scott Limited, 1960.

———. *The Writings of Henry David Thoreau*. Journals. 8 vols. Ed. John C. Broderick. Princeton: Princeton UP, 1981.

———. *Walden*. Ed. J. Lyndon Shanly. Princeton: Princeton UP, 1971.

———. "Walking." *This Incomparable Lande: A Book of Nature Writing*. Ed. Thomas J. Lyon. Boston: Houghton Mifflin, 1989.

———. *A Week on the Concord and Merrimack Rivers*. 1849. Orleans, Massachusetts: Parnassus, 1987.

Tichi, Cecelia. *New World, New Earth: Environmental Reform in American Literature from the Puritans through Whitman*. New Haven: Yale UP, 1979.

Tuan, Yi-Fu. "Geopiety: A Theme on Man's Attachment to Nature and Place." *Geographis of the Mind: Essays on Historical Geosophy*. Ed. David Lowenthal and Martyn J. Bowden. New York: Oxford UP, 1976.

———. *Space and Place: The Perspective of Experience*. Minneapolis: U of Minnesota P, 1977.

———. *Topophilia: A Study of Environmental Perception, Attitudes and Values*. Englewood Cliffs, N.J.: Prentice-Hall, 1974.

U.S. Bureau of Reclamation. *The Story of Hoover Dam*. Washington: U.S. Printing Office, 1961.

Vale, Thomas R. "Nature and People in the American West: Guidance from Wallace Stegner's Sense of Place." *Wallace Stegner and the Continental Vision*. Ed. Curt Meine. Washington: Island, 1997: 163–81.

Vesilind, Pritt J. "Why Explore?" *National Geographic* 193.2 (1998): 43.

Vizenor, Gerald. *Manifest Manners: Postindian Warriors of Survivance*. Hanover: Wesleyan UP, 1994.

Walsh, Mary Ellen Williams. "*Angle of Repose* and the Writings of Mary Hallock Foote: A Source Study." *Critical Essays on Wallace Stegner.* Ed. Anthony Arthur. Boston: G. K. Hall, 1982: 184–209.

Watkins, T. H. "Introduction." *Report on the Lands of the Arid Region.* By John Wesley Powell. 1879 Facsimile. Ed. T. H. Watkins. Harvard: Harvard Comm. Press, 1983: xi–xx.

Weiskel, Thomas. *The Romantic Sublime: Studies in the Structure and Psychology of Transcendence.* 1976. Baltimore: Johns Hopkins UP, 1986.

West, Elliot. "Stegner, Storytelling, and Western Identity." *Wallace Stegner: Man and Writer.* Ed. Charles Rankin. Albuquerque: U of New Mexico P, 1996: 61–72.

Wheat, Carl I. *Mapping the Transmississippi West.* 5 vols. San Francisco: Institute of Historical Cartography, 1957–1963.

White, Jr., Lynn. "The Historical Roots of Our Ecological Crisis." *The Ecocriticism Reader.* Ed. Cheryll Glotfelty and Harold Fromm. Athens: U of Georgia P, 1996.

Wilford, John Noble. *The Mapmakers: The Story of the Great Pioneers in Cartography from Antiquity to the Space Age.* New York: Vintage, 1981.

Wilkins, Thurman. *Clarence King: A Biography.* 1958. Albuquerque: U of New Mexico P, 1988.

———. *Thomas Moran: Artist of the Mountains.* 1966. Norman: U of Oklahoma P, 1998.

Williams, Rob. "'Huts of Time': Wallace Stegner's Historical Legacy." *Wallace Stegner: Man and Writer.* Ed. Charles Rankin. Albuquerque: U of New Mexico P, 1996: 119–44.

Wilson, E. O. *Biophilia.* Cambridge: Harvard UP, 1984.

Wood, Denis and John Fels. "Designs on Signs: Myth and Meaning in Maps." *Cartographica* 21.4 (1986).

Wood, Denis. *The Power of Maps.* New York: Guilford, 1992.

Woodward, David. "Medieval Mappaemundi." *The History of Cartography.* Ed. J. B Harley and David Woodward. 2 vols. Chicago: U of Chicago P, 1987: 287–370.

Worster, Donald. *A River Running West: The Life of John Wesley Powell.* New York: Oxford UP, 2001.

———. *Under Western Skies: Nature and History in the American West.* New York: Oxford UP, 1992.

———. *An Unsettled Country: Changing Landscapes of the American West.* Albuquerque: U of New Mexico P, 1994.

———. "The Wilderness of History." *Wild Earth* 7.3 (Winter 1997): 9–13.

Zelinsky, Wilbur. *The Cultural Geography of the United States.* Englewood Cliffs, N.J.: Prentice Hall, 1973.

INDEX

Note: Italic page numbers refer to illustrations.

and language, 19–20; literary pursuit of, 18; map of, 175
Lewis, Merriwether. *See* Lewis and Clark expedition
Lewis, R. W. B., 150
literary cartographers: inclusion in this volume, xvii, 3, 25
literary cartography, 6, 174, 177, 182; defined, 3; function of for Stegner, 155
literature. *See* place
Lopez, Barry, 171, 180, 195 n. 9; and maps in *Arctic Dreams,* 1–2; and New World optimism, 161; and scale of geographical perception, 178
Love, David, 180–81
Luther, Kem, 195 n. 3
Lutwack, Leonard, 188 n. 8
Lyell, Charles, 80, 193 n. 10

Machine in the Garden, The (Marx), xvii
Magoon, E. L., 27
Maine Woods, The, 39–56, 64–65, 68, 78; "The Allegash and East Branch," 40–41, 52, 53, 56; Burnt Lands passage, 43–46, 48, 64; "Chesuncook," 40–41, 47, 52; and Joe Polis, 52–56; "Ktaadn," 20, 40–41, 43, 46–47; maps in, 42–45, 56; physical signs in, 50–51; relation to *Walden,* 40
Manifest Destiny, 34, 159, 196 n. 12
Man in Landscape (Shepard), 92, 136
Mapmakers, The (Wilford), 8, 26
Map Making (Debenham), 13
Map of Virginia (Smith), 14, 174
mappaemundi, 8, 55
Mapping it Out (Monmonier), 13
Mapping the Invisible Landscape (Ryden), xvii, 3
maps: authored nature of, 10; in

bioregional knowledge, 184; blank spots on, 6, 13, 16–17, 79, 105, 149, 180; and colonizing objectives of, xvii, 98, 175; as communication media, 7; economic and political advantages of, 26–27; epistemological consequences of, 12–13; as expressions of geographical knowledge, 12; failures of, 5, 7, 13; and literature, 13, 25, 74, 188 n. 8; as mnemonic device, 2, 32; and narrative, 143; and Native Americans, 31–33, 53; and postmodernism, 179; and property, 6, 7, 26, 42; showing routes of explorers, 125, *126,* 194 n. 15; subjectivity of, 8
Marcos de Niza, Fray, 21
Marx, Leo, xviii
Mason and Dixon (Pynchon), 179
Mather, William, 103
Mazel, David, 189 n. 12
McClintock, Harry, 159
McPhee, John, 82, 179–83. Works: *Annals of a Former World,* 181–83; *Assembling California,* 182; *Coming into the Country,* 180; *The Pine Barrens,* 179–80; *Rising from the Plains,* 180
Melville, Herman, 1, 12, 17
mental maps, 15, 50, 152–53, 178, 187–88 n. 3
Merchant, Carolyn, 12
métis, 163–64
Miller, Perry, 17
Milton, John, 45
Mitchell, Elisha, 171–77; death of, 173; early trips, 172
Mitchell, Mount, 171–73
Modern Painters (Ruskin), 83
Moldenhauer, Joseph, 72
Monmonier, Mark, 9, 13

spirit of place, 7, 31, 35
Stanton, Robert Brewster, 108
St. Armand, Barton, 193 n. 10
Stea, David, 187 n. 3
Stegner, Page, 144
Stegner, Wallace, 142–70, 173; biographical sketch, 146–47; career of, 143; and
fiction to present facts, 153–55; and
"geography of hope," 144, 168; geography to, 144, 159; on history, 151–52; and
importance of place in the works of,
144–46; and imprinting, 150; on King,
160–61; and life in the Cypress Hills
region, 148; and métis, 163–64; and
"middle ground," 154; and motion as
hindrance to placedness, 145, 170; and
Native Americans, 167, 195–96 n. 12;
and place knowledge, 148, 150–51, 164–
65; and sense of place, 152–53, 166, 178;
and surveyors, 147–48, 163, 167; and
the West, 159–62; and wilderness, 169,
196 nn. 15, 16. Works: *All the Little Live
Things,* 145; *American Places,* 161;
Angle of Repose, 145, 153, 157–59, 168;
Beyond the Hundredth Meridian, 154;
The Big Rock Candy Mountain, 144,
147, 149; "History, Myth and the West-
ern Writer," 151; *Joe Hill,* 153; "Living
Dry," 161; *Mormon Country,* 147; *The
Sound of Mountain Water,* 168;
"Thoughts in a Dry Land," 162; *Where
the Bluebird Sings to the Lemonade
Springs,* 159; "Wilderness Letter," 143–
44, 168, 194 n. 1; *Wolf Willow,* 144, 146–
53, 162, 165–66, 168, 169
Stevens, Wallace, 51
Stewart, George R., 144
Stewart, William, 133
Stilgoe, John, 16

Stone, Julius, 108
story maps, 31
Stowell, Robert, 39, 189 n. 3
sublime, 177; Abbey on, 138; as aesthetic,
101, 188 n. 6; and American landscape,
24, 27; American version of, 29; animism and, 31; and Burke, 28, 29, 46;
conflict with surveying, 6; decentered,
37, 116; defined, 24; and Jefferson, 28–
29, 117; and Kant, 29; and King, 84–85;
and Powell, 115–17, 177; relation to
maps, 28, 33–35; reverence for land, 30;
and Thoreau, 46
surveying: and aerial perspectives, 29;
early, 10; institutional objectives of, 23;
and land ownership, 25; political and
economic advantages of, 25. *See also*
birds-eye view; maps; sublime
surveyors, 4, 5, and explorers, 92; Stegner
on, 147–48, 163, 167

Tall, Deborah, 32
Tallmadge, John, 24, 81, 83, 84, 106, 112,
114, 115, 192 n. 8
Tennyson, Alfred Lord, 112
Territorial Disputes (Huggan), 3
*Tertiary History of the Grand Canyon
District* (Dutton), 117, 126
theolodites, 4, 11
Thoreau, Henry David, 4–5, 9–10, 13, 20,
22, 25–29, 33, 35–36, 38–72, 115, 142, 146,
174; and cartographic metaphors, 63;
and Joe Aitteon, 52; and Joe Polis, 52–
56; and lostness, 50, 64; and maps, 39,
41–42, 50, 66; and sense of place, 72;
and science, 59; and sublime, 46, 48;
and surveying, 38, 56–57, 62–63, 65–
66, *70,* 72, 189 n. 1; and walking, 40,
66–70; and wilderness, 40–41, 45, 48–